Unmasking the Sexual Offender

This book unmasks the sexual offender by providing clear, comprehensible information about the motivations, techniques, and dynamics of sexual offenders and their behavior. It not only explores the biases and myths that the reader may rely upon to understand deviance but also explains pathways to offending, the distorted thinking and relating that offenders engage in, and the ways offenders manipulate and exploit others. Sexual offenders are surrounded by mythology, fascination, and revulsion. People who commit sexual offenses present difficult and complicated issues interpersonally, as well as in treatment and management; denial, victim-blaming, aggression, and blatant chronic deception are inherent in interactions with them. Unfortunately, the failure to truly understand their motives and techniques helps provide excuses for and further camouflage of their deviance.

The first part of the text explores the presumptions commonly adopted about sexual offenders and shows how misinformation supports the inappropriate behavior of the sexual offender. The second section focuses on exposing the sexual offender using straightforward language and tangible examples. A final, third section includes safety and management strategies for dealing with sex offenders for those both inside and outside the realms of law enforcement and offender supervision.

This book is intended for anyone interested in learning about sexual offenders. It is useful for both professionals and non-professionals, including students, paralegals, victim advocates, and others involved in the criminal justice system or mental health field.

Veronique N. Valliere is a licensed psychologist. She has her doctorate in clinical psychology from the Graduate School of Applied and Professional Psychology of Rutgers University. She has over 30 years' experience in the field and has worked clinically with violent offenders and their victims, adult and child. She is the owner and director of Valliere & Counseling Associates, Inc., an outpatient treatment center for mental health and interpersonal violence, with offices that treat victims and offenders, as well as provides consultation, training, expert witness services, and evaluations. She serves on the Pennsylvania Sexual Offender Assessment Board, reappointed continuously since 1997. She has published on the topic of sexual assault and presented on the same at international, national, and local conferences. She has trained for the FBI, DOJ, DOD, Bureau of Indian Affairs, Ontario Police, Alberta Crown Prosecutor's Office, Amber Alert, Army JAG Office, Pennsylvania State Parole, National Center for the Prosecution of Violence Against Women, and other agencies. She been a guest presenter at many forensic and violence related conferences. She is recognized as an expert on victim behavior and offenders, testifying nationally and internationally. She has testified before the US Congress and Judiciary Committee regarding sexual assault in the military, as well as consulted with the Department of Defense and the US Department of Justice. She has been interviewed for popular magazines on sexual assault and domestic violence, including *New York Times*, *The Atlantic*, *People*, *Self*, and *Good House-keeping*. She has appeared on "PBS News Hour," "CBS This Morning," and other programs and radio shows. Dr. Valliere was used as an expert in the sexual assault trial of Bill Cosby. In 2009, she established an annual conference on the investigation, prosecution, and treatment of violence entitled "Right From the Start." Dr. Valliere is the author of *Understanding Victim Response to Interpersonal Violence: A Guide for Investigators and Prosecutors*, published by Routledge Press.

Unmasking the Sexual Offender

Veronique N. Valliere

Routledge
Taylor & Francis Group

NEW YORK AND LONDON

Designed cover image: Marccophoto

First published 2023
by Routledge
605 Third Avenue, New York, NY 10158

and by Routledge
4 Park Square, Milton Park, Abingdon, Oxon, OX14 4RN

Routledge is an imprint of the Taylor & Francis Group, an informa business

ISBN: 978-0-367-74153-2 (hbk)
ISBN: 978-0-367-74124-2 (pbk)
ISBN: 978-1-003-15628-4 (ebk)

DOI: 10.4324/9781003156284

Typeset in Bembo
by KnowledgeWorks Global Ltd.

To those who supported and loved me through this process. I dedicate this book to the possibility that it will help us understand what threatens us, arm us against danger, and have courage to face what scares us.

Contents

Acknowledgments

I owe a great deal to others who have taught me, supported me, and contributed to my knowledge and ability to complete this book. First, I would like to acknowledge my husband who has firsthand dealt with some of the hardships that this field creates for us who are in it. Sometimes we have nightmares, fears, and intrusive thoughts that affect our relationships and our sex lives. Sometimes we impact the carefree interactions with others because we are vigilant or notice something unseen by others. Sometimes it is just no fun. Thank you and all the other partners out there who support the mission and are willing to see some unpleasant truths.

Second, I would like to acknowledge Dr. Bradley Beckwith, Dr. Aaron Myers, Mr. Anthony Mondello, and my mother Veronica. Dr. Beckwith and Dr. Myers read and edited my manuscript through a clinical and professional lens, as both have worked with me and the offenders we treat. They added their own insights and experiences in our discussions throughout the writing of this book. Mr. Mondello provided me insight into his experience as a career parole officer supervising sexual offenders. Through the years, Anthony has shared with me what happens outside the therapy room – incidents with families, friends, employers, and other treatment providers of sex offenders. He provided the narrative regarding being a part of the treatment team in Chapter 12. My mother also read and commented on the manuscript, offering her suggestions as a layperson (and avid mystery buff)! I truly appreciate all the gifts I have received from these people in my life, especially the gift of their time and expertise.

My team as a whole, both past and present, deserve special acknowledgment. They have chosen a difficult career path that is not lucrative or easy. They work hard with a difficult population. And they have stuck around to teach others – Toby Nicolosi, Trista Dashner, Vickie Moyer, and others, including Dr. Beckwith and Dr. Myers, are part of a team that keeps me motivated and fulfilled.

Finally, I have to thank Diane Dombach, who in 1997, helped select me for the Pennsylvania Sexual Offenders' Assessment Board. Through this Governor-appointed position, I have had the privilege of assessing and learning about sexual offenders. I have honed my knowledge through my peers and the court system. My position has afforded me many opportunities for which I am grateful. Thank you for believing in me, Diane!

Introduction

"You are born, and you have all this potential. Then something happens. Someone takes their perversions out on you. Then things change. You never become who you were meant to be," the 55-year-old victim of grandfather-child sexual abuse said to me, explaining how profound the impact of sexual abuse was when she heard I ran a group of sexual offenders. Later, I sat at the front of the same group, unaware that I was about to undergo my own life-changing event. Sounds dramatic, doesn't it? I was a young doctor, unexpectedly tasked with running an outpatient sexual offender program after the last director walked off the job. It was in early 1994. (The company would never fill the position.)

The group was filled with men, 15 or 18, almost all white and mandated to treatment. They looked and acted "normal," chatting with each other before group about work and sports, looking like guys I was used to seeing, being white myself. (That might have been the first lesson I learned – sex offenders are more "normal" than not.)

I was just getting to know each of them. We began by addressing Bill. Bill was a 35-year-old arrested for attempted rape of his neighbor at knifepoint, a nurse he had acquainted himself with and attacked in her home. As we explored his sexual history, he revealed other sexual offenses, something I would learn that most, if not all, of the clients in the program had (another lesson). Bill began describing what I thought of as a "recreational rape" of a woman he called a "friend." The woman was disabled and in a wheelchair. Bill would use the guise of assisting her, like running errands for her, to invite himself over to her house. At times, if the mood was right, Bill would rape her, mostly orally, forcing his penis into her mouth. He would then thank her and compliment her oral skills. He knew she dreaded this.

This night Bill was describing a particularly disgusting and demeaning assault of this victim. He was forcing his penis into her mouth as she sat in her wheelchair. At some point, he was not getting particularly aroused and decided he had to pee. So he pissed in her mouth. As she drew back and spit, he continued to pee on her face, chest, and wheelchair, laughing at her. He smirked while relaying this story. The group was horrified. I was livid. The men in the group began confronting Bill, as did I. How could he be so callous? What was the turn-on of that? How many times had he assaulted this woman? Why would he demean her like that?

After being challenged and having to explore his behavior for at least a half-hour, Bill began to have an emotional reaction to his actions. He started to cry. In truth, I was not responsive to his crying – I was angry and shocked. Instead of offering solace, as my training might have dictated, I asked him harshly, "What are you crying about?" He said, "I am so ashamed," muffled by his hands in front of his face. I did not buy this, again going against my training. "Really," I asked, "Ashamed about what?" Bill responded, sobbing, "I'm ashamed I fucked someone so ugly."

DOI: 10.4324/9781003156284-1

I hope that answer made your blood run cold, as it did mine at that moment (and still does). The group was stunned into silence. After 10 seconds or so, group members started to protest this, not in the way you might think, but to offer alternatives or plead with Bill to be different. "Oh, you don't mean that," one said. "Is that all," another queried, "Are you sure?" It was difficult, even for the offenders, to see someone offer such brazen truth, be exposed, and be someone different from expected. That response changed me because I was willing to accept it as truth. It changed my expectations, the way I listen, and what I am willing to believe. It made me understand that my training did not prepare me for the "truths" I would encounter in this work. Bill glaringly revealed that my assumptions and willingness to "fill in the blanks" with my own experience and expectations when working with people were wrong.

Since then, I have never assumed I knew what any of my clients were crying about, always asking. I learned a profound lesson of the egocentricity of empathy – that what we call empathy is often filling the space with ourselves and not the other. I learned the importance of curiosity and acceptance, truly needing to understand who a person is to intervene effectively and the necessity of acceptance, no matter how jarring the truth. I have learned to sit with being uncomfortable, disgusted, enraged, and hopeless to work with perpetrators and victims. Let me be clear, none of these words imply allowing someone to be harmful or sympathizing with the elements of their character and needs that motivate victimization. Acceptance here means putting myself aside – how I want to see someone, how I want the world to be – and acknowledging that people who commit sexual offenses are motivated by things I will never understand. This is what I ask of you to do reading this book.

On the other side, too, I never accept superficial answers that I cannot empathize with or make sense out of, answers that (to me) are readily accepted, used, and abused by offenders and those who do not understand what it takes to assault another person sexually. It is never "an accident" or a "mistake." Sexual assault is not a result of drinking or drugs (though both influence the behavior). Sexual assault is not a result of depression, an unresponsive spouse, intimacy deficits, or cognitive limitations. Again, all of these elements might factor into acting out sexually for sexual offenders, but that is different. Sexual assault is not about being "horny" or "lonely." Men do not assault because they struggle with their sexual identity or "can't get laid." Another thing I ask you to keep in mind, when offered "causes" for sexual offending, if you or the people you (think) you know would not sexually assault when they are (fill in the blank … drinking/depressed/lonely), then it is not a cause. All these things might be elements; we will discuss those. If drinking too much does not make you want to suck the penis of a three-year-old, how come it is different for that offender? That is what you need to understand and look for when seeking clarity. Look for those things that make offenders different and able to harm another person.

Sexual abuse is one of the most profound, destructive, life-altering events that one human can exact on another. Rates are rising. Prosecution, reporting, and intervention rates remain low. It is imperative that we, as a society, get better at identifying and intervening in sexual abuse and the behaviors of sexual offenders. It has become a primary mission in my life. I will share my lessons, my insights, and my knowledge through the book, all the things I have learned from offenders themselves. I will share some personal experiences that have been devastating and affirming. I have worked in the field of abuse for 30 years. I became a psychologist because people were the most fascinating topic I could imagine. My background contributed, fraught with chaos, psychopathy, and maltreatment. But over the years, I have been honored with the most dramatic, sorrowful, sordid, and transformative life stories. In this book, I want to make people understand the struggles for victims and the victories of offenders. I hope to help people make sense of offenders without excusing them.

I have seen a three-year-old teach me how to give a "blow job." A four-year-old has demonstrated graphically what "weenies" do to little girls. I have looked at crime scene photos (some call it pornography) of infants being anally raped. I have been called "honey" by the judge while he tells me I "make a big deal about nothing" after a pedophile sends Barney underwear to children. (Of course, the judge did not listen when I tried to explain that he used the name "Barney" when he was raping them.) I have worked with dozens of women who were sexually assaulted during a massage and now have significant trauma. I have been reprimanded not to use the word "fuck" by a man convicted of raping and murdering a child, a man who has found Christ (supposedly) but defends kissing and "feeling up" a 14-year-old because lust is "expected in man."

Throughout this book, I will refer mostly to men, because they are the most significant percentage of sexual offenders by far. Some of these concepts will not apply to children or young juvenile offenders. Their motivations and development are different, though I will say that you might encounter some at a very young age who are highly likely to become adult offenders and show the same issues. I want to write plainly, in ways that are easy to grasp, make sense of, and have concrete examples. I will not focus on the dramatic outliers that we have come to expect sexual offenders are – psychopaths, rampant pedophiles, or sexual sadists – though I will use some examples and explain them. I will stress both the insidious normalcy and the covert deviance of the offender.

Mostly, I am going to ask you to challenge yourself. Can you accept the "real" reasons that people hurt others? Does hope or a commitment to seeing the "good" in all people blind you?

Can you accept all the parts of a person, or must it be all or nothing? Do you struggle with a "victim" or "monster" dichotomy with the offender? Are you willing to explore the different sources of deviance that gratify people sexually – that deviant arousal is not about "sex" per se? Finally, are you willing to learn about something you might not ever be able to understand? Without finding a familiar, comfortable explanation that makes you feel better, but might compromise your safety, the safety of others, and the offenders' well-being? These are the things you will need to challenge. Sometimes, you will not be fun at a party.

Pseudonyms are used throughout the book for the individuals described. However, the events and quotes are actual, taken from verbatim notes or recordings.

The Offender's Best Weapon: Society as the Audience to the Offense

Chapter 1

The Co-Defendants

The Role of the Audience to a Sexual Offense

On October 13, 2021, a man harassed, sexually assaulted, and ultimately raped a woman on a crowded SEPTA transit car in the Philadelphia area (Vella & Palmer, 2021). It was before 10 at night. The man was a stranger to the woman he harassed for more than 40 minutes. The woman verbally and physically resisted, pushing the man away repeatedly. The man escalated to pulling the victim's pants down, and his own and vaginally penetrated her in the open on the train. He raped the woman for *six minutes* before a transit police officer saw him through the window, identified something was happening, entered the train, and pulled the man off the woman. The perpetrator told police that the woman initiated the "encounter." While the crime was striking enough, what brought international attention was that the perpetrator was surrounded by bystanders, at least one of whom recorded the assault. Not only was the brazen nature of the rape shocking, so was the fact that no one intervened for such a long time. Police Superintendent Timothy Bernhardt decried the lack of action of bystanders, commenting that the lack of intervention reflected "where we are in society" as "troubling." While the narrative of voyeuristic and callous spectators is not entirely accurate (people were coming and going, not aware of or watching the assault), this event has become a horrific symbol of society's role in being an audience to sexual offending.

Despite reform, education, and awareness, rates of sexual violence have been steadily rising in the US through the last decade (Statista, 2021), with an average of over 460,000 people victimized a year (RAINN, n.d.). Global statistics demonstrate the same trend of rising rates. A recent report by World Health Organization [WHO] indicated that one in three women globally had been a victim of physical or sexual violence. Reports referring to violence against women as endemic worsened during the COVID pandemic to 45% of women (Emandi et al., 2021; Goody, 2021; WHO, 2021). While this might represent a silver lining – the increased reporting of sexual violence – it also represents a significant incidence of sexual violence. On top of that, successful prosecution of sexual violence in the US remains low, with only less than 1% of reported assaults resulting in felony convictions (RAINN, n.d.; Van Dam, 2018). How is this happening? Why is this happening? Unfortunately, as the audience to sexual violence, we are partly to blame.

The Role of the Audience in the Facilitation of Sexual Violence

Larry Nassar was described as a nerdy, awkward doctor dedicated to the well-being of his gymnasts. When he was sentenced in December 2017 for having illegal images of child sexual abuse, then sentenced again in 2018 for seven counts of Criminal Sexual Conduct, the world was finally ready to accept that he was responsible for the sexual abuse of around 500 young victims over 20 years. The 499 victims of Nassar were praised in the media for

DOI: 10.4324/9781003156284-3

"breaking their silence." The problem was they were never really silent. There were repeated reports of abuse and concerns about Nassar's behavior. The children told everyone – parents, coaches, police, therapists, psychologists, administrators, USA gymnastics – over and over again (Howley, 2018; *USA Today*, n.d.). As Howley (2018) wrote in a *New York Magazine* article, "The story of Larry Nassar is not a story of silence. The story of Larry Nassar is that of an edifice of trust so resilient, so impermeable to common sense, that it endured for decades against the allegations of so many women." Even though the first report against Nassar was made in 1998, it was only when Nassar was caught nearly 20 years later with 37,000 illegal images of child sexual abuse that he viewed and collected for over a decade that Nassar was finally brought to court. He assaulted children in front of their parents and under blankets in the gym, people all around. He was seen as kind and selfless. He preyed on children, camouflaging his offending as alternative methods and medicine. He helped the victims, some said "tirelessly." Nassar repeatedly abused victims over the years, multiple victims in a week.

This story is only unusual because Nassar had so many victims, some famous. The storyline here has been repeated over and over in the last few years. Jeffrey Epstein was accused in 2005 of sexually assaulting a 14-year-old girl (McLaughlin & Frias, 2019). The investigation into the complaints revealed five victims he had assaulted and paid for sexual contact. After a grand jury in 2006, Epstein was charged with a count of solicitation of a prostitute. He pled guilty to one count of solicitation of prostitution and one count of solicitation of prostitution with a minor in 2008. The 14-year-old was *that prostitute*. R. Kelly married a 15-year-old in 1994. He was investigated in 2000 for sexually abusing a girl and in 2002, for a video of him sexually abusing a minor. He was indicted in 2002 but later acquitted. He was not convicted of any sex crime until 2021 (France, 2021). Harvey Weinstein, who abused women for decades, was not exposed until 2017 (Kantor & Twohey, 2017). Bill Cosby was first exposed in 2005 (Giles & Jones, 2015).

In the last few years, we have repeatedly seen how these high-profile sexual offenders have continued to offend successfully for years after being reported for sexual assault and abuse. How did it happen? Is the fact that these offenders had money and status the only explanation for their immunity and success?

Sadly, I wish I could say that this is true. It would certainly limit the number of repeat sexual offenders. However, nearly all reported sexual offenders get away with it. And the audience plays a significant role in reporting, investigating, prosecuting, and treating sexual offenders. Judith Herman (1997) gives one compelling explanation for our orientation toward sexual offenders. She writes, "It is very tempting to take the side of the perpetrator. All the perpetrator asks is that the bystander do nothing. He appeals to the universal desire to see, hear, and speak no evil. The victim, on the contrary, asks the bystander to share the burden of pain. The victim demands action, engagement, and remembering."

Gerry was about 60 years old when I met him. He was in a treatment group I took over. Gerry had been convicted for assaulting a 10-year-old girl. He was her foster father. In fact, Gerry was voted "foster father of the year" the year before he was investigated for abusing his victim. This was even though three other foster children had reported him for sexually abusing them. Three. When he was confronted, Gerry would cry. He would lament that no good deed goes unpunished. However, he would persevere in being a foster parent to the most challenging children – girls who had been sexually abused. That was the population he took into his foster home. Unfortunately for him, sexually abused girls often accused innocent people of sexual abuse – didn't they? This was the lie that he promoted that caseworkers believed. All three times, the investigation went nowhere, despite the victims' allegations. What was different the fourth time? The child had a new caseworker who had not been groomed by Gerry nor schooled in the disbelief of victims or the lie that sexually abused children "accuse everybody." She believed the victim. Gerry was convicted. During treatment, Gerry admitted to the sexual abuse of many other victims, including the three that reported him. He also described his other favorite foster children – babies. He sexually abused 60–70 babies he was never convicted for, victims that could not report.

This case is a glaring example of the role of the audience. When it comes to allegations of abuse, especially sexual abuse, we *immediately* take it upon ourselves to decide whether to believe or not believe. This is true for who the victim reports to, who hears about the allegations, who investigates the allegations, and on and on. Whenever there is an allegation, people opine rapidly about the perpetrator and victim, without knowing the facts, without investigation, and relying on assumptions, beliefs, and misinformation. When my colleagues and I train investigators and prosecutors, we ask them to believe the victim. Oh, the calamity that ensues! As if this is not what everyone does with each other all the time! Can you imagine going to your doctor to report a sore throat or chest pain? What if the doctor immediately said you "didn't look sick," so did not believe you? Or that if you really had a sore throat for three days, you would have come in right away. What if you went to the police to report a stolen car, and the officer decided you misunderstood what happened or gave consent to loan your car out so it was not stolen? Or that the borrower returned it with an empty gas tank, so you are reporting it stolen for retaliation. We can do these things to victims, without investigation, without consideration, or even without admitting that we do not know what happened. Whenever I hear the term "he said, she said," I am confident that "he said" will be believed over "she said." The perpetrator's word or version of the offense almost always holds more weight than the victim. The motive to lie is attributed to the victim for some specious reason, like jealousy, retaliation, or custody. Someone would rarely consider that being caught for a sexual offense is a motive to lie. When we ask the audience to believe, we do not ask for an unquestioned statement without investigation. We ask for a report to be valued, considered, and examined without the barriers of bias, misinformation, disregard, or dismissal.

Offenders rely on us to succeed in sexual offending – all of us. The prosecutor who does not take the case because it is not winnable. The jury who believes the victim brought it on herself. The judge who thinks that sexual assault is an issue of "boys will be boys." Family members that blame the offender's history of abuse. Spectators that believe the offender "isn't like that." A society that harbors deep misogynistic beliefs. Anyone who blames something else without holding the offender accountable. All of us are co-defendants with the offender. As a society and community around the victim and offender, how do we facilitate sexual assault?

Societal Building Blocks for Construction of a Good Offense

Societally, we maintain some insidious beliefs and values that enable the distortions of sexual offenders, the blaming of victims, and the normalization and acceptance of sexual violence. Generally, we are unaware of these underlying and persistent tenets and how they impact our perceptions and response to sexual violence.

Acceptance of Rape Myths

Rape myths are a complex set of false beliefs and values maintained and perpetuated in our society (Lonsway & Fitzgerald, 1994). These myths profoundly impact how society perceives and reacts to sexual violence. In general, rape myths excuse sexual violence, shift the responsibility of sexual violence from the perpetrator, and blame the victim for being assaulted. Some examples of a rape myth include the idea that women lie about being assaulted, that a drunk victim is partly responsible for what happens, that resistance is necessary to label something a rape, and that victims "ask for it" if they act or dress a certain way. The myths capture the ideas that the victim is to blame, that the offender did not mean it, that the act was not "real" rape, or that victims often lie about being assaulted. An example of a survey of some of these myths is the Acceptance of Modern Myths about Sexual Aggression (Gerger et al., 2013).

Rape myth acceptance and its influence have been studied for decades. Although there has been information available in the media and online, educational efforts, and social outcry to challenge and debunk myths about rape and sexual assault, they persist. Not only do these beliefs persist, but they are also held more tightly and overtly by men (See, 2017). They influence law enforcement attitudes and actions (Constantinou, 2021; Garza & Franklin, 2020). They affect jury perceptions and decisions – all in favor of the perpetrator and against victims when they are maintained. Jurors who uphold these myths are more likely to find a perpetrator not guilty of a sexual crime (Booth et al., 2018). Some studies show that men who adhere to rape myths are more likely to commit sexual violence (Yapp & Quayle, 2018). Rape myths are so powerful that they even impact crime lab personnel's decision-making, as one recent study discovered. Campbell and Fehler-Cabral's (2020) research revealed that crime lab personnel requested that police only submit DNA evidence for "real" sexual assault cases (violent stranger assaults) while indicating that "shady" cases were not worth testing (which included known assailants and assaults of adolescents and sex workers).

Notably, rape myths are not just embedded in our psyche societally; offenders use them to deny, minimize, manipulate, and get away with the offense. Wrote one offender in a treatment assignment,

> I have heard that society blames victims by saying it was their fault because they drank too much or because they went to a party. Society says victims "ask for it" by putting themselves in situations. Society also blames alcohol for behaviors offenders do – "you were drunk when it happened," "It's okay because you were drunk," "the alcohol made you do it."

Another wrote, "In the jail, women were being sexually assaulted by the C.O. (corrections officer) and captain didn't say anything. Captain said she shouldn't have come to jail." One offender described how rape myths helped his case. "My lawyer said he would blame her and not me," he explained, "I said, no it is me all the way. He said by the way she look and act to you, it would have made you do it. She was 12 to 14 years old." If offenders are acutely aware of these myths and use them to their benefit, we as a society should be able to confront and challenge them.

Rape Culture

Rape culture is a term used to describe an environment where sexual assault is normalized or trivialized by the prevailing attitudes. The term was first used in the 1970s but is still relevant today. It is clear that rape myth acceptance is part of rape culture, but so is victim-blaming, the idea of victims having the responsibility to avoid being raped, and the unwillingness or failure to hold perpetrators accountable. There is normalization or minimization of rape through lyrics, jokes, or media humor. People are objectified and humiliated sexually. When rape culture exists, women live in fear of rape, limiting opportunity and impacting access. Men, too, can be socialized to fear rape, especially in particular contexts, like prison. Rape is an effective threat used to silence and control victims and potential victims. Rape culture is created in a myriad of ways.

Victim Blaming

Rape culture supports victim-blaming, the transfer of responsibility for the crime from the perpetrator to the victim. The victim "asked for it" in some way – drinking, dressing a certain way, acting sexually, or being alone. The victim made bad choices that made her vulnerable, which a predatory person expectedly exploits. "What did she think was going to happen," an acquaintance said to me while we were discussing the assault allegations against a pro football player by a teenage girl. He went on, "She snuck into a bar! She shouldn't have been there! What did she think would happen?" My response was, "Oh, maybe that she would get grounded. Maybe an autograph? Not taken into the bathroom by a man and assaulted." Victims I have worked with who were sexually assaulted during a massage by a licensed massage therapist have been asked the same question, "Well, you went to a man. What did you think would happen?" Those are examples of how rape culture dictates perception.

 People try to soften the blaming with professed empathy, saying things like, "Not that she deserved it, but …" followed by comments about the victim's drinking, friends, and choices. Some researchers termed this thinking "benevolent rape myth acceptance" (Davies et al., 2012). We see the same dynamic in "prevention" programs that suggest that women drink less, have a "buddy" wherever they go, or try not to attract attention. There is the idea that the victim should "know better" and assumes the risk of being raped if she makes certain choices. Whenever I am approached in trainings about these issues, the person who questions me assures me that the suggestions only reflect the best intentions. Even Malcolm Gladwell (2019), in his analysis of the Brock Turner case, wished to focus on alcohol intoxication as the issue for both the victim and perpetrator, recommending that both victims and perpetrators watch their drinking, respecting the influence of alcohol on sexual assault. He is right about one thing, people who rape when they drink should not drink.

Idealization and Exaggeration of Male Sexual Interest and Desire

"There's no such thing as a bad blow job," the psychologist joked while we waited for a hearing about a sexually aggressive juvenile who assaulted another youth by sucking his penis, minimizing the sexual offense. The idea of uncontrollable sexual desire and an unremitting sexual appetite of men is woven into the fabric of rape culture. This belief leads to many underlying presumptions that fuel rape myth acceptance, mitigation of responsibility for male perpetrators, and permission for male sexual entitlement that women must manage successfully. Many excuses or justifications for sexual assault are embedded in the premise that men cannot control themselves, that sexual aggression is a natural part of the male makeup. "Boys will be boys" is a refrain that reflects this. The idea of "blue balls" being a terrible condition is another. A third is the idea that once a man is aroused or has an erection, he cannot stop himself. "What did you expect," one offender said, "She threw her vagina right on me! I couldn't help it!" He was talking about a 6-year-old. Others profess to be unable to resist any flirtation or supposed seduction. "She wanted it! She asked to see it," the stepfather said about his 14-year-old stepdaughter, "I don't know – I just got so turned on." When I asked him if he would have given her his car keys when she was so young and inexperienced, he looked aghast. "No, that would be irresponsible – she can't drive," he said. "But you gave her your penis," I reflected. Beliefs about the power and value of male sexual arousal force victims into the role of managing themselves and the arousal of men to avoid being raped.

These same beliefs exonerate perpetrators if there is any way to portray sexual assault as a natural consequence of this powerful sexual drive. People excuse perpetrators who persist in penetrating an unconscious, vomiting, or barely functioning victim, especially if the perpe-trator portrays the victim as consenting before becoming sick or unconscious. Review the Brock Turner case. You will discover his version of events is one of engaging consensually with the victim and assaulting her while she was unconscious because he simply could not stop or did not understand that he was raping her. In these perpetrators' minds, they are entitled to persist because they had presumed consent, which apparently is not time-limited. This entitlement for sexual gratification is magnified when there is a prior sexual relation-ship. In a trial involving multiple marital rapes, the accused testified that he thought when he was married, he "could have all the pussy [he] wanted for free!" He admitted to raping his wife four times. He was acquitted. That is rape culture.

Sexual Socialization of Children to Unhealthy Sexuality and Aggression

Even child-friendly movies and shows make rape jokes or use unhealthy, degrading sexual humor. "SpongeBob SquarePants" is notorious for being replete with sexual innuendo and assault jokes. Disney filmmakers have been confronted repeatedly in the media for sexual jokes embedded in the movies. It is not the sexual jokes in and of themselves – some can be harmless. However, they can be careless and promote objectification, aggression, coer-cion, misogyny, and toxic masculinity, all contributing to rape culture. At the same time, the power of children's media is praised for introducing diversity, tolerance, and healthy boundaries into the content, the influence of the sexual content that supports rape culture is dismissed with the assertion that children "don't get" the references. The information that children receive early, positive and negative, forms their openness and initial understanding of what forms values and beliefs. Exposure to rape jokes, sexual objectification, "funny" sexual assaults, and likable characters acting in a sexually aggressive manner is meaningful. SpongeBob tells his friend not to "drop the soap" while winking at him. While many of the supposed sexual things in Disney movies are not there (Bradley, 2015), there are many things in child movies that are there, including Disney movies (Dorsi, 2017). There is sexual coercion in *Beauty and the Beast*. There is a rape scene in *The Nutty Professor* – not just anal rape, but anal rape by an animal. Fairy tales themselves depict gruesome, violent sexual events, like in the original "Sleeping Beauty" when she is raped while unconscious or "sleeping." "Family Guy" has been repeatedly criticized for overt jokes about sexual aggression (e.g., see De Moraes, 2013). It is not only that media offers material about sexual aggression in a "funny" context, but also that the response to the events by the others in the show does not offer an alternative or corrective experience. For example, when Belle in *Beauty and the Beast* is sexually harassed in a coercive way by Gaston, he is viewed and supported as a viable suitor by others.

Rape as a Weapon or Threat

Rape culture supports the use of rape as a threat. Even on a show like "Law and Order: Special Victims Unit," which attempts to promote victim sensitivity and awareness of sexual assault, the officers threaten the offenders with sexual assault in jail, using their fear of being raped to leverage confessions. Rape is seen as an acceptable "payback" for bad guys or men who rape. Threats of rape are used to silence women, or comparisons to rape are used to minimize sexual assault. A victim is asked "how far" the massage therapist put his finger in her vulva to prove that she was not "really" penetrated or not "really raped." Online trolls threaten rape as a way to harass victims or others who speak out. This includes me, who did a Tedx Talk on sexual assault (Valliere, 2016). The comments included disparagement of my point, intelligence, and looks but also included rape threats. "Ill rape u if that is what ur into. bend over bitch," wrote gotcha bitch. Mug Numps added the racism of rape threats, writing, "Just look at how phat this bitch is, NO white man would touch this krap. Maybe she can get a drug dealer nigro to take care of her business." Another wrote about how being raped is the only way someone "would fuck" me. Others cite rape as the fantasy of women. Rape is used in war to punish and control. Rape threats are used to control, threaten, and silence because rape is a real weapon in our culture. Amanda Jones, a journalist, writes about her experience (2021), noting that surveys of women journalists, television presenters, columnists, and other public figures attract "disproportionately aggressive and misogynistic responses." Rape is a serious threat because the threatener knows the shame is with the victim, not the perpetrator.

Rape Jokes

There has been a great deal of controversy about rape jokes in the era of #MeToo. Rape jokes are being explored, analyzed, and reconstituted. While there is a recent recognition of the destructive nature of some rape jokes about women victims, rape jokes persist and are defended (Cooke-Cornell, 2018). Where rape jokes are still used and thought humorous, hilarious even, is in the comedic depictions of rape and sexual assault of men. McIntosh (2019) offers a critical analysis of the use of rape of men as a joke in the Pop Culture Detective YouTube Channel. Over and over again, movies and television shows reference anal rape of men, especially in the context of prison and "drop the soap jokes." Jokes about male rape appear in children's movies. These jokes are emasculating, portraying the victim as weak or small, promoting issues of power and racism in the portrayal of the rapist. The movie *Get Hard* (2015) is almost entirely based on Will Ferrell's fear of being raped in prison. The vulnerability of the victims is mocked. The subjugation of the victim being forced into a submissive role – being someone's "bitch" – reinforces the idea of violence against women at the same time. Being like a woman is weaker, lesser, and an invitation to sexual dominance. Women sexually assaulting men is also used as a trope in the media. Rape culture fosters the idea that men should consider themselves lucky if they have any sexual opportunity, as men want sex all the time. Additionally, the joke again relies on reinforcing gender role stereotypes and the degradation of women. It's funny because only deviant women act in a sexually assertive, dominant way, and it is extremely humiliating and degrading for a man to be treated like a woman (McIntosh, 2020). When a woman rapes a man with an object, he always walks funny the next day. Hilarious.

Lyrics or Other Popular Depictions of Sexual Aggression

Not only is humor a vehicle for normalizing rape and sexual assault, so is music. Many articles are calling out hip-hop and rap lyrics for the perpetuation of rape culture, lyrics that include rape, drugging women, getting women drunk, sexual entitlement, and ignoring women's resistance (Gray, 2019). Eminem brags in his song "Medicine Man" that he is so good sexually he "can even make the bitches I rape cum." However, these two genres are not alone in promoting rape culture and sexual violence. Pop music has its share, by both female and male artists and groups. Popular songs desensitize people to rape culture, combining music with words we absorb and repeat. We never really attend to the true meaning of what we are saying but cognitively rehearse and internalize them nonetheless. Music is influential. It is also disturbing that several singers with highly misogynistic songs with sexually violent or demeaning lyrics have been accused of sexual assault.

Misogyny

Misogyny is the contempt for and prejudice against women. In a society, misogyny is demonstrated by demeaning humor, hostility toward women, judging women for transcending gender boundaries, and punishing women who challenge male dominance. We have seen misogyny come roaring into the forefront as more women join the political arena. Women candidates are critiqued for their looks, wardrobes, "aggressiveness," moods, and "bitchiness," and other things that their male counterparts are not, including direct hatred and trolling online, with specifically sexualized, demeaning comments and threats. Misogyny is not sexism. Misogyny is retaliation toward women who threaten the norms, status quo, and power structure (Manne, 2018). Women demonstrate misogyny as well as men. Women express judgmental and demeaning opinions, including distrust and contempt for other women. This is referred to as "internalized misogyny," in which women turn on themselves with self-hating and contemptuous thoughts about their worth, body, and value compared to other women (Balestrieri, 2021).

Misogyny is reflected in the persistent beliefs that women are liars, vengeful, malicious, and capable (even eager) to shatter a man's life with a false allegation for such benign reasons as money, custody, or regret sex. These beliefs contribute to dismissing victims' allegations if the victim is not the "ideal victim" or makes an allegation in any context a motive for lying or fabricating can be inserted. Divorce or custody are two of them. Instead of assuming that a woman might divorce because she is being beaten or raped, the notion that she would make a false allegation because she is getting divorced is promoted. (And yet victims are castigated for not leaving an abusive relationship). Women as evil and vile, wielding sexual power with malice is an idea overtly promoted online, with groups like Incels (involuntary celibates) promoting male supremacy (Chokshi, 2018). These groups can advocate rape and killing women, often trolling women online with harmful comments and memes. Threats of rape are so common the term Rapeglish has been coined, as explained by Jane (2017). Sexist humor aimed to demean women is correlated with a self-reported proclivity for sexual aggression in men who enjoy this humor (Romero-Sánchez et al., 2016). The labeling of women's anger, assertiveness, or emotions negatively while demeaning their successes is misogynistic. Nike's (2020) ad with Serena William's voiceover "Dream Crazier" catalogs a number of these double binds women are in, specifically some of the ways women are labeled "crazy" when striving and feeling. For a good array of misogynistic postings and memes that show beliefs and reasons for allegations reiterated readily by offenders, google "bitches be crazy." Weekly, my colleagues or I hear these assertions about women and victims, both by offenders and their defenders.

Language of Lies

Language is powerful. Language forms the basis for thought, for conceptualization. When you examine the language around sexual assault, it is fraught with falsehood. There are many phrases I regularly encounter that have no place in the discussion or documentation of sexual assault and other sexual crimes. Yet there they are – over and over again. Here are some of the ones I most despise:

- Non-consensual sex
- Child prostitute
- Sexual relationship with a minor
- Child pornography
- Depicts a child having sex with an adult
- Oral sex with a victim
- Forced sex
- Fondle
- Molest
- Incest with a child
- Sex to describe sexual assault

Let's go through the list. Non-consensual sex? No such thing – it's rape. How can a child be a prostitute? The child is a victim. No one can have a "sexual relationship" with a child if it is a crime – it is abuse. It is not child pornography. It is crime scene photos of child abuse or images of child sexual exploitation. No image "depicts a child having sex with an adult." The image depicts an adult raping a child. You cannot have sex with a victim and be criminally charged, it is an assault of a victim. Fondle means to stroke or caress lovingly, not sexually assault. One definition of "molest" means to pester. Incest is a soft word for father-daughter or mother-son rape. Perpetrators do not have sex with victims during a crime.

Why is this language so important? It frames the issue cognitively and consciously. Numerous therapeutic interventions, including many techniques in cognitive therapy, rely on changing the internal language and self-talk to change beliefs and feelings. The internal "self-talk" of victims, perpetrators, juries, and society needs to be modified to understand the gravity, impact, and criminality of sexual assault. In our program, the offenders are confronted with their use of language. They must change any word they use that minimizes, sanitizes, or romanticizes their sexual offense. The offender must say, "I assaulted her by forcing her to suck my penis," rather than "I had her give me oral sex." It is much more difficult for an offender who uses sterile crime language that highlights the seriousness of the behavior to become aroused or sidestep his culpability and intention. It is essential for us to eschew this language of lies to help change the culture surrounding sexual assault.

The Glorification of Power, Status, Position

"For one thing, I used my office as a means for my offending. I appeared to be helpful to others while I was really setting them up for my own use," said the convicted priest who abused adolescent boys. Our society is enamored by status, power, and wealth. These things protected many who have been accused and/or convicted of sexual assault. When the accused has status, power, fame, and/or wealth, they benefit in many ways, like having legal resources and clout, having friends in high places, getting the presumption of trust, and having support for the illusion created by the public persona. During the first Cosby trial, spectators engaged in a back and forth of "Hey, hey, hey" with him during breaks, when he came out to yell in his Fat Albert voice. Fans yelled out about their love for "Dr. Huxtable," and he was referred to as "America's dad" in reports. The crowd was in love with the character. Our ability to love an illusion is profound.

When a perpetrator has status, they are of value to their community. This is perhaps no place more evident than in athletics. Despite confessions, evidence, and convictions, sports players are repeatedly given a pass for assault and sexual violence, especially if it is against women. The list is long. Players like Josh Brown or Ray Rice, who either were seen or admitted to assaulting their wife, were re-signed. Larry Nassar was loved by his team, the parents, and the organization. Jerry Sandusky was beloved by the community.

Two of the more insidious beliefs about offenders with status, power, or wealth are the assumption of their desirability and the amplification of a victim's motive to lie. When we assume an offender is desirable, we question their "need" to rape or that a victim would ever resist. "Oooh, he could rape me anytime," I recently overheard after sexual abuse allegations against Chris Noth were reported. "Why would he need to rape anyone? He can get laid anytime he wants," said someone to me when discussing the allegations against Kobe Bryant. We maintain a fantasy that famous men have readily accessible sex partners wherever they go, however they look, and however they act. In a 2012 interview with Andy Cohen, Katie Couric revealed that Matt Lauer "pinched [her] ass a lot" amid laughter, as if this was fine because of his fame and likeability.

This idea that the accused is desirable because they are attractive, wealthy, or can provide an opportunity promotes the idea that their victims are enviable. Who wouldn't want to have sex with that guy? It also bolsters the idea that the victims are lying. Not only is the perpetrator overvalued, but the victim is also undervalued. Combined with pervasive misogyny and distrust of women (I mean, Eve ruined everything with the apple), victims are immediately discounted. Victims are "gold diggers," attention-seeking, or motivated by some other nefarious reason. If more victims against a famous person come forward to support another victim, they are just "jumping on the bandwagon." Christine Blasey Ford has been attacked thoroughly in the media and online, so much so that books were written on why she should not be believed! The President of Michigan State University, John Engler, first accused Larry Nassar's victims of getting "kickbacks" from lawyers to accuse him, then said that the victims were relishing the spotlight (Wagner, 2019). This statement came after Nassar's admissions. Fame is protective for the offender, while it magnifies all the doubt, distrust, and disbelief for their victims.

Summary

Society serves as a co-conspirator with the sexual offender. In all too many cases with which I have been involved, the victim's credibility and efforts were meaningless because the audience – judge, jury, prosecutor, supports – could not or would not believe. There are foundational problematic beliefs, values, and culture that allow the offender to go relatively unchallenged in his actions and distortions. The sexual offender is aware of the issues and consciously exploits them whenever possible. Until we actively and intentionally address rape myth acceptance, misogyny, rape culture, and other issues that normalize and minimize sexual assault, we will continue to have an unacceptable rate of victimization, offending, reporting, and prosecution of sexual crimes. As we progress in addressing the outlined issues, we, as bystanders to sexual offending, will become better able to understand and more empowered to intervene. Studies show that education works – with children, students, law enforcement – with all of us. If we, as the audience, are unable or unwilling to name and call out sexual assault and sexual offenders, what can we ask from the victims?

In conclusion:

- If the audience to the sexual assault adheres to problematic beliefs and values about victims, offenders, and sexual assault, the likelihood that appropriate intervention, investigation, and prosecution decreases.
- If we, as the audience, hold these inherently flawed ideas, we will fail to support victims and hold offenders accountable.

- Offenders exploit the collective misinformation and culture that overtly or covertly facilitates sexual assault. Misogyny, sexism, and rape myth acceptance in men increase their self-reported propensity for sexual aggression, as well.
- Changing our language will change our thinking.
- It is not enough to just choose not to be sexually assaultive. In this arena, doing nothing supports the continuing culture of violence. An educated bystander who is willing to confront, challenge, and intervene can profoundly positively impact preventing and addressing sexual violence.
- Education works. Awareness works. As a society, we all have a responsibility to prevent, not just be a collusive audience for the sexual offender.

References

Balestrieri, K. (2021, May 24). 7 Not-so-obvious signs of internalized misogyny. *Modern Intimacy*. https://www.modernintimacy.com/7-not-so-obvious-signs-of-internalized-misogyny/

Booth, N., Willmott, D., & Boduszek, D. (2018). Rape myths and misconceptions. *The Law Society Gazette*. https://www.lawgazette.co.uk/commentary-and-opinion/rape-myths-and-misconceptions/5068719.article

Bradley, B. (2015, January 14). Finally, the truth about Disney's 'hidden sexual messages' revealed. *Huffington Post*. https://www.huffpost.com/entry/disney-sexual-messages_n_6452666

Campbell, R., & Fehler-Cabral, G. (2020). "Just bring us the real ones:" The role of forensic crime laboratories in guarding the gateway to justice for sexual assault victims. *Journal of Interpersonal Violence*, 37(7–8). https://doi.org/10.1177/0886260520951303

Chokshi, N. (2018, April 24). What is an Incel? A term used by the Toronto van attack suspect explained. *The New York Times*. https://www.nytimes.com/2018/04/24/world/canada/incel-reddit-meaning-rebellion.html

Constantinou, A. (2021). *Applied research on policing for police*. Springer. https://doi.org/10.1007/978-3-030-76377-0_7

Cooke-Cornell, B. (2018). Rape jokes in the era of #MeToo. *The Journal of Popular and American Culture*, 3(2). https://responsejournal.net/issue/2018-11/article/rape-jokes-era-metoo

Davies, M., Gilston, J., & Rogers, P. (2012). Examining the relationships between male rape myth acceptance, female rape myth acceptance, victim blame, homophobia, gender roles, and ambivalent sexism. *Journal of Interpersonal Violence*, 27(14), 2807–2823. https://doi.org/10.1177/0886260512438281.

De Moraes, L. (2013, November 15). PTC blasts 'Family Guy' for jokes about rape, sexual exploitation of kids, and "internal defrosting of frozen hot dogs." *Deadline*. https://deadline.com/2013/11/ptc-blasts-family-guy-for-jokes-about-rape-sexual-exploitation-of-kids-and-internal-defrosting-of-frozen-hot-dogs-636005/

Dorsi, J. (2017, October 27). Why these Disney films may help perpetuate rape culture. *Teen Vogue*. https://www.teenvogue.com/story/disney-films-rape-culture

Emandi, R., Encarnacion, J., Seck, P., & Tabaco, R. (2021). Measuring the shadow pandemic: Violence against women during COVID-19. *UNWomen*. https://data.unwomen.org/sites/default/files/documents/Publications/Measuring-shadow-pandemic.pdf

France, L. (2021, September 27). A timeline of the case against R. Kelly. *CNN*. https://www.cnn.com/2021/08/18/entertainment/r-kelly-timeline/index.html

Garza, A., & Franklin, C. (2020). The effector of rape myth endorsement on police response to sexual assault survivors. *Violence against Women*, 27(3–4). https://doi.org/10.1177/1077801220911460

Gerger, H., Kley, H., Bohner, G., & Siebler, F. (2013). Acceptance of Modern Myths About Sexual Aggression (AMMSA) scale. Measurement Instrument Database for the Social Science. Retrieved from www.midss.ie

Giles, M., & Jones, N. (2015, December 30). A timeline of the abuse charges against Bill Cosby [Updated]. *New York*. https://www.vulture.com/2014/09/timeline-of-the-abuse-charges-against-cosby.html

Gladwell, M. (2019). *Talking with strangers: What we should know about the people we don't know*. Little Brown.

Goody, M. (2021, March 9). Nearly 1 in 3 women experience violence: Landmark report from WHO. *NPR*. https://www.npr.org/sections/goatsandsoda/2021/03/09/975358112/nearly-1-in-3-women-experience-violence-landmark-report-from-who

Gray, K. (2019). Evidence of rape culture in modern music. *CLA Journal*. https://uca.edu/cahss/files/2020/07/Gray-CLA-2019.pdf

Herman, J. (1997). *Trauma and recovery*. Basic Books.

Howley, K. (2018, November 19). Everyone believed Larry Nassar. The predatory trainer may have just taken down USA Gymnastics. How did he deceive so many for so long? *New York*. https://www.thecut.com/2018/11/how-did-larry-nassar-deceive-so-many-for-so-long.html

Jane, E. (2017). Systemic misogyny exposed: Translating rapeglish from the manosphere with a random rape threat generator. *International Journal of Cultural Studies*, *21*(6), 1–20. https://doi.org/10.1177/1367877917734042

Jones, A. (2021, June 8). Disagreeing with a woman: Threats of rape and violence. *Legal Feminist*. https://legalfeminist.org.uk/2021/06/08/disagreeing-with-a-woman-threats-of-rape-and-violence/

Kantor, J., & Twohey, M. (2017, October 5). Harvey Weinstein paid off sexual harassment accusers for decades. *The New York Times*. https://www.nytimes.com/2017/10/05/us/harvey-weinstein-harassment-allegations.html

Lonsway, K. A., & Fitzgerald, L. F. (1994). Rape myths: In review. *Psychology of Women Quarterly*, *18*(2), 133–164.

Manne, K. (2018). *Down girl: The logic of misogyny*. Oxford University Press.

McIntosh, J. [Pop Culture Detective] (2019). *Sexual assault of men played for laughs – Part 1 male perpetrators* [Video]. YouTube. https://www.youtube.com/watch?v=uc6QxD2_yQw

McIntosh, J. [Pop Culture Detective] (2020). *Sexual assault of men played for laughs – Part 2 female perpetrators* [Video]. YouTube. https://www.youtube.com/watch?v=uc6QxD2_yQw

McLaughlin, K., & Frias, L. (2019). A timeline of the sexual abuse cases against Jeffrey Epstein. *Insider*. https://www.insider.com/timeline-jeffery-epstein-sexual-abuse-cases-2019-7

Nike (2020, January 11). *Dream crazier* [Video]. YouTube. https://www.youtube.com/watch?v=zWfX5jeF6k4

RAINN (n.d.). *Victims of sexual violence: Statistics*. https://www.rainn.org/statistics/victims-sexual-violence

Romero-Sánchez, M., Carretero-Dios, H., Megías, J. L., Moya, M., & Ford, T. E. (2016). Sexist humor and rape proclivity: The moderating role of joke-teller gender and severity of sexual assault. *Violence against Women*, *23*(8), 951–972. https://doi.org/10.1177/1077801216654017

See, W. (2017). Differences in rape myth acceptance between genders: A systematic review. 10.31234/osf.io/8dns4

Statista (2021, September 29). *Reported forcible rape rate in the United States from 1990 to 2020*. https://www.statista.com/statistics/191226/reported-forcible-rape-rate-in-the-us-since-1990/

USA Today (n.d.) Who is Larry Nassar? A timeline of his decades-long career, sexual assault convictions and prison sentences. *USA Today*. https://www.usatoday.com/pages/interactives/larry-nassar-timeline/

Valliere, V. (2016, October 21). *Sexual assault and the "V" word* [Video]. https://www.youtube.com/watch?v=QBPgxdCBhYI&t=18s

Van Dam, A. (2018, October 6). Less than 1% of rapes lead to felony convictions. At least 89% of victims face emotional and physical consequences. *The Washington Post*. https://www.washingtonpost.com/business/2018/10/06/less-than-percent-rapes-lead-felony-convictions-least-percent-victims-face-emotional-physical-consequences/

Vella, V., & Palmer, C. (2021, November 1). What we know and don't know about the SEPTA rape case. *Philadelphia Inquirer*. https://www.inquirer.com/news/septa-rape-case-philadelphia-video-victim-fiston-ngoy-20211101.html

Wagner, L. (2019, January 15). Interim MSU President John Engler Says Larry Nassar's victims are having a blast in the "spotlight." Deadspin. https://deadspin.com/interim-msu-president-john-engler-says-larry-nassars-vi-1831774684

World Health Organization [WHO] (2021, March 9). *Devastatingly pervasive: 1 in 3 women globally experience violence*. WHO. https://www.who.int/news/item/09-03-2021-devastatingly-pervasive-1-in-3-women-globally-experience-violence

Yapp, E., & Quayle, E. (2018). A systematic review of the association between rape myth acceptance and male-on-female sexual violence. *Aggression and Violent Behavior*, *41*, 1–19. https://doi.org/10.1016/j.avb.2018.05.002

Chapter 2

Weaponized Humanity

Why We Offer Denial and Disbelief to Offenders

"I had to deny who he is to love him – so I denied what he did," the mother explained to me. Her husband had sexually abused her child, his stepdaughter, over the course of time. She was able to later identify things that made her uncomfortable in his behavior, as well as recognize her daughter's attempts to tell and avoid the abuse. Yet, when she was told the allegations, her first response was disbelief. When asked why he kept offending even after his victim disclosed, a different offender wrote, "No one did anything to make me fill [sic] like I did nothing bad."

Disbelief and denial of the offense and protection of the offender come very naturally to us, more readily than support of the victim, regardless of our relationship to the victim. At one time in my treatment program, we presented brand new clients with a typewritten list of "Excuses you shouldn't bother to use" during their first session. Over and over and over, offenders of all types would tell me the same things about why they did what they did, why they were innocent, misunderstood, or not responsible for their offenses. I began to question why I heard the same things repeatedly, complaining at times about the lack of creativity in the offenders, prompting the creation of the list that included terrible lawyers, bad childhoods, drinking, lying victims, or mistakes. I realized that the offenders did not need to be more creative because these things worked. The more important question became, "Why did they work so well?"

Humans can be terrible decision-makers, influenced by various social and cognitive issues of which we are not aware. Social science has been studying human decision-making, as have economists, marketers, and, well, sexual offenders, to capitalize on these influences and issues to achieve their goals. This chapter does not fully explore all the factors that influence our perception and decisions. Many good books and resources are available for a deeper dive into this arena (see authors Dan Ariely or Daniel Kahneman, for examples). The topic is fascinating and complex. This chapter will not be a treatise on dishonesty or denial, again complex issues. What I will do in this chapter is introduce some concepts for you to explore and challenge within yourself and others to better your understanding of how offenders utilize and exploit some of our humanity. After all, we are the human audience.

I will often tell new therapists that choose to work with offenders that it can be the easiest job in the world if you do it wrong. They are pleasant (until you challenge them). They are prosocial (until you begin to uncover the deception). They will offer you information and participation, coming to therapy with something to talk about, like their depression, the death of a family member, or their feelings about missing their family. Offenders will bring their public face to therapy. They will pull from you the humanity you are trained to offer. And they will recreate the victim-perpetrator relationship where you will be deceived and controlled, using your humanity against you, just like they did their victims and their audience. They are very good at this. In a more formalized survey of 50 offenders in our

DOI: 10.4324/9781003156284-4

program, they confirmed what we had known forever, that the people in their lives believed their denial. They effectively fooled nearly everyone (83%), *even when they confessed or were caught in the act!* Except for one person, the only time the family or loved ones did not believe their denial was when they were caught in the act, or there was evidence, like digital images. What about us makes us want to believe them? What about us embraces their denial?

Biases – Constructs of Complacency

Merriam-Webster dictionary (n.d.) defines bias as "an inclination of temperament or outlook, especially a personal and sometimes unreasoned judgment, prejudice." Biases are some of the "hidden forces" that impact our perceptions and decision-making, sometimes causing problems in our ability to see the truth or make "logical" decisions (Ariely, 2008). There are scores of biases identified in the literature, which can be found easily on the Internet (see Wikipedia) and described more thoroughly in books like *Thinking and Deciding* (Baron, 2007). Some biases, however, are highly relevant when it comes to understanding how the human audience contributes to successful sexual assault.

Loss Aversion

Loss aversion is one of the most potent biases impacting our behavior and decision-making. Loss aversion describes the intense reluctance we humans have for losing something, creating a pressure that could be twice as powerful as our need to gain something (Kahneman, 2011). We vividly experience pain more than we experience joy – loss is one of the most painful things of all (Brafman & Brafman, 2011). Imagine the forced choice of having to lose a family member, spouse, beloved figure, or idol to believe a victim, one who might not be known to you or who can be dismissed or maligned. Even when a sibling sexually assaults another sibling, it is not the victim child that the parent faces "losing," it is the perpetrator child. The perceived loss can be real, like if a spouse goes to prison, or more symbolic, like the loss of a cherished memory or fictional character on television (like Dr. Huxtable).

Accepting someone is a perpetrator of an offense pervasively reviled in society, we experience loss on many levels. We must acknowledge that someone can be bad or evil, that the world is dangerous, that our judgment of character is faulty, that we were fooled, and ultimately the loss of control and invulnerability. It is easier to make excuses, blame the victim, or engage in other defenses to avoid our pain, to avoid these losses.

Denial Bias/Normalcy Bias/Status Quo Bias

The need to avoid pain contributes to denial bias, the tendency to reject unpleasant or unsettling information. The normalcy and status quo bias reinforce denial through our tendency to underestimate risk for the sake of normalcy and the need for things to stay the same. There is perhaps no more disorganizing or shocking event than to find out that someone is capable of violence, especially someone close. As Heller (2019) eloquently wrote in her article about evil,

> We simply deny that which causes us distress. Given that evil calls into question our fundamental trust in the order and structure of our world, we are compelled by our instinct for self-preservation to deny evil's existence and construct a reality that offers an illusory sense of safety and predictability.

Again, to accept that people can do evil things, especially those who look and act like us, we lose a sense of control and safety. We must face the vulnerability inherent in love, trust, and relationships. We want to believe that we live in a safe and just world, where only bad things happen to people who deserve it or ask for it. Hence the seduction of victim-blaming. When we believe things are beyond our control, we are more fearful (Gardner, 2008).

Hindsight Bias and the Just-World Fallacy

Hindsight bias is the bias that tells us, "I knew it all along." It is a persuasive partner to victim-blaming as it biases us to think that the outcome was much more predictable than it was ("Hindsight Bias," 2021). It allows a retroactive examination of victim choices in the context of a known outcome, the sexual assault. When the audience asks, "What did she think was going to happen," the message is that any fool could see the danger and outcome. However, this hindsight bias is generally applied only to the victims, not the perpetrators. Hand-in-hand comes the faulty presumptions about drinking, what the victim wore, where the victim was, or what choices the victim made, like rapists rape because the victim wore certain clothing. Again, this bias leads us away from accountability for the perpetrator, transferring the assumption of risk to the victim. The victim's responsibility is to make "good" choices to avoid being raped.

This hindsight bias allows us to maintain the fallacy of a "just world," which is the belief that the world is predictable, karma is inevitable, and that people get what they deserve ("Just-world Hypothesis," 2022). It is frightening to realize that a just world does not exist and that offenders create disorder because they do not follow the rules. If the rules include the ability to prevent sexual assault by following them, then only those who do not follow the rules will be in danger, protecting the rest of us. Victims of assault struggle with a profound alteration in their worldview when they are sexually assaulted, especially if they have not engaged in behavior that could be perceived as risky behavior, for instance, women who were sexually assaulted during a massage. "I did everything right, every step of the way," one victim said in defense of herself, "Sometimes doing the right thing doesn't come out right." She went to church. She helped disadvantaged children. She was a virgin until her wedding night. She went to a licensed, well-known massage franchise that used licensed massage therapists. The therapist sexually assaulted her. Some of these same victims were confronted about being unclothed in front of a man. "What did you think was going to happen," they were asked, then told, "Well, at least you didn't get raped."

Confirmation Bias

There are other things at play as well, like confirmation bias. This bias ensures that once the belief is in place and we are invested in it, we collect information biased to confirm that belief (Kahneman, 2011). If we believe in someone or wish to deny something about someone, we easily can. Offenders understand confirmation bias. They will use it to "prove" themselves. "Ask anyone," multiple offenders have challenged me, "I never touched their kids!" Offenders will provide character references and point out all the times they were around others without abusing them. Mel Gibson's ex-wife supported his denial of domestic assault when he was accused, saying he had never physically assaulted her (Lee, 2010). If the audience believes that "down deep" the offender is good, kind, loving, misunderstood, or has other good qualities, we will look for evidence to confirm that belief. If the audience is attached to or invested in the offender, we will look for information to maintain the attachment.

The biggest problem with confirmation bias is that it is so easy! Especially with such a private crime as sexual assault, we can almost always only confirm the accused's innocence. What information is available to the audience to disprove the offender's claims of innocence? Unless there is direct evidence, like a witness or digital evidence, the offender can simply trot out the dozens or hundreds of people he did not assault. The information that the audience relies upon for their confirmation is meaningless. The meaningful information is not available – typically, only the offender and the victim have it. When it comes to sexual assault, we call this "he said, she said." We do not think this through with logic. It is obvious that an offender does not assault everyone. That in no way proves anything. Coupled with the fact that offenders often choose victims with vulnerabilities or issues, the offender can focus the audience on confirming faults about the victims. Children who are sexually abused have behavioral problems. The offender requires that the victim lie to keep the abuse a secret, then proves that the victim is a liar. This will be discussed more fully in another chapter, but the conditions of sexual assault provide plenty of fodder for the confirmation coffer.

Anchoring Bias

"Did you try to control the information or get ahead of the spin," I asked the offender, who had been an up-and-coming attorney. "Oh yeah, yeah, yeah – absolutely," he said, "so, that's why I went into the office and tried to call – I was calling higher-ups trying to get my story out before they got the story from the police." He explained that he was "trying to shade" and minimize what he had done. Other offenders "prep the battlefield" by telling friends, family, and co-workers that the victim is a problem, a liar, a drunk, Bipolar, or crazy. Offenders talk about marital issues or set up displays and confrontations involving victims and the audience. Offenders who rape their victims will go and brag about how they "got with" a girl/woman, humiliating her again. I have spoken to numerous women who were raped in high school that also had to suffer the humiliation of being labeled a slut after the offender bragged about "bagging her" or "tapping that." This behavior is more than just a tactic to alienate and isolate the victim. This is an offender's utilization of anchoring bias.

Anchoring bias is the tendency we have to affix our perceptions and decisions on the initial information we get on something. It is powerful and guides our decisions toward the initial information (Kahneman, 2011). While most of the research examines anchoring in terms of prices and economic decision-making, it is undoubtedly at work in interpersonal interactions. Anyone who has relied on "first impressions" is using anchoring. In the context of sexual assault, we may have already received the initial information. The priest gave a moving sermon about sexual modesty and prudence. The coach was patient and kind – the children loved him. Jerry Sandusky was a goofy, childlike guy who might have had boundary issues but was really harmless. The initial information that the audience gets about victims is that she waited to tell, kept in touch with the offender, was drunk at the time of the allegations, or was passed out beside a dumpster. Often the "anchor" about the victim is in direct contrast to the anchor about the offender. It is essential for the offender to control the narrative, thereby dropping the anchor.

Halo Bias or Halo Effect

"So, when you meet new people, right away with me, I was right into the mode of I got to show these people I'm a nice guy, show them that I would do anything for anybody," said the ex-coach who assaulted a ten-year-old family member. Another offender explained,

"Someone who is really over helping, really go out of their way for you." He continued, "I'm the guy down the street, though, you know, if you needed a ride, I would purposely go out of my way to give you a ride just to impress you." A good soldier. A good Christian. A great doctor. An attractive defendant. A great athlete. Established a charity. All these things contribute to what is known as the "halo effect" or halo bias.

The halo effect is the bias that causes us to globally attribute positive qualities to someone who is deemed positive, good, or attractive in a particular area ("Halo effect," 2022). This is another powerful bias that appears in some significant arenas in our society. For example, in a study about attractive male defendants, the research found that attractive defendants were acquitted more often and were given more leniency in sentencing (Gunnell & Ceci, 2010). Imagine how this plays out in a sexual assault trial where attractiveness is equated with sexual success. As one offender told me, bragging about his attractiveness, "I get more pussy by accident than most men get on purpose!" Other comments reflect similar biases, like "do I look like I need to rape anybody?" Brock Turner's swimming accolades were mentioned during his trial. That many sex offenders do not have a known criminal record, hold a job, and are "good" family men are continuously mentioned in sentencing hearings I have attended. The halo bias allows us to generalize if someone is good in one area, he is good all the way through, hence incapable of sexual assault.

The Need to Be "Good"

People have many basic needs – safety, affiliation, control, influence. We need to feel good about ourselves and others. Our society is saturated with the expectation that we be good and the expectation or even demand that we see others as good. Religious and spiritual tenets require that a "good Christian" or a "good" human adopt the values and principles of forgiveness, sympathy, hope, kindness, redemption, charity, and belief in another's ultimate value in the eyes of God. We are required to reject the notion of evil or that others are bad, lest we face the same judgment and condemnation. "I wore the white hat in my capacity of volunteering with the church youth group," explained an offender who assaulted a child from the group. He went on,

> There is a level of trust in that community that's, you know, just inherent in some of the values and principles that are taught in the church community, like forgiveness and redemption, just some of the things that are inherent (in religion) that lend a certain level of trust to people.

Another offender got the words "forgiveness" and "redemption" tattooed on each forearm before his release from prison, anticipating the challenges he might face after his conviction for raping his wife's young sister. These tattoos were about 10 inches long and 2 inches wide and faced out, so they were boldly visible to whoever he was speaking to (especially his therapist and parole officer). He always wore short sleeves until I confronted him about these tattoos. He sheepishly stated that they were reminders to others about what he should be afforded for "doing [his] time."

It is incredibly difficult for us to decide that someone should not be forgiven, excused, or have our affection or love. Offenders require decisions and actions from their victims and society that go directly against our human tendency toward affiliation. A victim must ultimately decide that there are no more chances for the offender. A victim has to turn into a "bad" person to report the offender, deciding to no longer excuse, forgive, be kind to, or wish to protect the offender. Given that most victims are victimized by someone they know and maybe even love, this is an extremely difficult decision. Holding others accountable for their actions and decisions is hard. It is uncomfortable. It requires us to set and maintain boundaries, be firm and unyielding, and be willing to challenge ourselves and our natural tendency to accept, yield, and submit to the pull of sympathy, affection, and simplicity. Offenders require us to betray our commitment to the values of living in a kind society to promote peace and kindness truly. Ironically and tragically, we will more easily side with the offender than the victim to maintain our sense of goodness. To believe the victim, we must confront the fact that not everyone is good and make the changes required. Victims are tough on us – they require that we be angry, uncomfortable, scared, and helpless. Offenders make it easy for us to feel good about ourselves.

Our Narcissism

"Doc, I asked to come to you specifically; I know you are the best," an offender said to me, "I know, the guys in prison said you were really tough and hated men, but I know you're the best." Another offender, a highly antisocial drug dealer and child rapist, said to one of my psychologists, "You're not like the other ones, I mean, you listen, man. You get me. I can really open up to you." Are these statements reflections of the good work we are doing? Unfortunately not. They are statements stroking our narcissism, egocentricity, and need to be liked, helpful, and successful. Offenders manipulate the audience by helping us feel good about ourselves, making us feel special, knowledgeable, and the people who know the "truth" about them and the world they face.

Our egocentric needs both dictate our perceptions and willingness to see the offender clearly and make us vulnerable to the manipulations and machinations of the offenders, who are exceedingly good at identifying our needs. "They had a lack there, something I could step in and fulfill and make them feel good about themselves," an offender explained to me. Being useful, fulfilling people's needs protected him when his victim became public with her allegations. "That was one way to gain trust and also to just shield myself from being ever suspected of anything," he said, "Actually, I would always ask them how they were doing, listen to what they were talking about, take their side." His stroking of the ego of his audience had long-term, fascinating results. When he was released from prison and admitted his offending to his friends and family, they did not believe him. He said,

> Yeah, it worked – it worked with a lot of people. So much so that when I came out on parole and reconnected with some and sat down to tell them, 'Look, this is really what happened,' they still did not believe it. [Me, "Really?"] Yeah, they were like, 'Ahhh, you are letting these guys in therapy brainwash you. That's not what happened, Jesus. That's not what happened – I can't believe that happened.' I've had to cut ties with a lot of people because they could not let go of the lie that I built up so great in their heads.

How are other ways offenders use our narcissism against us – our own need to be right, feel liked, be special? They ask us for support because we are the ones who "know" them. They pit us against one another. They make us feel like we are the ones helping them, especially effective with therapists who would otherwise feel helpless or incompetent. They show us their pain, tears, and victimization, telling only us for the "first time" about it. They convince the audience that they can be changed through redemption, forgiveness, love, and focusing on their strengths instead of being challenged on their issues and decisions. It benefits the offender to make us feel good about us, just as they do their victims. Because then it will cost us something to see them differently – now we have invested hope, effort, and trust, so do not want to be betrayed. If we are wrong about the offender, we lose a sense of our competence. We must be disappointed. We have to admit we are not a "good judge of character."

Similarly, our narcissism gets in the way of truly viewing the world as the offender does. Most people think that empathy is putting ourselves in someone else's shoes. This is not the case. This leads to a projection of things we might do or feel, not what the offender thinks or feels. Much like Bill in the introduction, we would project that his shame was about hurting someone else, not "fucking someone so ugly." Inaccurate empathy leads us to conclude that the offender made a mistake, only did it because he was drunk, was only curious, and was driven to his stepdaughter out of loneliness or his cruel wife. Inaccurate empathy and projecting ourselves onto an offender's experience leads to outright disbelief and denial. The offender is too old to be dangerous, too attractive to need to rape, or too famous to risk a career. All that denial because we could not imagine doing what they do. When we see the distress of the offender who is caught, we attribute it to remorse. We do not remember that during his confession, he said, "I felt guilty every time I did it," which means that guilt never prevented the next time. We must not let our empathy and hope blind us, used as a tool by the offender. We must remember that true empathy is putting ourselves aside to experience the world through the other person's view, especially when that other person thinks and feels differently from us.

Misapplied Social Rules and Understanding of Deception

"I'm trying to explain and you keep interrupting," he said, "You just keep interrupting, Jen – will you just listen? You keep interrupting." "I'm fucking listening," she responded. "You just keep interrupting. You're not listening," he reiterated and continued, "Like I was saying, I don't know – she just grabbed it and – she's just a little girl, Jen! She doesn't know what she's doing!" "So you just gave it to her," the mother demanded. This is part of a recorded interchange between a husband and wife, who the wife caught with his penis in his four-year-old daughter's mouth. Throughout the conversation, Riley silences his wife, tells her to calm down, reprimands her for interrupting and not listening, and forces her to listen to his "explanation" (while he blames the victim and blames her) without challenging him. It is an excellent example of how the offender uses social rules to control others, in this case, the actual audience to a sexual assault, the wife who caught him in real-time.

Social rules are powerful. Gavin de Becker, in his book *Gift of Fear* (1997), does an excellent job of educating us on how offenders use these social rules and expectations to decrease our suspicion, manipulate us, and deceive us. Social rules place demands on the audience to adhere to certain expectations and display certain behaviors that most people use to make society function. This includes being polite, not asking too many questions, not interrupting, being "nice," and being cooperative. Offenders exploit these social rules to control others. An example that we encounter regularly is the handshake. Most of us struggled mightily in the COVID pandemic to change this social behavior, feeling awkward and rude when we had to reject a handshake before not touching became normalized. Rejecting an outstretched hand feels wrong in our society. Yet, one of the first things I teach new therapists to do is never shake hands with a client. Why? Isn't this a failure in rapport building? Isn't it rude? It is not a failure in rapport building, as the relationship will grow regardless. It is a clear message – social rules will not control us during your treatment. We will do what we need to, including foregoing the need to be liked and polite. A handshake is a gesture known for social messaging. It is related to dominance and an implicit agreement that we are collaborators, even friends. Therapy, which will require some discomfort and self-exploration, is not a friendship. A therapist is not in the role of a friend. An offending client, who will almost always present a hand immediately, should not be in the dominant role. This is one of many examples of social rules that the audience must be aware of in understanding and unmasking offenders.

Another area where social rules and knowledge are misapplied is applying deception rules to offenders and victims. Typically "deception detection" techniques rely on interpreting the meaning of body language, identifying verbal and non-verbal indices of deceit and lying. There are many books about lying, interrogation techniques, and catching deception, both popular and professional. See, for example, Rudacille (1997), Gordon and Fleisher (2002), or Navarro (2008) for some examples. The problem with typical tenets of deception detection is that they do not work well with experienced offenders or victims. What many of the "signs" of deception reveal is *distress*. For many people, lying causes distress, so the signs accurately reveal the distress associated with lying. However, many of the signals that are interpreted as signs of lying are demonstrated by victims experiencing distress about the memory or disclosure of sexual assault or the cognitive impact of trauma (Valliere, 2019). Soothing and blocking behaviors (like crossed arms) help the victim cope with shame, fear, and avoidance of the issue. Inconsistency in details or disorganized, changing memories can result from trauma in the formation of memory or through other defense mechanisms. People who are ashamed may avoid eye contact, while offenders who understand the social expectations of what honesty looks like will lie while looking you straight in the eye. It is important to be cautious when assessing a victim's credibility with traditional techniques – they will inaccurately guide your decision-making.

In his book *Talking to Strangers,* Malcolm Gladwell discusses two phenomena that contribute to our failure to identify deception that apply to understanding how we, as the audience, are fooled – default to truth and mismatch. According to Levine (cited in Gladwell, 2019), people have a truth default, or default to truth when trying to detect lies. If the lie is not obvious or is complicated by other influences (confidence of the liar, for example), we assume someone is telling the truth. Pair this default to all the other is issues I have described, including our inexperience with deviance and lack of knowledge about what motivates sexual offenders, then you can see why it is so easy for offenders to lie successfully. The more you lie, the more comfortable you get with it.

Mismatch is the other issue. When someone does not act as we presume a truthful or guilty person should act, we interpret their behavior as matching our expectations. A stuttering, avoidant victim must be lying. A confident, righteous offender must be truthful. Offenders are good at lying. Jesus explained,

> You believe it – it becomes part of who you are. So when you meet new people, right away with me, I was right into the mode of I got to show these people I'm a nice guy. Show them that I would do anything for anybody, I wouldn't hurt anybody, and, in fact, I was just taking advantage of everybody's trust.

Ariely, in a podcast by the Knowledge Project (Parrish, 2018), explains several relevant issues about deception. He explains how the brain is in part used for detecting novel or surprising information. So a liar's brain reacts initially to lying, but when the liar keeps lying, the brain stops reacting. Imagine living in the home where you are sexually assaulting someone right under the nose of your spouse – the number of lies that have to be told! Accompanied by how offenders justify, rationalize, and minimize their behaviors to make themselves feel better, they become very skilled at hiding distress and comfortable with their lies and denial. This creates a mismatch between what we think someone lying acts like and someone who presents as truthful. Setting aside presumptions about lying and liars in the assessment of interpersonal crimes is critical.

Confused by "Counterintuitive" Behavior

The term "counterintuitive" behavior is not a diagnostic or psychological term. It refers to behaviors or responses that seem to be a mismatch with our expectations of how "real" victims act. Some examples of behavior that are considered counterintuitive would include a not telling, inconsistent disclosure, failure to forcibly resist an assault, failing to escape when an opportunity presents itself, having continued contact with the offender even including consensual sex, or acting "normal" following a sexual or physical assault. The audience is confused by victim behavior that does not match our expectations. The refrain, "s/he didn't act like a victim," has been used not to investigate allegations, fail to prosecute an allegation, acquit offenders, or overturn convictions. The original prosecutor in the Cosby case, Bruce Castor was quoted as saying that Andrea Constand's behavior was "inconsistent with a person who had been sexually assaulted" (Paquette, 2016). Victims who "didn't act right" were cited as a cause of case attrition in a report by a program of the US Department of Justice (Morabito et al., 2019). An op-ed by a victim of military sexual assault described the expectations of victim behavior, as well as her behavior when she was sexually assaulted (Dostie, 2019), an op-ed triggered by an overturned conviction of a West Point cadet. In that case, because the victim did not yell during the rape, in a field surrounded by other cadets, the judges believed she colluded to avoid detection, making the sexual contact consensual. In full disclosure, I was involved in that trial. There was a conviction by a military panel (jury) who heard the evidence and believed the victim, who explained she was terrified and frozen (Taylor, 2019).

The case was not just overturned on an assessment of the victim's "mismatched" behavior but the accused's behavior (Taylor, 2019). The judges cited Cadet Whisenhunt's lack of action to hide his behavior or clean up his semen as an indicator of his innocence. Because he did not seem afraid to be caught, the act must have been consensual. As the audience, we look for offender behavior that matches a guilty person. Would a rapist ask the victim out on another date? Would an offender of children be so loved and good with kids? Would a guilty man go from friend to friend, asking for letters about his character for the judge, openly discussing the allegations against him? As discussed, Larry Nassar offended children in a full gym or with their parents in the room. Jerry Sandusky took a victim from the classroom, sexually assaulted the boy, then returned him. Who does that?

Richard offered an excellent example of how even educated people can be confused by an offender's counterintuitive behavior. He was caught by a police officer in the process of raping his victim, a prostitute, at gun point. The officer heard the woman screaming from Richard's parked car. When the officer came up to the car to question Richard, Richard calmly rolled down the window and greeted him. The victim was screaming for help, saying she was being raped. Richard explained that he and his date were having "a row," apologizing for the trouble. The officer chose to put the woman in his police car, asking Robert to follow him to the police station. The officer allowed Richard to keep the gun and never asked him for identification. Richard followed the officer to the station, but was released without charges or an investigation, as the officer determined the allegations were false.

Offenders are well-skilled at acting "normal" while contrasting their behavior with the victims. The 50 offenders surveyed in my program identified how they fooled their audience, what expectations the audience had of the victim, and what they – the offenders – knew about victim behavior. Almost 80% admitted to presenting as a "nice guy," knowing that people think sex offenders are "the guy on the corner with his shades drawn," as Scott, an offender, explained. To confuse the audience, 44% "acted like nothing happened," while another 20% entirely and successfully denied the abuse when confronted. Many offenders said that others offered "proof" that the offending did not happen, like that the victim "acted normal," did not fear the offender, or did not scream or fight. The overturned conviction described above reveals that this type of proving is persuasive and effective for the offender.

Offenders understand the power of their post-offense behavior. Offenders are aware of how victims are judged. In fact, there is no such thing as "counterintuitive" victim behavior. All victims respond to assault in individualized ways for a myriad of reasons (Valliere, 2019). What is consistent is that the only people who deeply understand and exploit our faulty expectations of victim and offender behavior are the offenders themselves.

Need for Ideal Victims

The concept of ideal victims includes an archetype of blameless victims for their victimization and who act as expected during and after the victimization (Randall, 2011). A "good" victim is not an addict, a prostitute, or mentally ill. She is not an angry wife who "suddenly" reports being anally raped by her husband after their separation. She or he has not been drinking. The victim is not a sexual being who may have had sex with the perpetrator or others before or after the assault. Research continues to demonstrate social adherence to the "ideal victim construct" (Lewis, Hamilton, & Elmore, 2019), where a "legitimate" victim that meets the construct gets more sympathy and credibility than an "illegitimate" victim. Again, offenders understand this construct. They choose victims who are not ideal, both because the victims have vulnerabilities and because they know we, the audience, will blame the victim.

Summary

Our humanity is weaponized by offenders, used against the victims and us to succeed in sexual offending and self-gratification. Offenders are able to use the audience to activate the blaming of victims, to transfer the burden of the offending to the victims, and to judge the victim's credibility, deflecting their own responsibility for the offending. To unmask the offender, the audience is forced to think and act outside psychological and social barriers that exist in all of us. Believing victims and unmasking the sexual offender *takes work*. It is easy to deny. It is easy to believe in good. It is easy to follow social rules and expectations. It is easier to blame victims than accepting that offenders cause chaos to our well-constructed order, making the world more dangerous. It is easier to be lazy because doing the right thing, the truthful thing, can be challenging, upsetting, unsettling, and uncomfortable.

However, we can change this. We can unveil the truth and see more clearly and accurately when we understand what might be impacting our perceptions and judgments. We can make better decisions by addressing and challenging the problematic biases and assumptions under which we operate. We do this through education. In conclusion:

- There are naturally occurring biases in our thinking, perception, and decision-making that offenders can easily exploit.
- Our need for safety, predictability, and control of our world is potent. Threats to that need, like truly understanding and accepting offender behavior, can be denied or rejected.

- Offenders use our need to be good people and avoid conflict to their benefit.
- Offenders are adept at uncovering what is important to us and manipulating us through our narcissism.
- Dealing effectively with offenders requires us to break social rules and be willing to be uncomfortable and make others uncomfortable.
- Understanding victim behavior and rejecting the ideal victim construct will improve our understanding of offenders and support for victims.

References

Ariely, D. (2008). *Predictably irrational: The hidden forces that shape our decisions.* Harper Collins, Inc.

Baron, J. (2007). *Thinking and deciding* (4th ed.). Cambridge University Press.

Brafman, O., & Brafman, R. (2011). *Sway: The irresistible pull of irrational behavior.* Doubleday.

De Becker, G. (1997). *The gift of fear: Survival signals that protect us from violence.* Little Brown.

Dostie, R. (2019, July 22). She didn't act like a rape victim. *The New York Times.* https://www.nytimes.com/2019/07/22/opinion/armed-forces-rape.html

Gardner, D. (2008). *The science of fear.* Plume.

Gladwell, M. (2019). *Talking with strangers: What we should know about the people we don't know.* Little Brown.

Gordon, N., & Fleisher, W. (2002). *Effective interviewing and interrogation techniques.* Academic Press.

Gunnell, J., & Ceci, S. (2010). When emotionality trumps reason: A study of individual processing style and juror bias. *Behavioral Sciences and the Law, 28*(6), 850–877. https://onlinelibrary.wiley.com/doi/pdfdirect/10.1002/bsl.939

Halo effect. (2022, March 6). *In Wikipedia.* https://en.wikipedia.org/wiki/Halo_effect

Heller, S. (2019, August 21). Blinded by darkness: The collective denial of evil and its impact on psychiatric treatment. https://medium.com/invisible-illness/blinded-by-darkness-the-collective-denial-of-evil-and-its-impact-on-psychiatric-treatment-573bd19b26c8

Hindsight Bias. (2021, October 19). In *Wikipedia.* https://en.wikipedia.org/wiki/Hindsight_bias

Just-world hypothesis. (2022, January 16). In *Wikipedia.* https://en.wikipedia.org/wiki/Just-world_hypothesis

Kahneman, D. (2011). *Thinking fast and slow.* Farrar, Straus and Giroux.

Lee, K. (2010). Ex-wife supports Mel Gibson in battle with Oksana. *People.* https://people.com/crime/ex-wife-supports-mel-gibson-in-battle-with-oksana/

Lewis, J., Hamilton, J., & Elmore, J. (2019). Describing the ideal victim: A linguistic analysis of victim descriptions. *Current Psychology, 40*(1), 4324–4332. https://doi.org/10.1007/s12144-019-00347-1

Merriam-Webster (n.d.) Bias. In *Merriam-Webster.com dictionary.* Retrieved March 11, 2022, from https://www.merriam-webster.com/dictionary/bias

Morabito, M., Williams, L., & Pattavina, A. (2019). *Decision making in sexual assault cases: Replication research on sexual violence case attrition in the U.S.* Office of Justice Programs' National Criminal Justice Reference Service. https://www.ojp.gov/pdffiles1/nij/grants/252689.pdf

Navarro, J. (2008). *What everybody is saying: An ex-FBI Agent's guide to speed-Reading people.* Harper Collins.

Paquette, D. (2016, February 2). A new wrinkle in the Bill Cosby saga. *The Washington Post.* https://www.washingtonpost.com/news/wonk/wp/2016/02/02/the-reason-a-prosecutor-didnt-charge-bill-cosby-in-2005-might-crumble-today/

Parrish, S. (Host). (2018, May 25). Dan Ariely: The truth about lies (No. 33) [Audio podcast episode]. In *The Knowledge Project.* https://fs.blog/knowledge-project-podcast/dan-ariely/

Randall, M. (2011). Sexual assault law, credibility, and "ideal victims": Consent, resistance, and victim blaming. *Canadian Journal of Women and the Law, 22.* https://doi.org/10.3138/cjwl.22.2.397

Rudacille, W. (1997). *Identifying lies in disguise.* Kendall/Hunt.

Taylor, D. (2019, June 9). West Point cadet's rape conviction is overturned, drawing criticism. *The New York Times.* https://www.nytimes.com/2019/06/09/nyregion/west-point-cadet-rape-case.html

Valliere, V. (2019). *Understanding victims of interpersonal violence: A guide for investigators and prosecutors.* Routledge.

Chapter 3

Myth-Information
Our Misinformed Beliefs about Sexual Offenders

Because sexual assault and motives behind sexually harming someone can be so bewildering, we continue to rely on misinformation to fill the gaps in our knowledge and experience. If you are someone who could not conceive of sexually abusing a child or being able to get or remain sexually aroused in the context of maltreatment, you can only rely on your own experiences to make sense of behavior alien to you. In our efforts to make something incomprehensible make sense, we can rely on or accept information that is faulty, that superficially makes sense, or that seems familiar to us. This leads us to relying on myths, justifications, rationalizations, and excuses for sexual offending that are inaccurate. Here are some of the persistent conventional misunderstandings of sexual offenders and sexual assault.

Not Always Monsters – The Insidious Normalcy of the Sex Offender

"Oh my God! Now that's a real predator," says the mother, comparing the media portrayal of the stranger child abuser with her husband who "only" tried to meet a 15-year-old online. The words "pedophile" and "psychopath" are thrown around casually and synonymously with sexual offender, eliciting images of scuzzy men with puppies and clown vans or cold, sexually sadistic serial killers. The media constructs the narrative of the sexual predator as older, violent, and preying upon small children, especially boys (DiBennardo, 2018). The term sexual predator evokes grim, horror movie images of easily identifiable rapists.

These words are titillating. Accurate even at times. But the exaggerated imagery and stereotyping of the sexual offender actually helps them hide – because most offenders look and act like us. They are us – soldiers, fathers, co-workers, brothers, lovers, friends. The vast majority are not ghoulish or violent looking people, though that would make it easier to avoid them. "The perception out there is trench coat or the odd looking person," explained the man who violently raped his victims, "It wouldn't have been that unusual to see me walking there." [Because you don't look like a criminal?] "I lived there, too," he explained, "Yeah, if I'm knocking on your door, you don't think, 'ew, a rapist.'" Offenders hide in plain sight.

The Most Feared – The Pedophile and the Psychopath

Only a small portion of people who sexually assault children are exclusive pedophiles, meaning individuals who are strongly and only attracted to prepubescent children (Kesicky et al., 2014). Yet, the word pedophile is casually used to label offenders of adolescent minors or dismissed when the offender "proves" he has a "normal" sex life. Most offenders of children have arousal to appropriate partners. However, they are capable of assaulting children,

DOI: 10.4324/9781003156284-5

for a variety of reasons – opportunity, indifference to age or relationship, severe objectification of children, or arousal to another dynamic that is not reliant on a victim's age or development. Pedophilia is not synonymous with child sexual abuse; sex offenders who do not profess an arousal to children are the most frequent abusers of children.

Another overused word is the term psychopath. A psychopath is an individual who is highly antisocial and narcissistic, with severe personality pathology characterized by callousness, a lack of empathy, aggressive egocentricity, and other significant features. Psychopathy is not a diagnosis, but a clinical condition that combines the features of the antisocial personality with the malignant, aggressive features of the narcissistic personality (Hare, 2003). Only a small portion of sexual offenders are psychopaths. When a psychopath is also a sexual offender or has deviant sexual interests, that person is considered the most dangerous type of sexual offender (Seto et al., 2016). But what is the effect of using the term sexual offender and psychopath interchangeably? Again, it forms an inaccurate perception and internalized image of a sexual offender as a cold, callous, unempathic, criminal individual who is incapable of love, empathy, attachment, and prosocial behavior. This, too, leads to erroneous conclusions about sex offenders are not psychopaths.

Lack of Empathy?

It is intuitive to conclude that offenders do not have empathy. After all, sexual assault is such a heinous, destructive crime. Wouldn't it take someone without empathy to commit such a crime? How can a sex offender be a good father, a good husband? How can they be outstanding mentors, priests, or coaches? "I really can't say enough good about Larry," said Nassar's neighbor (Howley, 2018). "It's like he was put on this earth to work with kids. I don't know if I have ever met another man that was as caring and compassionate with children," said the assistant director of The Second Mile about Jerry Sandusky (Manfred, 2011). A closer look at both of these men reveals boundary violations, excessive interest in children, and other interpersonal issues. However, both showed kindness, compassion, concern, and friendliness. Neither were callous nor lacked empathy, *except in the context of their offending*. When it came to their self-gratification, they were able to rationalize, justify, and compartmentalize their behavior, to hide it from others. They did not need to ignore empathy until it interfered with their desire. Sandusky referred to himself as the "Great Pretender" (Mann, 2011). Talk about hiding in plain sight!

Sex Maniacs?

Another "monster" like stereotype is the idea that sexual offenders are sex maniacs that indiscriminately pursue targets, the idea of the creepy pedophile who will snatch up any child or animalistic offender who has no control over their lust. This concept of the offender underlies the defense that he "didn't do it to me/my kids," so is not a "real" sex offender. In at least three cases I have been involved with, the offender was acquitted because *he stopped* sexually assaulting the victim when her resistance was earnest enough. One offender had drugged the victim. When she jumped up to throw up as he was assaulting her, he stopped and went to help her. Another offender was digitally raping a victim while her toddler laid asleep on the floor beside the couch. When she finally yelled stop after trying to tell him in a whisper and pushing him away, he stopped. Another offender was penetrating the victim until she was able to get her legs up enough to push him off with her feet. He stopped raping her then. All these men admitted to what they were doing. All three claimed that they stopped when they realized the victim "really" meant no. All three were acquitted.

I believe that they were acquitted because no "real" rapist would stop or be able to control himself. "Real" sex offenders will use all opportunities to offend. "Real" dangerous offenders wouldn't stop. What the jury failed to see in all these cases was that the assault *was already in progress – it had already been committed*. A rape does not start when the offender stops. In combination with some of the other myths below, this portrayal of the offender was powerful enough to get him acquitted. They were not monsters.

The Mythos of False Allegations

"I'd say that it is a very scary time for young men in America, when you can be guilty of something that you may not be guilty of," said the then President of the United States Donald Trump, following multiple allegations against Brett Kavanagh of sexual misconduct (Bump, 2018). Trump's pronouncement reflects the conviction that false allegations are common and successful, resulting in the wrongful prosecution of innocent men. The #MeToo movement allowed tens of thousands of victims of sexual assault to disclose. Instead of resulting in greater awareness of sexual assault, the backlash has increased skepticism of victim disclosure (de Roos & Jones, 2020).

The belief that there is a high rate of false allegations of sexual assault has been repeatedly debunked by research. Despite this, the public, especially males and law enforcement, remains certain that victims are fabricating reports of assault at a very high rate (Huntington, Berkowitz, & Orchowski, 2020; McMillan, 2018). When the research is rigorous and informed, the rate of false allegations is consistently between 2% and 10% of the studied allegations (Lisak et al., 2010). False or fabricated allegations of sexual assault rates are similar to fabricated allegations of other crimes. Unfortunately, the trope of false allegations is common in the media, and, when it is believed to have happened, false allegations receive tremendous media attention. Stories about false allegations wrongly reinforce the idea that false allegations are common, which may have further-reaching effects. A recent study (de Roos & Jones, 2020) showed that when men were exposed to a story about false allegations, they were more likely to blame the victim and minimize the impact of sexual assault.

What has led to the belief that there are so many false allegations? In part, the research itself has contributed to this idea. When "false" allegations are not consistently defined, it can cause confusion. "False" allegations are fabricated allegations. However, some research labeled allegations as false under other conditions. When no investigation occurred, the allegations were labeled as false. If the victim recanted, the allegation were labeled as false. When the allegations were unfounded or unprovable, they were labeled false. If the victim did not cooperate with the investigation or prosecution or when a victim reported to some authority, but not to police or law enforcement (like campus police), these have been considered false. Not only are fabricated allegations rare, but they also are easy to detect, have similar features, and rarely make it through the criminal justice system (De Zutter, 2021; Newman, 2018). Allegations that are messy with confounding elements like consensual acts, reports of intimacy, and victim cooperation with the offender are more likely to be dismissed; yet, these messy facts are the elements that are associated with true allegations (De Zutter, 2021)!

The reality is that sexual assault is underreported. Fears of not being believed keep victims from reporting. Offenders deny very well. We are making another cognitive error by not believing victims – ignoring the base rate. The base rate of allegations suggests that about 95% of them are true. We need to treat allegations as we would anything else. We would undoubtedly investigate if we had a lump that the doctor said was 95% likely to be a problem.

"Boys Will Be Boys" and Myth of the Unmanageable Arousal

The man on the phone was urgently explaining to his wife why she saw him with his penis in their four-year-old daughter's mouth, catching him when she came home early from work. After bathing the kids, he insisted that he was wet and was changing his underwear when he was sexually surprised by the child. "So I turned around and I told her to get her stuff on and she grabbed it and put it in her mouth … I don't know – I just lost for a minute. I don't know, you know what I mean," he said. This offender fully expected his wife to believe that men "lose it for a minute" and are incapable of ration when a child touches their penis.

Sexual assault is not a natural result of male sexuality and arousal. However, offenders capitalize on this idea that excuses or mitigates male sexual aggression as "natural." Offenders would like us to believe that their arousal is unmanageable. They are unable to stop themselves once aroused. It is the responsibility of women and children to prevent male arousal. This belief is demeaning and limiting to men. Most men are not sexual offenders. No one has ever died from "blue balls."

"The Devil Made Him Do It" – The Fable of "It Wasn't Me"

"Hate the sin, not the sinner," said a father at the trial of his father, who sexually assaulted the grandchildren. This excuse, separating the deed from the doer, appears in many forms. It was an accident, a mistake, curiosity, a misunderstanding, or only one time. It was "out of character" or an impulse. These are simply excuses that try to separate the offender from the motivation and intention to offend. When we believe these excuses, we become blind to the offender's characteristics that serve as the impetus for their behavior and decision-making.

Curiosity and Impulse

It is vital to adhere to common sense when evaluating an offender's excuses. Curiosity can be genuine, but it only explains once. "I didn't know what it was," an online offender explained, "I just clicked the pop-up, and there was this video of two kids doing it." It seems reasonable, right? Until you read further and find that he was "curious" for months, downloaded and saved illegal material, and masturbated to the images. That is not curiosity. The same analysis is relevant when an offender describes something as an impulse. Think of your last impulse. An impulse always reflects something that we desire, like, or think we will like, something that serves us. We do not act impulsively to choose something we know we will hate. I buy stuff I like impulsively – I do not stick a fork in my eye impulsively.

It is always important to recognize a sexual assault as a choice or, more accurately, a series of choices that result in a sexual offense. They are not accidents. You don't trip into a child's vagina. A penis doesn't just fall out of someone's pants or into someone's mouth. All of our behavior reflects an aspect of our character, something that we have the potential for doing. Accepting and owning that is critical for self-management. Yet offenders will do their best to disavow their choices.

Alcohol and Sex Offending

This is true for the effect of alcohol on sexual offending as well. Drinking serves as a ready excuse for many offenders. Alcohol use is correlated with sexual assault for a variety of reasons. But it *does not cause* an offender to commit a sexual offense. Alcohol intoxication can decrease inhibitory controls. Inhibitory controls are those external factors that help us manage behavior, like fear of embarrassment or consequences. When we begin to lose sight of these controls, it is a phenomenon called alcohol myopia (Giancola et al., 2010). When we get "near-sighted" with alcohol and can only attend to our strongest urges or states, we do not attend to the inhibitory controls, making us more likely to act out on our urges.

Alcohol use makes a person at risk for sex offending at greater risk when he drinks. When an offender blames alcohol, he is saying that he cannot manage his otherwise controlled deviance or desires when he is intoxicated and has an opportunity to offend. Remember, a cause is a straight line to that event. Substance use might be a factor for an offender, but not a cause. Another factor is alcohol expectancies, or our expectations of how alcohol will affect us psychologically, socially, and behaviorally (Davis et al., 2013). We hold numerous expectations about how alcohol impacts sexual arousal, sexual behavior, and sexual availability. If we have the expectation that we are more social when we drink, we become more social. The most important link between expectancies and sexual offending is the idea that someone drinking is less responsible for his poor behavior. If we believe drunk people are less responsible for bad acts, offenders can use this as a way to mitigate culpability. Finally, a victim is more likely to be blamed for a sexual assault when she was drinking, both by others and herself (Grubb & Turner, 2012). Offenders are aware of being able to "blame the booze" and be held less accountable for their crimes. This is so successful that I have seen offenders ordered to AA or substance abuse treatment instead of sex offender or batterer's treatment.

The Fiction of Low Self-Esteem, Immaturity, or Sexual Deprivation

"If we could just pay a prostitute to come in and show these boys what sex is," the psychologist said to a stunned group of us during a training. She promoted the myth that sexually aggressive adolescents and men could be fixed if they just got "fucked the right way." There is a persistent notion that sexual inadequacy, low self-esteem, social immaturity, or sexual deprivation are root causes for sexual offending. People thought the "cure" for pedophilic priests was to allow them to be married. "When his wife went through menopause, she lost her sexual desire," the evaluator wrote (paraphrased), "Out of loneliness and frustration, Mr. Jones turned to his stepdaughter. He did not want to cheat on his wife." In an article for *The Daily Mail* in 2017, Dr. Catherine Hakim wrote about the dangers of "sex-starved" men who are compelled to commit sexual assaults, something their wives caused by withholding sex.

Most of the offenders I have treated or evaluated had appropriate sexual partners or had access to other appropriate sexual partners. Sexual deprivation was *never* the issue that drove an offender to offend a child or commit rape of an adult. More accurate is that the offender became so involved with and aroused by the deviant arousal that he could no longer be satisfied sexually by an appropriate partner. The offender withheld sex because he was unable to be aroused. "Yeah, I still had sex with my girlfriend," Scott said, "But mostly after I would touch her daughter. Then I would get aroused and like, go masturbate in [his girlfriend's] vagina." Scott was always fantasizing about the victim when having sex with his lover. Troy said when he was deep into his offending, his sex life with his wife improved. "I would say it got better," he explained, describing his increased level of arousal and fantasy life.

Offenders will blame their "low self-esteem" for why they assaulted their victim. Therapists and others will buy this excuse. Some offenders say they are shy or anxious. Some say they are inadequate, "scared" of women, or have "intimacy deficits. Again, I will ask you to think through the validity of some of these assertions. It is essential to differentiate between what *causes* or motivates a sexual offender to offender versus the state an offender is in when he presents himself to treatment, especially after being caught and facing consequences. An offender might present as depressed, suicidal, or anxious only after he is discovered. This is not necessarily a reflection of who he was when he was offending.

Let's examine the idea that offenders are motivated to offend because they have "low self-esteem." Often that catchphrase is ill-defined and taken at face value. Self-esteem is a fluid concept, a state, not a trait. It is defined at least in part by the context. For instance, a victim might have great esteem as a student but feel terrible about herself as a girl or woman. Victims' self-esteem issues are generally *preyed upon* by offenders. Low self-esteem is characterized by a poor feeling of worth and value, a lack of confidence, overvaluing others while undervaluing oneself. It is NOT associated with entitlement, valuation of one's rights over others, and taking what does not belong to you from others.

To violate and manipulate a victim for self-gratification, an offender has to feel entitled. A feeling of inadequacy or that the world is not making you feel good about yourself might lead to the idea that you deserve to feel better and will make yourself feel better at the expense of others. This is not low self-esteem. It is a result of narcissistic depletion leading to the right to self-indulgence. An offender might not have the power, influence, or admiration he thinks he deserves. It might be too difficult to impress an adult or fulfill the responsibilities of a healthy relationship. This is immaturity but does not cause sex offending. Offenders have intimacy issues, but offending necessitates secrecy and duplicity that destroy intimacy. "It was a bad time for me," explained an offender who abused his stepdaughter, "Me and my wife were fighting all the time. I thought she was cheating. I just wanted someone to love me." Steve explained in detail how he created intimacy issues in order to have the space to offend. He began going to bed and getting up at a different time than his girlfriend. He would be vague about telling his friends where he was going or what he was doing. It is very important to specifically assess the esteem and intimacy issues in the context of the offending and not as the cause.

The idea of offending because someone feels badly about himself does not have logic. First, I am not sure how it improves anyone's self-esteem to choose to become a child sex offender. Second, self-indulgence, power, and the ability to manipulate a child and retaliate against a partner might make you feel better, but not because you are addressing your low self-esteem. It is more about gaining power, "getting over," and self-gratification. Finally, the timing of when the offender professes to have low self-esteem is important. They will offer this explanation after they are caught and facing consequences. Or offer it when they are in treatment and benefit from a sympathetic therapist interested in bolstering them so they feel better about themselves.

The link between esteem and aggression is complicated. The connection between aggression and self-esteem, either high or low, is not consistently found in the literature. One recent study showed that lower esteem helped prevent aggression following narcissistic provocation (Hart et al., 2019). Boldness, something characteristic in many (if not all) sexual offenses, is correlated with narcissism and higher esteem (Miller et al., 2019). People with high narcissism and low esteem related to perceived rejection are more likely to endorse sexual coercion (Lamarche & Seery, 2019). I have found the problem to be the offenders' narcissism (discussed more later) than their self-esteem. As Abraham Lincoln said, "When I do good, I feel good. When I do bad, I feel bad. That is my religion."

"He Is Crazy/Sick/Sex Addicted" – The Myth
of Mental Illness and Sexual Offending

When the public thinks of mental illness, we generally think of those disorders that disrupt the ability to function and perceive reality, like psychotic disorders or serious mood disorders. We do not generally think of paraphilic disorders or personality disorders. However, we readily ascribe the words "crazy" or "sick" to people who engage in behaviors that we cannot understand, like sexually abusing children or engaging in violent sexual crimes. In discussing mental illness in sexual offenders, it is essential to differentiate between the presence of a diagnosable disorder and the culpability or ability to form intent for behavior. In that context, it is important to understand a disorder as a factor in sexual offending, rarely a cause.

"They came yesterday with the fridge," he exclaimed, "I just wanted a new microwave too!" A group home resident with schizophrenia described why he was arrested for indecent exposure. He was caught for openly masturbating on the front yard of his group home. He had the magical belief that because he was masturbating when the appliance was delivered, he made it happen. This is an example of when an active acute mental illness causes a sexual offense. This is rare. The offense was not characterized by instrumental choices to groom a victim, keep the offending secret, cover-up and protect the offending, or engage in secretive offending for a prolonged period. Another person in a full-blown manic state ran around a baseball field naked, where children were playing softball. He was immediately caught. He was having delusions about being a famous player and the magical powers of his nudity. An unmanaged psychotic or mood disorder *in a person with a history of sexual aggression* will raise the risk of recidivism. But that is the key to the relationship between major mental illness and sexual offending and violence – it makes aggressive people more at risk for further aggression. In and of itself, acute mental illness is not a common cause of violence.

Many sexual offenders have other disorders, like substance abuse disorders, mood disorders, anxiety disorders, or attention-deficit disorders. These disorders might be factors that affect an individual's decision-making, impulse control, or emotional regulation, contributing to risk factors for offending. They must be addressed in treatment and management. However, none of these concurrent disorders are to blame for the sexual offending. An evaluator must carefully evaluate whether the disorder pre-existed the consequences of offending though; many offenders get depressed when caught and anxious when they are lying.

Some sexual offenders have a diagnosable disorder according to the DSM-5 (American Psychological Association [APA], 2013) that is directly related to their offense behavior. These disorders are related to the offenders' motivation to offend. Some personality disorders and paraphilic disorders are directly related to the sexual victimization of others. These are the disorders underlying civil commitment and sexually violent predator laws. I will discuss these later in this book.

Another "explanation" for sexual offending is sex "addiction." Sex addiction is not a diagnosis in the DSM-5 (APA, 2013) but has been a term used to describe individuals who engaged in excessive sexual behavior. This sexual behavior is more accurately described in ICD-11 (World Health Organization [WHO], 2019) as "compulsive," characterized by sexual preoccupation, problematic and less discriminate sexual choices (like infidelity), and excessive masturbation to the degree an individual's functioning is impaired. It is not associated with sexual offending, nor does it cause sexual offending. If someone with a propensity to harm others sexually or with deviant arousal that involves victimization becomes sexually preoccupied and sexually dysregulated, that person will be at risk of targeting a victim of choice. When engaged in the course of their sexual offending, many offenders become sexually preoccupied, masturbating and fantasizing often, sometimes obsessed with their victim or their offending. This preoccupation is a result of being invested in and reinforcing their arousal. These offenders do not have a disorder that causes the behavioral problem. The behavioral problem results in the compulsive disorder. The danger of focusing on the addiction is that this focus conveys the message that the problem is outside the offender's locus of control or agency, as opposed to the offender's choices and motivation to offend. When a person addicted to heroin relapses, she uses the drug again. When a sexual offender rapes a child, it is not the same type of "relapse."

"That's Not His Type" – The Problem with Typologies

Richard was a stereotypical pedophile aroused to boys, preferably between 10 and 12 years old. He worked in a carnival, where he would meet boys, lure them into a meeting, and assault them by sucking their penises. He also would grope children's genitals while lifting them onto rides. He had countless victims. Richard was difficult to work with but began making progress in treatment. He cleaned up. He got a job. He stopped wearing clothes that would attract children that we had to confiscate. He was doing so well the treatment team assigned Richard to help a new group member, a younger adult man who had trouble reading. Richard sexually assaulted this man when the man fell asleep on Richard's couch. Richard taught me two lessons. When he was confronted in prison about how "good" he was doing in treatment and asked why he reoffended, Richard made it clear that he always "cleaned up" before offending, reminding us that no one would come near him when he looked unkempt and poor. Richard also explained that, despite his professed disgust for adults, he would exploit any opportunity when he was motivated to offend, even if his preference was not available. "Any port in the storm," Richard said. We failed in managing Richard because we were managing him by victim type, not his sexual offending patterns and ability to transgress boundaries.

Typologies of sexual offenders have defined categories of offenders and offensive behavior in an attempt to classify offenders. Some of the ways that typologies classify offenders are by their victim choice (child versus adult, boy versus girl), their offense behavior (rapist versus molester), or their relationship to the victim (family/incest versus extra familiar). There are many problems with typologies. They are simply unreliable. While typologies may capture an offender's preferences, means of offending they are comfortable with, and some of what gratifies them, offenders are a highly heterogeneous group (Wojcik & Fisher, 2019). Research has been unable to capture the individualistic nature of the sexual offender.

Additionally, some research relies on characteristics of the known offense or what the offender was convicted of, not what the offender has actually done. It is well known that the self-report of offenders is unreliable and that most offenders have committed far more and varied types of offending than what is documented. When polygraphed on sexual history, sexual offenders consistently report more victims, more types of offenses, and more sources of deviance than their records or self-report demonstrate (Grubin, 2008; Jung et al., 2021). Crossover offenses, which vary in victim age, gender, and relationships, are common in offenders, contradicting the belief that offenders are stable in their choice of victim choice or preferences (Heil et al., 2003).

Failure to understand these facts leads to poor decision-making in treating and managing offenders. Unfortunately, I have seen and made this error time and time again, relying on "types" to protect victims. Offenders who assault one child are allowed to parent another. Before an offender is known to the treatment people or supervising agents, decisions about contact with potentially vulnerable people are allowed. It is critical to see an offender's full potential for deviance, or at least as close as we can, and understand the offending dynamics and arousal to non-sexual stimuli, like violence, power, or cruelty, when making treatment interventions and management decisions.

I have worked with offenders aroused to domination who have adult, child, male, female, and animal victims. The same is true for those aroused to cruelty. Bob was sent to treatment for sexually assaulting his daughter after his wife died. She was 14 when it started. She had a younger sister. Bob was cruel man. On all assessment tools, he was deemed low risk and needed minimal supervision. He had no known criminal history. He assaulted a family victim with secondary sex characteristics. The problem was is that no one knew him. Through treatment, we found that he had assaulted his daughter after bringing her into his bed, making her sleep in his bedroom on her dead mother's side of the bed. He would force the child to do things to him sexually to feed her little sister. Bob pretended to go into the woods to shoot himself when she would resist. He was too miserly to buy his wife pain medication while she was dying of cancer, so would split her pain medication into thirds to dole out. He did not get her medical treatment for her radiation burns on her breasts but photographed them and displayed them for the children to see, along the picture of their mother in her casket. He read the Bible at the table with a gun. He was heartless and manipulative. Bob bought the book *Courage to Heal,* professing that it was to gain empathy. He would masturbate to stories of the victims' suffering. His only comment about abusing his daughter was, "At least she won't forget me." Get to know each offender for who he is, not what typology he fits into neatly.

"Hurt People Hurt People" – The Problem of the Victimized Victimizer

The term "hurt people hurt people" has been overused by offenders to justify their behavior and activate our empathy. It is true that trauma dramatically impacts interpersonal functioning, sometimes resulting in reactive aggression, destructive behavior, and a propensity for callousness. It is also true that sexually abused children show more sexualized, sexually reactive, and sexually aggressive behavior. These behaviors tend to disappear as the child ages. Most sexually aggressive youth do not become adult offenders (Lobanov-Rostovsky, n.d.), even if many adult sexual offenders begin offending as adolescents. Studies suggest that adult male sexual offenders have been sexually abused somewhat more often than males generally, around a third of them instead of 20% of adult males (Glasser et al., 2001). While there is a link between adverse childhood experiences to other issues, there is not an established strong link between abuse and sexual offending (Kahn et al., 2021).

It is important not to see the sexual offender primarily through the lens of victimization for several reasons. First, offenders lie about being abused. Anna Salter (2003), in her book *Predators*, addresses this issue directly. She writes, "The offender who claims he himself was a victim gets seen as less of a 'monster' than one who wasn't a victim, and he gains much more empathy and support" (p. 73). Second, we often see people as victims because we refuse to see them as perpetrators, refusing to accept who they are and hold them accountable. We see them as victims for ourselves, selfishly, so we can care for and value them. Third, seeing the offender as a victim reinforces their sense of victimization and persecution, helping them feel unfairly and unjustly punished for their behavior, making intervention and accountability more difficult. Finally, if the offender is a victim of abuse and this trauma is addressed first in treatment, the therapist may create a risk situation. The offender might not have the tools to understand and cope with trauma, leaving treatment feeling vulnerable, weak, angry, and disempowered. Individuals who seek to resolve these feelings destructively are at risk for problematic, possibly victimizing behaviors.

We should respect all trauma. However, we must hold the offender accountable first, eradicating the justifications he used to hurt someone else. This is healing for the offender who is a victim as well – no excuses for offending applies to the offender and his offender the same, relieving that offender from the blame of his victimization.

Myth: Consent Is Too Complicated

"No means yes. Yes means anal." This was a chant heard on the Yale campus in October 2010 (Bonus, 2010). You can still buy a t-shirt online with the chant as of March 2022. "No means yes. Yes means harder" memes fill the Internet. There persists a myth that consent is complicated. Acceptance of this myth has led to continual issues involving "mistake of fact as to consent," a legal argument that posits that the offender misunderstood, accidentally, or unintentionally sexually assaulted the victim. This myth attempts to shift the burden onto the victim to resist "enough" to be clear or to reject any advances vociferously. Again, the offender is not held accountable for not getting consent or for overriding resistance, either physically or psychologically, by persuasion, coercion, intoxication, or other means.

Consent is not and should not be confusing. As John Oliver (2015) said, "Because sex is like boxing. If both people didn't fully agree to participate, one of them is committing a crime."

Offenders use the issue of consent in many ways to manipulate the victim and others into believing that the sexual assault was an accident or a result of miscommunication. If a victim once consented, offenders assume ongoing consent. This is one of the things that complicate sexual assault in a relationship as if saying yes once eliminates the right to say no. Offenders have argued that prior consent explains sexual assault when the victim is asleep, intoxicated, or not interested. The offender justifies assault if he feels entitled to the partner or act. "Well, we talked about it once – she said she would try it," explained an offender who anally raped his girlfriend. Suppose a victim was "making out" with the offender before throwing up and passing out. In that case, the offender could use this prior involvement to explain the sexual assault, as Brock Turner and so many others have. The idea that "anything short of a firm no is a 'yes' or 'keep at it'," something Schwyzer (2011) calls "male legalism," is a real problem. And it impacts victims as well as the entire criminal justice system. Even therapists fall prey to this myth.

We have to remember some issues about the idea that consent is complicated. There is miscommunication between sexual partners. Sometimes, men and women have sex when they are not really into it. This is not rape or assault if there is no coercion, force, or fear. These cases are not before us – they are cases for discussion and self-reflection. Even though offenders present as confused or mistaken about consent, they rarely are. They can identify the coercive or manipulative techniques they used – the emotional blackmail, bribery, grooming, isolation, or induction of fear. They know the force they use but just lie about it. They know when the victim is unconscious. The offenders I have worked with can identify their victims' resistance, despite professing that the victim did not resist. But they have to be asked. In our survey, 19% of the offenders acknowledged that their victim "tried to talk them out of it." Another 37% said that the victim tried to avoid them, pretended to be asleep, or acted physically passive, doing things like turning their heads. These subtle types of resistance are things that the offenders ignore but do not report. Victims do not think that these acts qualify as resistance.

Consent is not complicated. I demonstrate this in trainings by approaching a participant and taking her cellphone. I tap on the home button. Sometimes I push it farther, telling her to give me her unlock code. It becomes very uncomfortable. There is never the presumption that I can pick up and use someone's phone without permission. Why is there the presumption that someone can sexually touch another person without the explicit affirmation of that act? This is not about leaning in for a kiss or making the first approach to someone you are attracted to, as some would like to portray sexual assault. As Sara C. (2018) writes, men are not such "bumblers" as to not understand that they are committing a sexual assault. This idea goes back to the myth that all men are capable of and willing to commit sexual assault. It seems that what we have a problem with is confusing the difference between implication and consent (Valliere, 2008). The offenders can distort the perceived implication of sexual interest into consent and participation. This distortion can become so profound that offenders who abuse small children will claim that the child was consenting and the aggressor. A repeat offender of children wrote in his confession (transcribed as he wrote it),

> Then she pulled her pants down and told me to due [sic] her. But I didn't, then she put my hand on her. I told her I couldn't due her because she was to [sic] young. She said I might as well that it would be the last I ever will have. So like a nut I eat her out.

Summary

As humans, we love to make sense of things, especially behaviors we cannot understand. We apply concepts and connections that are familiar, that superficially make sense. We attribute motives and explanations flawed and inaccurately, replete with assumptions and projections. Our inaccuracy at understanding others increases as we are less familiar with the issues. Very few of us understand deviance or understand what motivates someone to commit a sexual assault. It is hard to imagine being gratified by harming someone sexually. Our error rate in attributing motive and causes is very high.

In conclusion:

- Myths cloud our judgment and true understanding of sexual offending and sexual offenders. Believing misinformation can have serious consequences, hinder cases and investigations, and result in bad judgments.
- Offenders utilize these myths readily, sometimes interchangeably depending on the victim and the circumstances. If we don't buy that the victim consented, we will hear that he was drunk too. If that does not work, he was confused, depressed, or just does not understand how he could do such a thing.
- Acute mental illness does not cause sexual offending. There are diagnosable disorders that can serve as the impetus for offending, but these are chronic and pervasive conditions, like personality disorders or paraphilic disorders. Unmanaged mental illness in those individuals who are at risk for committing a sexual assault can add risk issues. However, the most important thing to remember about mental illness is that it is much more highly associated with being victimized. Up to 40% of women with mental illness have been sexually assaulted.
- Being educated, challenging myths, and not reacting emotionally in evaluating sexual offenders or assault allegations will decrease our error rates.
- Remember to rely on your common sense instead of getting distracted by your other needs, including a lack of understanding of deviance.

References

American Psychiatric Association (2013). *Diagnostic and statistical manual of mental disorders* (5th ed.). https://doi.org/10.1176/appi.books.9780890425596

Bonus, A. (2010, October 18). Fraternity pledges' chant raises concerns at Yale. *CNN*. https://www.cnn.com/2010/US/10/18/connecticut.yale.frat.chant/index.html

Bump, P. (2018, October 2). Trump says it's a 'very scary time' for young men – but that women are 'doing great.' *Washington Post*. https://www.washingtonpost.com/politics/2018/10/02/trump-says-its-very-scary-time-young-men-that-women-are-doing-great/

Davis, K., Kaysen, D., Gilmore, A., & Schraufnagel, T. (2013). Alcohol and sexual violence. In P. Miller (Ed.), *Principles of addiction*. Academic Press.

de Roos, M., & Jones, D. (2020). Empowerment or threat: Perceptions of childhood sexual abuse in the #MeToo era. *Journal of Interpersonal Violence*, 37(7–8), NP4212–NP4237. https://doi.org/10.1177/0886260520925781

de Roos, M., & Jones, D. (2020). Self-affirmation and false allegations: The effects on responses to disclosures of sexual victimization. *Journal of Interpersonal Violence*, 1–24. https://doi.org/10.1177/0886260520980387

De Zutter, A. (2021). True and false allegations of rape. In N. Deslauriers-Varin & C. Bennell (Eds.), *Criminal investigations of sexual offenses: Techniques and challenges*. Springer.

DiBennardo, R. (2018). Ideal victims and monstrous offenders: How the news media represent sexual predators. *Socius*. https://doi.org/10.1177/2378023118802512

Giancola, P., Josephs, R., Parrott, D., & Duke, A. (2010). Alcohol myopia revisited: Clarifying aggression and other acts of disinhibition through a distorted lens. *Perspectives on Psychological Science*, 5(3), 265–278. https://doi.org/10.1177/1745691610369467

Glasser, M., Kolvin, I., Campbell, D., Glasser, A., Leitch, I., & Farrelly, S. (2001). Cycle of child sexual abuse: Links between being a victim and becoming a perpetrator. *Br J Psychiatry*, 179, 482–494. https://doi.org/10.1192/bjp.179.6.482

Grubb, A., & Turner, E. (2012). Attribution of blame in rape cases: A review of the impact of rape myth acceptance, gender role conformity and substance use on victim blaming. *Aggression and Violent Behavior*, 17(5), 443–452.

Grubin, D. (2008). The case for polygraph testing of sex offenders. *Legal and Criminological Psychology*, 13(2), 177–189

Hakim, C. (2017). Academic who says wives who deprive husbands of sex are wrecking society. Reward chaps for doing the washing up! *Daily Mail*. https://www.dailymail.co.uk/femail/article-4228560/Hidden-toll-starved-sex-husbands.html

Hare, R. D. (2003). *The hare psychopathy checklist–revised* (2nd ed.). Multi-Health Systems.

Hart, W., Richardson, K., & Breeden, C. (2019). An interactive model of narcissism, self-esteem, and provocation extent on aggression. *Personality and Individual Differences*, 145, 112–118. https://doi.org/10.1016/j.paid.2019.03.032

Heil, P., Ahlmeyer, S., & Simons, D. (2003). Crossover sexual offenses. *Sexual Abuse: A Journal of Research and Treatment*, 15(4), 221–236. https://doi.org/10.1177/107906320301500401

Howley, K. (2018, November 19). Everyone believed Larry Nassar. The predatory trainer may have just taken down USA Gymnastics. How did he deceive so many for so long? *New York*. https://www.thecut.com/2018/11/how-did-larry-nassar-deceive-so-many-for-so-long.html

Huntington, C., Berkowitz, A., & Orchowski, L. (2020). False Accusations of sexual assault: Prevalence, misperceptions, and implications for prevention work with men and boys. https://www.researchgate.net/publication/343240574_False_Accusations_of_Sexual_Assault_Prevalence_Misperceptions_and_Implications_for_Prevention_Work_with_Men_and_Boys

Jung, S. H., Jin, M. J., Lee, J. K., Kim, H. S., & Ji, H. et al. (2021). Correction: Improving the quality of sexual history disclosure on sex offenders: Emphasis on a polygraph examination. *PLoS One*, 16(8), https://doi.org/10.1371/journal.pone.0256993

Kahn, R., Jackson, K., Keiser, K., Ambroziak, G., & Levenson, J. (2021). Adverse childhood experiences among sexual offenders: Associations with sexual recidivism risk and psychopathology. *Sexual Abuse*, 33(7), 839–866. https://doi.org/10.1177/1079063220970031

Kesicky, D., Andre, I., & Kesicka, M. (2014). Pedophiles and (or) child molesters. *European Psychiatry, 29*(1), I. https://doi.org/10.1016/S0924-9338(14)77731-4

Lamarche, V., & Seery, M. (2019). Come on, give it to me baby: Self-esteem, narcissism, and endorsing sexual coercion following rejection. *Personality and Individual Differences, 149*, 315–325. https://doi.org/10.1016/j.paid.2019.05.060

Lisak, D., Gardinier, L., Nicksa, S., & Cote, A. (2010). False allegations of sexual assault: An analysis of ten years of reported cases. *Violence against Woman, 16*(12), 1318–1334. https://doi.org/10.1177/1077801210387747

Lobanov-Rostovsky, C. (n.d.). *Chapter 3: Recidivism of juveniles who commit sex offenses* [Report Sex Offender Management Assessment and Planning Initiative]. Office of Sex Offender Sentencing, Monitoring, Apprehending, Registering, and Tracking (SMART). https://smart.ojp.gov/somapi/chapter-3-recidivism-juveniles-who-commit-sexual-offenses

Manfred, R. (2011, November 16). *10 Deeply disturbing pre-scandal quotes about Jerry Sandusky. Business Insider.* https://www.businessinsider.com/jerry-sandusky-quotes-2011-11

Mann, T. (2011, November 19). Jerry Sandusky called himself "The Great Pretender." *The Atlantic.* https://www.theatlantic.com/national/archive/2011/11/jerry-sandusky-called-himself-great-pretender/335272/

McMillan, L. (2018). Police officers' perception s of false allegations of rape. *Journal of Gender Studies, 27*, 9–21. https://doi.org/10.1080/09589236.2016.1194260

Miller, J. D., Sleep, C. E., Crowe, M. L., & Lynam, D. R. (2019). Psychopathic boldness: Narcissism, self-esteem, or something in between? https://doi.org/10.31234/osf.io/5mfyr

Newman, S. (2018, September 18). *I've studied false rape claims. The accusation against kavanaught doesn't fit the profile.* Vox. https://www.vox.com/first-person/2018/9/18/17874504/kavanaugh-assault-allegation-christine-blasey-ford

Oliver, J. (2015, August 10). *Sex education: Last week tonight* [Video]. YouTube. https://www.youtube.com/watch?v=L0jQz6jqQS0

Salter, A. (2003). *Predators: Pedophiles, rapists, and other sex offenders.* Basic Books.

Sara, C. (2018, January 15). *On bumbling men, consent, and the myth of the "accidental" rapist.* Medium. https://medium.com/@QSE/on-bumbling-men-consent-and-the-myth-of-the-accidental-rapist-f325374f4fc0

Schwyzer, H. (2011, September 16). *The accidental rapist.* The Good Men Project. https://goodmenproject.com/featured-content/the-accidental-rapist/

Seto, M. C., Harris, G. T., & Lalumière, M. L. (2016). Psychopathy and sexual offending. In C. B. Gacono (Ed.), *The clinical and forensic assessment of psychopathy: A practitioner's guide* (pp. 403–418). Routledge/Taylor & Francis Group.

Valliere, V. (2008, January 29). Consent shouldn't confuse in non-stranger rape cases. *The Morning Call.* https://www.mcall.com/news/mc-xpm-2008-01-29-3972941-story.html

Wojcik, M., & Fisher, B. (2019). Overview of adult sexual offender typologies. In W. O'Donohue & P. Schewe (Eds.), *Handbook of sexual assault and sexual assault prevention.* Springer.

World Health Organization (2019). *International statistical classification of diseases and related health problems* (11th ed.). https://icd.who.int/

Chapter 4

"I Know Him – He's Not Like That"
The Struggle to Believe

"I was the all-around good guy in the neighborhood," Shawn said. "So, I guess no one really believed it when you were caught," I commented. He responded, "No, nobody did. Even as much as, uh, the deputy police chief." We struggle to believe that anyone we "know" could be a sex offender. "It was a double life – the great guy that everybody knew. I went to the judge with a stack of letters – 'please don't send him away! You don't know him like we know him,'" said Brandon, an offender with images of child sex abuse. The Internet is replete with statements of people struggling to navigate the complexities of the impact of the relationship on our perception of sexual offenders. "He's NOT a sex offender," wrote Anonymous on *Quora,* "Yes, he has the label. But he's not predatory. He just made a stupid mistake and has been paying for it for the past almost 17 years." Anonymous believed the victim lied about her age. Another writer FranklinV on the same site asserts, "Most people on the sex offender registry are guilty of 'crimes' like taking a pee on the side of the road. A startlingly small number of people on the list are there for actual violent crimes."

Sex offenders are monsters – vile people we could never like or love. Right? That would be easier and make us safer. But the problematic fact is sexual offenders are more like us than not like us. This does not mean we "know" them. Most offenders are significantly invested in not being known because being known will make them accountable. In my program, 80% of the offenders surveyed admitted that they relied on the idea "I knew people would not think I was 'like that'" to deny their offense behavior successfully. What makes our disbelief about people we think we know so readily available for exploitation?

Public, Private, and Secret Selves

We all have a public self, a private self, and a secret self. Many of us are open and consistent, with the variance between public and private or secret selves minimal. We all have secret thoughts or opinions that we do not share or personal thoughts and behaviors that we only show to the few or one person closest to us. The levels of self-expression we engage in depend on a few things – how accountable we want to be, the damage we can do to others, shame or fear of judgment, or how we wish to protect our behavior. Somehow, we forget this fact when it comes to a sexual offender.

"You are only as sick as your secrets" is a well-known adage in Alcoholics Anonymous, capturing the idea that the person cannot hide the addiction or related behavior to have genuine recovery. Imagine that the secret is extremely sexually gratifying, subject to significant judgment from society, and relies on duplicity and a lack of accountability to flourish. Sexual offending is not just a private behavior. It is a secret behavior, known entirely only to the offender. The victims may share the secret but do not know its full definition and expression.

DOI: 10.4324/9781003156284-6

Offenders live double, even triple lives. They hide from everyone in their lives, destroying true intimacy while presenting as "nice," open, honest, misunderstood, unlucky, or unfortunate. They have an excellent capacity for presenting themselves in a prosocial way. Shawn explains it well. He began sexually abusing children as a teenager himself, peeping on girls, taking them to isolated areas to sexually coerce them with threats of abandoning them in the woods, and sexually abusing his girlfriend's young daughters, ages 12 and 14. He said,

> To me, it was the same thing. Everything was secretive. You know, my girlfriend was sleeping. The kids were sleeping. I was the only person awake in the house. I would, you know, sneak about, you know, feed my deviancy. And then, when the sun come up, I was, you know, Shawn, the good guy in the neighborhood. Shawn's a great guy, but he drinks too much.

Shawn was eventually reported and convicted for one assault, touching the victim on the breast while she slept. He had assaulted the children hundreds of times. The oldest decided to report him when Shawn escalated and assaulted her when she was not asleep (or pretending to be). She got scared when he digitally penetrated her during the day, going to school the next day and telling about one nighttime assault. In her documentary *Truth, Lies, and Sex Offenders* (1996), Anna Salter revealed the offenders' double life, further discussing it in her book (2003). Despite the popularity of true crime, despite knowing that offenders rely on duplicity, we continue to deny that the offender WE know is "like that."

What makes us blind to the fact that we truly "know" very few people? Why do we prefer to believe that the offender we know is really on the sexual offender registry for "peeing on the side of the road" or because the girl "lied about her age," when these are both rare events that result in a sexual offense conviction? According to the public sentiment, "most" people on the sexual offender registry are not "real" sexual offenders and have been caught in a broad and meaningless net – look at threads related to sexual offender registries or dating a sex offender. The Internet is full of endless defenses of offenders, men who have been wrongly punished for "just one picture," public urination, being 19, and dating a 16-year-old, or a false allegation. The contrived massive numbers of falsely identified sex offenders are just not real. I have evaluated thousands of sexual offenders and treated hundreds. It only takes some challenging and educated questioning to reveal information closer to the truth. The urinating against a tree in the park was public masturbating next to a high school running track. The accidental downloading of one illegal image was a collection of hundreds of images saved to the subject's phone. The unfortunate mistake of online chatting with a victim who was 13 but lied about her age was a several months' long enticement by the offender who sent pictures of his penis and lured the girl (who said her age repeatedly) to a meeting.

A secret life, or double life, exists in all of us. The secret life of the offender takes more effort, as their secret is precious to them, worth vigorously protecting. A secret life affords the offender control, a lack of accountability, and an absence of judgment. As Dr. Carter (2020) states in his video about secret selves, "The more I let you know who I am, the less I can be who I want to be." It is important to accept an offender's investment in their deviance. They protect it for many reasons. As wikiHow (2021) outlines, keeping a double life requires keeping quiet, being extra professional/prosocial, being cautious about what information is shared, and addressing concerns and conflicts quickly. This is intuitive to the offender. Most of our surveyed offenders (74%) kept quiet, private, and isolated. Most were helpful or "nice." Our offender clients are often solicitous, volunteering to meet their parole officer anytime, or go to the office to save time. These behaviors, including the offender who immediately starts telling everyone about a problem or accusation, give the offender control. Control of information and others, especially others' perceptions, is a way to protect the secret life. Remember these things when you think you "know" someone.

"Stranger Danger" Myth – The Impact of a Relationship on Denial

Even though most victims of sexual assault are assaulted by someone they know, we continue to overestimate the danger of strangers and underestimate the threat and risk of people we know. In general, women fear being sexually assaulted by a stranger as opposed to an acquaintance (Dos Santos, 2021; Scott, 2003; Wilcox et al., 2006). Parents fear that a stranger will pose a risk to their children instead of someone known. Sex offender registries and restrictions are appealing because they ostensibly protect the unknowing from the dangerous stranger.

A relationship is the best avenue to sexual offending. It is the path to love, trust, hope, and denial. An offender in a relationship with a victim has access to the victim and excuses for the allegations. What stranger rapist can claim that the victim is making accusations because of jealousy, custody issues, or because she was grounded? What stranger offender can tell the child's mother it was an "accident" during bath time or that he was "just wrestling?" It is critical to understand that a relationship with the offender serves the offender very well, not just in terms of getting access to victims but in terms of being protected by the audience.

An offender needs to groom the audience as much as he needs to groom the victim. Grooming is a term used to describe the process of preparing the victim to be a victim – to comply with the offense, protect the offender, and maintain an attachment to the offender despite the negative aspects of the offending. The exact process goes on with the offender's community. The offender grooms the audience through his relationships, building currency he can exchange for denial and protection. Suppose we are the offender's helpers, like his therapist or supervising agent. In that case, that currency is exchanged for our trust, investment in the offender, and unwillingness to see the offender clearly because we "know him." The offender engages in the same process with us as he does the victim and demands the same exchange. The offenders understand all the benefits the relationship affords. As one explained,

> Well, I knew my wife loved me. We had children. She had invested ten years in our relationship. No one wants to, you know, no one's going to jump to the first conclusion that 'this guy's offending – he is a sex offender.' She wanted to believe the best of me. She would not want to believe that she had been tricked. You know, uh, putting myself in her shoes now – you know, I would feel – I would feel dumb.

He added, "You know this person is invested. You know they are not going to want to believe the worst because then they would question themselves and blame themselves."

When we have a relationship with an individual, we presume to know how the person thinks and feels. We feel an affiliation to strangers who seem familiar (New York University, 2018) and discount facts or overlook reason to maintain affiliation (Sloman & Fernbach, 2017). Our ability to ignore facts may be related to an evolutionary need for cooperation and collaboration (Sloman & Fernbach, 2017). This can lead to dangerous errors – underestimating the risk of offenders we treat, failing to demand safeguards or restrictions for offenders we know or supervise, and disregarding signs that things are not as they seem. Especially if our own needs are being met by maintaining the alliance with the offender, we can explain away issues easily. Think of the needs the offender can fulfill for us. A therapist who feels incompetent can be reinforced by the offender who is "doing great." An over-worked probation officer can be untaxed by the compliant, helpful offender who regularly goes to work and therapy. An offender's wife can be groomed by a considerate, pleasant offender who does not demand sex. Offenders are keenly aware of the unspoken exchanges we make for affiliation.

Familiarity with the offender can provide a false sense of knowing as well. The "illusion of explanatory depth" is our overconfidence about our knowledge of things familiar to us (Sloman & Fernbach, 2017). Unless challenged, we feel confident we understand something in the world around us. When it comes to offenders we know, this is true as well. Regularly, I will hear vague explanations for behaviors or situations I find suspect in my work with offenders. "Oh, he's always like that, it doesn't mean anything," "he doesn't really understand that stuff," "his English isn't very good," "you make him nervous," or many other excuses well-meaning individuals offer who think they know the offender in question. Jerry Sandusky was viewed as "someone that goofed around with Second Mile kids all the time in public" (Gladwell, 2019). Even when colleagues thought he had "a boundary issue" with boys and cautioned him to wear shorts in the shower, they still did not truly believe the allegations against him (Gladwell, 2019).

As discussed earlier, empathy requires information about another's perspective, not utilizing our viewpoint. An interesting study revealed that even when subjects believed they knew the person whose perspective they were taking (e.g., spouse), the subjects were inaccurate at understanding the other person (Eyal et al., 2018). The study showed that interpersonal inaccuracy was present in predicting lying, activity preferences, emotions from body postures, and other areas when the predictor relied on old information instead of seeking new information. Given the inexperience, unfamiliarity, and denial of deviance and malintent in others most people have, it is easy to see how "knowing" the offender can be more blinding than not knowing.

Finally, the problem with accurately knowing an offender is compounded by the fact that the offender can present in a way that deflects accountability and examination. "Oh, I just default to dumb," an offender recently said when describing how he dissuaded his family from asking about his offending or treatment. Offenders have a variety of ways to distract us from attending to signs that something is not right or that they are being deceptive to control us and control their reactions to the examination of what they are saying. "George! Do you have cotton in your ears," one of my frustrated counselors said when we were challenging an offender who would go conveniently deaf when asked relevant questions. Because he was elderly, people thought he did not comprehend or had a hearing problem. After a time, people would give up on challenging him. In response to the counselor's question, George literally pulled cotton out of his ears. He later revealed that he would put cotton in his ears before coming to therapy to convincingly say he did not hear us and muffle the feedback and questions he would get. Offenders tell us what we want to hear, act in compliant ways, and don't fit our "real" offenders' stereotypes.

"He's Good Down Deep!" – All or Nothing Thinking

"All or nothing" or "black and white" thinking is a common cognitive distortion called dichotomous thinking. These terms describe the simplistic way we mentally categorize things, beginning in childhood, how we split things into two. Good/bad, dark/light, always/never are all examples of dichotomous thinking. Dichotomous thinking is a target of cognitive-behavioral therapy and is associated with anxiety and other disorders. It is destructive to have this thinking generally, but it is dangerous to us as the audience when we want to understand and work with sexual offenders.

"But I love him," she said, after learning that her husband sexually abused her daughter. "He is a good man! He is a good father! You people only see the bad," she lamented loudly, "That's what you want me to do – just see the bad!" My staff or I have heard this refrain or one very similar from spouses, family members, attorneys, caseworkers, or supporters of the offenders with whom we work. As treatment providers for the offenders, we are often disparaged by people who are sympathetic to the offender for challenging and holding offenders accountable.

Like all of us, offenders are not all good or all bad. It is critical to accept that the perpetrator sitting across from you is the one who seems remorseful, the one who is working in treatment, AND the one who raped his four-year-old daughter orally. This is the same individual who hid successfully from his wife and family for months while offending – the people who loved and trusted him. It is important to remember that the offender has already mastered maintaining a "normal" outside while acting upon his most secret desires. What we expect in treatment, a relationship, or supervision is something the offender already has the skills to do. We cannot assess an offender's progress or change based on typical measures. Employment is not meaningful if he had a job while he was offending. We need to measure change and compliance differently for the offender – one meaningful way is accountability. Secrets do not allow accountability. Accountability does not allow superficiality.

The same all-or-nothing thinking applies to the concept of trust as well. We usually describe trust as a blanket we cover another person with – they either have it, or they do not. However, trust is not meaningful in that paradigm. Trust should be allotted in small boxes, based on experience. Think about each person in your life. Aren't there things you trust that person with and other things you don't? You might trust your husband never to steal from the family, but do not trust him to be on time. You trust your sister to babysit, but you won't lend her money because she never pays it back. Trust is allocated in these ways, with solid knowledge and experience of another person. It should be fluid and flexible, changing with new information and suspended when it needs to be.

In some ways, trust becomes meaningless when working with offenders. This is similar to working with people with addiction issues. Reliability, consistency, and predictability are all characteristics that someone who is successfully navigating recovery demonstrates. In working with offenders, I do not measure anything on trust. I look for changes in behaviors (especially sudden ones), questionable stories, things that do not make sense, or surface information. Some examples are the uncooperative, hostile offender that suddenly becomes cooperative in treatment. The sullen, reticent group member that has a lot to say unexpectedly. The client who is suddenly sick frequently, gains weight, or gets a makeover. All these examples are related to cases that resulted in the offender's reoffense.

The critical thing to remember about trust is that no one brings it up as an issue until it is an issue. And it is usually the offender who questions it – "why don't you trust me?" or "when will you ever trust me?" Trust is not generally an issue in relationships until someone has broken it or is demanding it. Trust is a weapon. If you are questioning yourself or defending your trust in someone, take a closer look. Trust comes as a by-product of experience. It should be doled out in parcels. And when the cost and consequences are as high as a sexual offense, trust should not be the issue.

Summary

Why do we deny? What makes denial so powerful, especially for those we love or think we know? We need to go back and remember examples of the applicable biases, like loss aversion and confirmation or "myside" bias. All of us are in danger of denial. Therapists, supervising agents, law enforcement, family members, all of us are subject to the grooming, narcissistic investment, and blindness due to hope or care for an individual.

A relationship with an offender requires careful navigation, accurate empathy, and tempered hope and trust. We cannot become overly invested in the offender's well-being or acceptance of us. We must be realistic, as well as skeptical. We have to be willing to demand accountability, reject vagueness, and be resistant to compromising when the need for affiliation arises. We can still care for the offender and value what is real while rejecting the problematic behaviors, thinking, and choices. Detachment, accountability, and a "fearless moral inventory" are tenets of self-help groups like Al-Anon. We can practice the same when it comes to offenders. We do not have to "hate" or "love" the offender, but we must practice active acceptance – fully seeing, acknowledging, and understanding the offender for precisely who he is – not what we want or need him to be.

In conclusion,

- A secret self exists for everyone but is very deep and protected by the offender. They are skilled at duplicity and rely on our assumptions and projections to fill in the gaps of our knowledge. The more we assume, the more we enable the offender to hide.
- People fear strangers more than they fear people known to them. This contributes to denial and excuse-making for those offenders we know. We underestimate risk and forget about the offender's potential, in part to maintain affiliation and protect our investment in another person.
- All-or-nothing thinking is a harmful distortion, especially when it comes to offenders and trust. Challenging our dichotomous thinking is crucial for sound judgment and assessment.
- Offender will exploit what we offer, convincing us that they have changed and will never be dangerous again. Remember that the offender will always carry the potential to meet or exceed their past behavioral limits.

References

Carter, L. (2020, April 9). *A narcissist's 3 selves: Public, private, and secret* [Video]. YouTube. https://www.youtube.com/watch?v=kG1tAvjyiIE

Dos Santos, V. (2021). *Rape myth acceptance and fear of sexual victimization on college campuses* [Unpublished master's thesis]. University of Tennessee at Chattanooga. https://scholar.utc.edu/cgi/viewcontent.cgi?article=1903&context=theses

Eyal, T., Steffal, M., & Epley, N. (2018). Perspective mistaking: Accurately understanding the mind of another requires getting perspective, not taking perspective. *Journal of Personality and Social Psychology, 114*(4), 547–571. http://dx.doi.org/10.1037/pspa0000115

Gladwell, M. (2019). *Talking to strangers.* Little Brown and Co.

New York University (2018, January 29). *Why do we trust, or not trust strangers? The answer is Pavlovian, new psychology research finds* [News release]. https://www.nyu.edu/about/news-publications/news/2018/january/why-do-we-trust–or-not-trust–strangers–the-answer-is-pavlovia.html

Salter, A. (1996). *Listening to sex offenders part one: Truth, lies, and sex offenders.* Eastern Kentucky University.

Salter, A. (2003). *Predators: Pedophiles, rapists, and other sex offenders.* Basic Books.

Scott, H. (2003). Stranger danger: Explaining women's fear of crime. *Western Criminology Review, 4*(3), 203–214. https://www.westerncriminology.org/documents/WCR/v04n3/article_pdfs/scott.pdf

Sloman, S., & Fernbach, P. (2017). *The knowledge illusion: Why we never think alone.* Riverhead Books.

wikiHow (2021, December 9). How to live a double life. https://www.wikihow.com/Live-a-Double-Life

Wilcox, P., Jordan, C. E., & Pritchard, A. J. (2006). Fear of acquaintance versus stranger rape as a master status: Towards refinement of the shadow of sexual assault. *Violence and Victims, 21*(3), 355–370.

Chapter 5

The Theater of Sexual Assault

The Act versus the Production

"I would accidentally walk in the bathroom on them. I would accidentally walk into the pool house when they were changing ... I knew damn well they were in there," admitted Scott during his interview. He abused multiple adolescent girls. Josh, on the other hand, described a different way of offending. He explained, "Over time it happened, it wasn't right away. One thing at a time. It started out as wrestling to taking their clothes off, wrestling in bed, manipulating my victims into letting me orally assault them, tell them it's not homosexual, it's not gay. I put a lot of energy into that." Josh sexually assaulted about ten boys.

The two offenders and their offending acts above characterize how we generally conceptualize offending – one as a "mistake," accidental, or opportunistic act, the other as a prolonged, predatory process. Both are limited dichotomous conceptions of sexual offending that lead to inaccuracies of understanding the sexual offender and the sexual offense. Sexual offending encompasses a wide array of behaviors and schemes. While offenders might have a preferred way of offending, it is crucial not to maintain rigid expectations or conceptualizations of offenders or offense behavior. A two-pronged approach to examining and categorizing offenses and offenders contributes to errors in identifying, classifying, managing, and treating offenders.

Deviance: Criminogenic or Sexual Needs

To become a sexual offender, an offender must have a need or impetus that motivates the offense behavior. That need may be sexual, like a paraphilic interest. It may be criminal, like a need for gratification at the expense of others. It may be narcissistic, like an egocentric gratification through exploitation. I will discuss the need in more detail in a later chapter, but we must always consider the offender's motivation to offend.

The Stages of Criminal Behavior – Modified

Students of criminal justice are often taught that crime occurs in stages – intent, preparation, attempt, and accomplishment. This paradigm captures the process of a criminal act, from the formation of the desire, to the act itself. I find a modification of this model helpful in analyzing and understanding sexual offense behavior. For sexual offenders, examination of their process would include investigation of the following: need (criminogenic or sexual); fantasy/preparation; victim access; victim/audience preparation; the offense; and post-offense behavior.

DOI: 10.4324/9781003156284-7

The Prologue: Fantasy/Preparation

An offender's fantasy of the crime is not the same as a "typical" sexual fantasy. In the offender's fantasy, he can prepare. He can construct rationalizations and justifications for his offense behavior. The offender can identify and reinforce sources of his arousal and gratification. He can manage his anxiety and mentally compartmentalize to suspend what he must, like empathy, compassion, or shame. It is essential to understand that an offender's fantasy includes the pre-offense behavior, which is arousing, and the post-offense behavior, important to helping cover up the crime.

The Setup: Victim Access

How do offenders get access to their victims? Is she a school teacher who selects awkward 7th grade boys to "romance"? Is he an Uber driver who assaults intoxicated passengers? Is he a stepfather who marries a woman because he is aroused to her seven-year-old daughter? Offenders tend to prefer a particular method to getting victim access. Some offenders take jobs that offer limitless opportunities to offend. Some offenders use the access they have, offending within a family. Others form relationships with victims. Some seek strangers while others exploit their power and position.

"But it's not like he planned it," an attorney colleague of mine stated during a discussion about offender types, "He couldn't know there would be a drunk girl there he could rape." This area can become muddied and confuse us about who the offender is. Victim access is the act of the play when we start to label the offender as a predator or an opportunist, as someone who is instrumentally hunting a victim versus the offender who "made a mistake." It is imperative to identify how an offender prefers to get access to a victim. It is essential information, but it must lead to a more nuanced understanding of the offender and *always* be flexible enough to incorporate new information and possibilities about the offender. Generally, an offender labeled a predator is perceived as far more dangerous than an opportunist, whose offense behavior can be minimized as a mistake, accident, or curiosity, whose victim can be blamed for being drunk or otherwise vulnerable.

What is crucial to keep in mind is that the opportunist is *always ready to offend*. Otherwise, what would define an opportunity? What kind of person sees a sexual opportunity in a passed-out victim who has peed her pants? An opportunity in a woman walking down the sidewalk? A pop-up window promising young girls? The offender's needs/desires and motivation define the opportunity. They are not flukes or aberrations in the offenders' behavior. These offenders are more unpredictable and more challenging to manage than those who engage in a longer process to attain victims. I responded to my attorney friend that both spiders and lions are predators. They just hunt differently.

Setting the Stage: Victim Selection and Victim/Audience Preparation

As we have discussed throughout the book, the offender is masterful at setting the stage for the final act. To be successful in offending, the offender must select the right victims. The victims that offenders choose are highly likely to have a vulnerability that the offender exploits. Suppose the offender knows the victim, possibly desiring an ongoing abusive relationship with the victim. It is better for the offenders if the victims have vulnerabilities that make them more accessible, like a single-parent household. Some of the vulnerabilities that are meaningful to the offenders include things that compromise the victims' credibility, increase the chance the victims will become attached to or dependent on the offenders, or decrease the likelihood that the victims will disclose. These include:

- Behavioral problems in children
- Social isolation or rejection
- Homelife compromised by lack of love, attention, or supervision
- Life compromised by abuse, poverty, mental illness, or addiction
- Physical or cognitive disability
- Prior history of abuse
- Intoxication or substance abuse
- Personality traits, like passivity, introversion, willingness to comply, and secret-keep
- Prior history of compromised credibility and poor performance/reputation
- High-risk jobs or situations, like sex workers
- Lack of knowledge or lack of access to services and resources
- Fear of consequences for disclosure

Remember that offenses occur with the backdrop of a society that makes it difficult for victims, the scenery to the play. As the offender has already pre-prepared the audience to disbelieve and deny that such a thing could be true, the victim has even more barriers to overcome to report. Michael was a boy in a home for troubled boys run by priests. He was raped by one of the priests and went to seek solace from a second priest. Fr. Johnson, instead of comforting the boy, told the boy to "show him what happened." He proceeded to victimize Michael again, touching the boy's penis. Not only did Fr. Johnson not report the initial assault, he continued to abuse Michael weekly for years. Imagine the barriers this victim faced to report! He was a perfect selection for the predatory priest.

Not only do the offenders identify and prey upon victims' vulnerabilities, but they also *create vulnerabilities in the victims*. The creation of vulnerability can happen close to the crime – getting the victim intoxicated, physically isolating the victim, drugging the victim, threatening the victim. More insidiously, the offender can create vulnerability over time. Remember the concept of weaponizing humanity? The feelings of love, care, sympathy, and trust are human. Offenders purposely foster these feelings to make their victims vulnerable. Examples would include the pain management doctor who gets his female patients addicted to pain killers then sexually assaults them, the school teacher who convinces the student they are "in love," and the stepfather who supports the family and is "nice," especially compared to the biological father who was violent. We will further explore grooming techniques but keep this in mind when examining offender behavior.

The Climax: The Offense

One of the fascinating things I learned during my years of working with sexual offenders is how unimportant the actual sex part of the offense was to the offender. For many offenders, the sexual act is not very gratifying as a sex act. How fun and satisfying can it be sexually to penetrate an unresponsive partner who just vomited? A crying victim? One who is complaining that it burns? The build-up, fantasy, manipulation, and exploitation of the victim, the power and success all mean as much if not more than the offense itself. Obviously, the offender receives sexual gratification from the offense – the source of the gratification is not solely from genital stimulation. However, it is the act that we focus on and make meaningful, especially in the criminal justice system. The act is the crime. The act is what defines the offenders criminally and legally. The act is the path to prosecution. But remember, the act is only part of the play.

The Final Act: The Post-Offense Behavior

Post-offense behavior is an essential component of offending as well. The offender's post-offense behavior provides a great deal of information to the audience, guiding the interpretation and resolution of the offense for both the victim and the audience. An offender who walks calmly from the bedroom, describing how "she's asleep now" or that he was "just checking on him" after assaulting a child, constructs the guise of normalcy to his spouse. The teacher who keeps a failing student after class to help him with his homework then brags to colleagues about his improved performance while abusing the student builds a reputation as a stellar teacher. The rapist who assaulted his date after she passed out drunk, then texts her about the great time he had, asking when they can see each other again, is acting to have his behavior interpreted as consensual or drunk sex.

The offender's post-offense behavior steers the victim's post-offense behavior as well. Josh, an offender of a dozen boys ages 8 to 11, explained,

> Every time I offended, I tried to make it as peaceful and non-violent as possible. In my head, I'm like, "Don't scare them or traumatize them or anything, so there's no detection when they go home." Make it like a fun thing so that when I'm done victimizing, I kid around with them, joke with them, so by the time they get home, they're in a good mood again, and in my mind, they forgot about what happened. So, by the time the parents see them again, they're like, you know, "How did it go? Did you have fun?" He says, "Yeah, yeah." That seemed to work for me.

An offender's post-offense behavior includes confronting the problem by soliciting character letters from friends to defend himself against an accusation, going on social media and announcing the allegations, acting righteous and hurt, or even confessing some of the offense behavior in a remorseful tone. "Minimization by the offender can be more effectively misleading than denial," Bancroft et al. (2012) write, "By expressing remorse while simultaneously portraying his victim as provocative and dishonest, a [offender] is sometimes able to persuade a professional that he has been wrongly accused (p. 21)." Remember, as we have expectations of victim behaviors, we also expect offenders to act guilty or suspect.

Mistakes in Understanding Offenses and Offenders

By maintaining fixed ideas of offenders and offending, we as the audience can get caught in simplistic concepts. By overlaying a template of assumptions based on a lack of experience or understanding of offenders and offending, we make significant mistakes in assessing sexual offenders. We do not understand sexual offending as an event. We do not understand where it happens, how long it takes, what situations are protective, or how the victim is selected. Most of us have little experience with committing a crime, nonetheless sex crimes. We ascribe "normal" arousal and behavior to a sexual offense, resulting in misguided interpretations of behaviors and circumstances.

The Idea of Opportunity

As we touched on above, opportunity is defined very individualistically and acted upon based on the offenders' needs and readiness to offend. What is an opportunity to one is not necessarily an opportunity to another. And the way we assess an opportunity is not based on the experience of the offender. For example, I had a recent discussion regarding offenders who sexually assault passengers during a rideshare. The idea that the offenders were experienced offenders who understood the prime opportunity of being a rideshare driver was foreign to my colleague. "What about the risk? I mean, I think these guys are just knuckleheads who see a drunk girl – it's not like they do it all the time," the colleague said. He was taking into account what most of us do when assessing an opportunity – risk, time, investment, consequences. However, offenders have greater knowledge of these things than we do. And, the more experience they have, the more knowledge they have.

If we know that sexual assault is far underreported, the offenders do too. Most offenders have multiple victims. Through testing rape kits, we are uncovering many more serial offenders than predicted, who have different victim selection and histories than expected (Lovell et al., 2019). In our survey of offenders, 80% of them simply thought the victim would never tell. That does not seem like much of a risk, does it? Disclosure rates go down when a victim was intoxicated at the time of the offense as does the likelihood that the victim will be able to physically resist (Kahn et al., 2003). In my experience, even when they are on GPS, offenders offend because they know that no one monitors them in real-time. They have plenty of time to set the stage for plausible deniability. So the rideshare drivers have picked the perfect occupation for risk-free (or almost) offending. They are unknown to the victim, and they potentially see where the victim lives, raising the fear of retaliation. Offenders assess opportunity differently than we do.

Overestimation of Time

"How long did it last," the prosecutor asked the victim about the sexual assault. "I don't know – 10 or 20 minutes," she guessed. This answer was a wild overestimation that resulted in a lengthy cross-examination about the comings and goings of roommates, why she did not call for help, and a confrontation about texting that went on during that 20-minute time frame. The offender later stated that the entire assault occurred in less than five minutes. The overestimation of how long a sexual offense takes presents a considerable problem in our ability to identify and understand sexual offending. An actual sexual offense can and does occur pretty rapidly. Even consensual penile-vaginal intercourse lasts, on average 3–5 minutes (Waldinger et al., 2005).

When was the last time you surreptitiously scratched your genitals in public? How long did it take? Did you do it in a crowded elevator? Train car? Meeting? That is how quick it can be to assault someone sexually. Groping a child's genitals while lifting them onto a carnival ride. Rubbing your groin against a woman who is waiting for a bus. Lifting your leg pumping gas while your penis falls out of the underwear with the missing elastic. A child can be assaulted when a mother leaves the room to go to the bathroom. Or in a supervised visit. When Jeff would sit with a child next to her mother in church, he could slip his hand under the child's dress and put his finger in her five-year-old vagina while they sang hymns. The offender who waits until victims fall asleep during their massage at a luxury hotel before he sticks his finger in their vagina or rubs his erection against their hands or heads. The offense can be very brief, especially when the offender does not have prolonged access to the victim in private. It might be 5 minutes in a locked bathroom, during the time they "check on" the drunk victim passed out in the dorm room or the car driving home.

Our failure to consider the potential brevity of a sexual offense disallows us from correctly predicting or identifying possible risk situations. Offenders can offend when we "just leave them alone for a minute" if the time is right. When victims are questioned about why they did not fight, scream, or escape, sometimes, by the time the victim realizes that an offense is happening and decides what to do about it, it might be over.

Sexual Assault Is Not Easily Identifiable

Another mistaken belief is that a sexual assault is readily identifiable to either the victim or the audience. Victims often label an event with an offender as something other than assault – a miscommunication, accident, or bad sex (Wilson & Miller, 2016). This occurs even with penetrative assaults like rape (Wilson & Miller, 2016). Nassar's victims were told he was performing a medical procedure. The victims I interviewed who were sexually assaulted during a massage struggled with labeling the assault, instead telling themselves they were mistaken, the offender "just had big hands," or that it was a technique different than what they had experienced prior.

There are numerous factors that make labeling an experience as assault difficult. When there is a relationship between the victim and perpetrator, recognizing an assault is more difficult (Kahn et al., 2003). When there is no physical force or violence during the assault, victims find it hard to characterize the event as an assault (Littleton et al., 2006). A lack of violence in the assault fools the audience as well. Stolzenberg and Lyon (2014) found that offenders were acquitted more often when their attorney argued a lack of force, even when the victims were children. Our acceptance of rape myths decreases our ability to identify what a sexual assault is.

Defining the "Sex" in Sex Offense – The Non-sexual Sex Offense

A victim can be assaulted in ways that are not even identified as sexual. Take Derrick, the father with arousal to feet who sexually abused his daughter. He would remove her socks and tickle her bare feet during supervised visits. She would have a traumatic breakdown after the visit, peeing her pants and having nightmares. No one saw the offense, but the offender was committing a sexually gratifying act in front of everyone. And the impact of the offense was the same for the victim, traumatized by the arousing nature of the behavior. Individuals with deviant arousal sources can be aroused to a myriad of non-sexual things and behaviors. Offenders like Josh above get sexually gratified by wrestling and horseplaying with their victims. The offender sexualizes the non-sexual elements.

Presumption of Protection

Because of our limited experience with sexual offending, we can presume that some situations are protective against being victimized. It is nearly inconceivable to think that rape can happen in a crowded McDonald's bathroom. Or that Larry Nassar assaulted his victims in a gym full of people. However, offenders can and do offend everywhere. This includes:

- In a doctor's office with a nurse nearby
- In a church pew during a service
- In the bed with her husband sleeping right next to her
- In a hotel room with six other people there
- In an airplane on a full flight
- In a field surrounded by 200 soldiers
- In a train car surrounded by other passengers

All of these were places where an offender committed a sexual offense. All admitted to the crime. Not all were convicted. When offenses occur in places where we presume we are protected, there is a tendency to default to the conclusion that the offense was actually a consensual act. Unless, of course, the victim is a small child, then we might just choose disbelief.

Summary

We need to be mindful and respectful of our inexperience and lack of information when it comes to sexual offending. We have to remember that the offender is not concerned about the victim of the sexual offense. Even stimulation of the victim is for the offender's pleasure and benefit. Inherently, a sexual offense is about the gratification of the offense, meeting whatever the offender desires. Offenses are not romantic, with music and candlelight. They are one-sided, meant to be successful, and designed to minimize risk to the offender. The offender is experienced in assessing the victims and the situation and directing the perception of the audience.

In conclusion,

- All stages of the offender's criminal sexual behavior should be explored and scrutinized.
- We need to challenge our ignorance and remain flexible enough to incorporate new information and insights into the offenders around us.
- We need to avoid presumptions and assumptions about offender behavior, opportunity, risk, and gratification.
- In our analysis, we must take into account the confusion of the victim and the camouflage by the offender.
- Finally, it is imperative to understand that each sexual offense involves many decisions, choices, and behaviors to actualize. We fail to understand this when we minimize an offense as a mistake or accident.

References

Bancroft, L., Silverman, J., & Ritchie, D. (2012). *The batterer as parent* (2nd ed.). Sage.

Kahn, A., Jackson, J., Kully, C., Badger, K., & Halvorsen, J. (2003). Calling it rape: Differences in experiences of women who do or do not label their sexual assault as rape. *Psychology of Women Quarterly, 27*(3), 233–242. https://doi.org/10.1111/1471-6402.00103

Littleton, H., Axsom, D., Breitkopf, C., & Berenson, A. (2006). Rape acknowledgment and post-assault experiences: How acknowledgment status relates to disclosure, copying, worldview, and reactions received from others. *Violence and Victims, 21*(6), 761–778.

Lovell, R. E., Williamson, A., Dover, T., Keel, T., & Flannery, D. J. (2020). Identifying serial sexual offenders through cold cases. Law Enforcement Bulletin (official publication of the U.S. Federal Bureau of Investigation), May. https://leb.fbi.gov/articles/featured-articles/identifying-serial-sexual-offenders-through-cold-cases

Stolzenberg, S., & Lyon, T. (2014). Evidence summarized in attorney's closing arguments predicts acquittals in criminal trials of child sexual abuse. *Child Maltreatment, 19*(2), 119–129. https://doi.org/10.1177/107755951453988

Waldinger, M., Quinn, P., Dilleen, M., Mundayat, R., Schweitzer, D., & Boolell, M. (2005). Multinational population survey of intravaginal ejaculation latency time. *Journal of Sexual Medicine, 2(4),* 492–497. https://doi.org/10.1111/j.1743-6109.2005.00070.x

Wilson, L. C., & Miller, K. E. (2016). Meta-analysis of the prevalence of unacknowledged rape. *Trauma, Violence, and Abuse, 17*(2), 149–159. https://doi.org/10.1177/1524838015576391

Unmasking the Sex Offender

Chapter 6

Defining Deviance

The Pathway to Offending

"But why? Why would he do that?" Why is the question continuously asked about sexual offenders – by their victims, family, and anyone who has not worked with the offender population. To be honest, I still encounter stories of offenders and offenses and wonder why. I will start this chapter by telling you two things immediately – the answer to why is because they like it; it gratifies them. This answer just leads to another "why?" Why do they like it? It would be impossible to explain why something inconceivable to you could be sexually gratifying to someone else. And if you are a victim asking "why," there will never be a good enough answer to explain why someone hurt you. There is not a good enough answer. A more answerable question to understanding offenders' motivation is the question, "What motivates them to offend? What lets them hurt others?"

Two Primary Pathways to Offending – Character and Sexual Deviance

When you google the word deviance, Google (n.d.) defines it as "the fact or state of departing from usual or accepted standards, especially in social or sexual behavior." There has been significant debate about the word deviance and its implications regarding what is "right" and "wrong." Deviation from the norm can create social change, define boundaries, and establish expectations. In the context of this book, deviance refers to the departure from the norm sexually, characterologically, and behaviorally, resulting in acts that are harmful to others or disruptive to one's own functioning, whether through criminal acts, negative consequences, or problematic interpersonal behavior. I use it as a word that captures how an offender diverges from prosocial behavior and consensual healthy sex acts into criminal, destructive, and damaging behaviors to meet their egocentric desires.

Most people have deviant urges or fantasies, whether to hurt another person, break a taboo, behave in a shocking manner, or engage in sexual behavior that is atypical for them. What is different for those who commit sexual offenses is that they allow deviant urges and problematic personality traits to combine to engage in self-gratifying behavior that harms others.

Research has demonstrated that two principal factors facilitate sexual offending – certain problematic character traits and deviant sexual arousal (Doren, 2002; Hanson & Morton-Bourgon, 2005). Throughout the United States, sexually violent predator laws reflect our knowledge that individuals who are more likely to recidivate have a mental abnormality or personality disorder correlated with repeated sexual offense behavior (see Felthous & Ko, 2018). The related conditions include diagnoses characterized by disordered sexual arousal patterns or character traits that facilitate the harm of others. The most frequently diagnosed disorders in sexual offenders include substance abuse disorders, personality disorders, and paraphilic disorders (Eher et al., 2019). The problem character traits would

DOI: 10.4324/9781003156284-9

encompass those traits that contribute to criminal thinking, disregard for rules and rights of others, exploitiveness, and a lack of empathy or callousness. Sexual deviance would include paraphilic arousal that leads to the victimization of others. Charles was a highly antisocial, criminal offender. "She was just layin' there. I thought, 'I could tap that,'" Charles stated, explaining his rape of a victim. He robbed a convenience store, pistol whipping the cashier to unconsciousness. While she lay on the floor unresponsive, her skirt pulled up, Charles raped her just because he could. Don was a pedophile, having a deep sexual arousal to prepubescent children. He violated his probation by standing in front of his living room window masturbating as children walked by for school. He was never criminal other than his sexual crimes against children. He was sexually deviant.

So Are They Sick? Are They Crazy? Are They Mentally Ill?

"He must be crazy," she exclaimed, "Who would do such a thing?" Much has been made in the media about mental illness and violence, both sexual and non-sexual violence, especially in light of the recent rise in mass shootings and domestic violence. When the term mentally ill is used colloquially, most think about someone who has severe disruptions in thinking, behaving, and relating – that the person has an illness that compromises the ability to function rationally and adaptively in the real world. Most people think that people with schizophrenia are dangerous, as schizophrenia is a disorder characterized by hallucinations, delusions, and other psychotic symptoms (American Psychological Association [APA], 2013). We imagine that the mental illness has compromised the individual's reality in a way that would be easily recognizable, making them illogical, erratic, or psychotically disconnected from reality. The media associates mental illness with mass shooters, conjuring images of identifiable and ignored dangerous people who should not have gotten a gun.

What is misunderstood is the true underlying cause of violence – a distorted belief system that maintains two primary tenets – (1) violence is a viable option or solution to a problem, and (2) the targets deserve the violence. People with character disorders are not "insane" or "crazy" like a person in an acute state of mental illness. However, they may have fantasies or perceptions that involve distortions related to their personality pathology, like feelings of persecution or entitlement that motivate their violence. Domestic violence offenders that kill their estranged wives because they believe she "is mine" or does not deserve to live because she left are not mentally ill in the layperson's understanding of mental illness. They can function in other areas of their lives successfully, rationally, and adaptively. But, their narcissistic belief system and fantasies of their own self-importance motivate them to target and kill people. They have not "snapped" or "lost it" – mass shooters have decided to act on long-standing thought patterns, making strategic plans and decisions to manifest their schemes for retaliation or vengeance.

Adam Lanza, the Sandy Hook school shooter, was repeatedly called autistic in news reports (Katersky & Kim, 2014; Salam, 2017). He had a history of developmental delays, learning problems, interpersonal difficulties, and anxiety/obsessive-compulsive symptoms. None of these things are related to the mass shooting. Adam also had an "obsession" with destruction, war, and guns. He had graphic fantasies of violence. His father spent time with him at shooting ranges. He had books on mass shootings. Adam had a spreadsheet detailing hundreds of spree killings and mass shootings. He had threatened to shoot up the school previously. Adam was given some mental health treatment through the years but was never diagnosed with an acute mental illness marked by psychosis – he was described as "troubled," not "crazy." His obsession with violence and killing showed his fantasy life and motivation for violence, not his diagnoses of Asperger's Syndrome, anxiety, or obsessive-compulsive disorder. His preoccupation with killing should have been the focus of his treatment, the brilliant red flag that needed speedy and intense intervention. Instead, he was treated for his social issues and anxiety (his mental "disorders"), while his "preoccupation with violence was largely unaddressed." This is not to say that acute symptoms of mental illness should go untreated, clearly. What this story illustrates is how we tend to attribute violence to mental illness versus to the deep, engrossing, and stimulating fantasies of violence in violent people.

Who comes to your mind when you think of the words "mentally ill" or "crazy?" Certainly not the kind priest, the well-spoken politician, the successful actor, or the loving husband, all common roles for sexual offenders.

Several points must be understood when discussing diagnoses or the terms mentally ill or mental disorders. It is *critical* to understand that:

- Mental illness is an umbrella term that encompasses many types of disorders and diagnoses.
- Most diagnoses do not cause the person with the diagnosis to disconnect from reality.
- Most diagnoses are not related in any way to violence or harming others.
- Most people with a diagnosis of a mental illness will never commit a sexual offense.
- Generally, severe mental health diagnoses are related to being victimized, and not being victimizers (Rossa-Roccor et al., 2020).
- A diagnosis does not explain the instrumental, calculated, and purposeful behavior of the offender that he uses to hide, trick, manipulate, and deceive to be a successful offender.

Labeling behavior as "crazy" or "sick" because we do not understand it is an easy shortcut that lends to excuse-making and relieving an offender of responsibility for behavior and choices. As a society, we continue to have misinformed stereotypes and biases regarding mental illness. One that benefits offenders is that if they are mentally ill, they are not competent, responsible, or intentional in their behavior. The offender cannot "help it." It is more sympathetic but inaccurate to view a person's choices and decisions to sexually harm another person as a result of "addiction" or illness. While a type of deviance may result in a diagnosis, this diagnosis might be the impetus for the offending but not the full explanation for all the other choices and decisions the offender makes to commit a sex crime. In other words, pedophilic interests might motivate the desire for sexual contact with a child. It does not account for all the choices and behaviors an offender executes to get his wishes met.

There are severely mentally ill people who do commit sexual offenses. However, neither the majority of sexual offenders are seriously mentally ill, nor the majority of the seriously mentally ill are sexual offenders. Rarely does a serious mental illness serve as the stimulus or drive for a sexual offense. Sometimes, individuals in a disorganized or dysregulated state can commit a sexual crime. An example is a man I evaluated who was arrested for Indecent Exposure to a group of children. He was in a severe manic state and ran naked through a park. He certainly exhibited himself. But it was evident that his intention was not sexual. I have worked with offenders with serious mental illness who were also sexual offenders. It was not their mental illness that motivated their offending; it was their sexual interest in children or their antisocial character.

If Someone Has an Atypical Sexual Interest or a Problem Personality, Will They Be a Sex Offender?

Most people with problematic character traits do not commit sexual offenses. Most people with paraphilic arousal patterns do not commit sexual offenses. However, *in those individuals who commit sexual offenses*, there is more likely to be a deviant sexual interest or characterological issues that facilitate the sexual offense. In my experience, the individual's character is more powerful in determining whether or not someone will commit a sexual offense than their sexual interest.

Additionally, many sexual offenses do not involve sexual deviance. Some people commit sexual offenses for motivations that include cruelty, punishment, retaliation, power, or convenience, like the husband who rapes his wife after battering her to prove she belongs to him. Offenders who are not truly pedophilic can still assault children, age being no barrier to them sexually. Others will commit sexual offenses simply because they can, like offenders who rape intoxicated victims who are passed out.

For another example, arousal to adolescents is not considered deviant. If the victim has secondary sex characteristics, like breasts and pubic hair, sexual arousal to the victim is considered "normal." Most female offenders I have evaluated or worked with sexually abused adolescents who had reached puberty, like the schoolteacher who sexually abused the 15-year-old boy. Predation on adolescents by adult males is common. Offenders who assault adolescent victims can be more challenging to treat. They benefit from some of the most effective ways to blame the victim – "she looked older than she was," "she lied about her age," "he came on to me," "he was bigger than me, if he didn't want it, he could have stopped it." The adolescent victim is held far more responsible for the offending than younger victims. They are older. They should "know better." They are less dependent and afraid.

The adolescent victims might have other things to blame as well. They might be sexually active, participate more in hiding the offense, and have distortions that feed the offender, like they were "in love" together. The victims might have cooperated with the offending, like texting or secretly messaging the offender or sneaking away to meet him. Social media and technology complicate this. The victims might be drinking or smoking pot with the offender, taking secret gifts, driving his car, getting privileges, sending nude pictures, or engaging in sexual chat. While finding an adolescent attractive might not be sexually deviant, the behaviors the offender must engage in, including the hiding, secrecy, distortions, and manipulation of a child reveal the offender's capacity to be socially deviant.

David was a 35-year-old man, a stepfather to Brittney. He began sexually abusing Brittney a year after marrying her mother, who had a significant addiction issue. She was 12 years old at the time. Brittney had spent years as a child taking care of her mother, selling toys on the street to buy food for her siblings, and engaging with adults to get cared for while her mother was high. She was parentified and pseudo-independent. David always pointed out to his friends how flirtatious she was, and how much older she acted than most kids.

When Brittney turned 14, David killed her mother in front of her, stabbing her mother in the throat with a large chef's knife. As her mother lay dying beside the bed, David forced Brittney to lay down, orally assaulting her while telling her how beautiful she was, how they could be together now, and how much he loved her. David was arrested and confessed. David's friends got up to defend him at his guilty plea and sentencing hearing. They described Brittney as a seductress, a whore who knew more than it seemed, the temptress who manipulated David into killing her mother. David was, in their eyes, a naïve, befuddled man in a bad marriage who was led astray by the child. Until David took the stand and began describing how he started lusting after Brittney when she was 11, that he was amazed at "how sweet such a young pussy could taste." That changed things for his witnesses – 11 was much different than 14.

David provides an example of a sexual offender who did not have a diagnosis of a severe mental illness or a deviant sexual arousal pattern. David had not been identified previously as having any mental health issues. He was functioning in the military. He was an active member of the military band with status. Yet, he sexually abused his stepdaughter for two years, then murdered her mother. Was he "crazy?" His behaviors are hard to fathom, but they were rational in the context of his narcissistic needs and his ability to hurt others to meet them.

Power of Deviance

To explain the intensity and allure of offenders' deviance to them is extremely difficult. "I thought about it all night and day," Steve explained, "I would masturbate at work. When I had sex with my girlfriend, I thought about it." Ted, a priest who abused children, described his offending. "I would touch, you know, touch the covers around their pubic area. I didn't masturbate to them," he said, "It was that act, the act was fulfilling – to me the act was what was fulfilling about it." He went on, "It gave me a feeling of power – that I could do something like that and get away with it." Earl tried to explain to his mother his deviance. "To this day, it's extremely tough," he said, "Because she doesn't understand. You know, she doesn't understand the things that motivate a sex offender to offend. She doesn't understand the core attraction to the wrong thing." Offenders will stay up all night searching for deviant stimuli on the Internet, masturbating time and time again. They will risk their careers, families, and lives in pursuit of the deviant gratification.

Deviant sexual arousal is more potent than appropriate "normal" arousal. It is not only extremely sexually stimulating and gratifying for the offender; it contains non-sexual elements that magnify the impact and satisfy other emotional and psychological desires. Someone who rapes his partner to punish her not only can achieve the physical reinforcement and satisfaction of sexual orgasm but also receives the desired psychological gratification from humiliating and dominating his partner. In a "goodbye" letter to his deviance, Nick writes, "The insidious way you wove yourself thought the fabric of my being was unconscionable. You tainted everything that I saw through my eyes to a hue of your liking, until what I was seeing was a vision of depravity."

The Thrill of the Process

Not only is the arousal extremely gratifying in itself, the interpersonal deviance is thrilling and potent. Offenders get physiologically and sexually aroused by power, control, exploitation, risk-taking, deception, and violence. Jamal, an offender in the program for shooting a woman, described his excitement about violence. When I asked him if he ever got an erection when he was violent, he said excitedly, "Yeah! At first I thought there was something wrong with that too. But then as time went on it just, it was just kind of a part of it." He further explained, "I used to get an erection before it (the violence) actually, just at the thought of it. Got me another one, just sitting there so happy and content with myself." Art, a violent offender who raped women described, "The best hard-on I ever had was when I had her hanging over the balcony by her neck. The look on her face ... I almost came in my pants." The violence and interpersonal interaction was sexually arousing.

Deception can be arousing for offenders. Duping delight is a term coined by Paul Ekman (1992) to describe the excitement and thrill some people feel when they lie. Juan described the satisfaction of being able to manipulate his child victim. Because he knew she was naïve and did "not have life experience," he worked on "trying to get her to play into" his scheme to abuse her. "It's like 'this is kinda cool,'" he said, "that I am able to manipulate her into thinking that it is normal. It is horrible, but at the time it was something that was really arousing to me."

Non-sexual Displays of Deviance

Another thing that is difficult to explain regarding offenders and their deviance is how offenders can become aroused to non-sexual targets, situations, and dynamics, as well as display their deviance in non-sexual ways. Remember, the word deviance indicates a deviation from the typical boundaries that define more normative behavior. In the personality and sexual deviance displayed by offenders, the sources of arousal and expression of the deviance are far expanded than most would understand. In working with and supervising sexual offenders, we must remain vigilant to identify sexual offending behavior that is occurring in non-sexual ways. Deviance itself is exciting and arousing. If it goes unaddressed, it can culminate in a reoffense.

Leonard was an offender who had victimized a crack-addicted mother and her two very young children, one of whom had a disease that stopped her growth when she was a toddler. Leonard was aroused to exploiting the vulnerabilities of others. He came into treatment to announce that he had made progress as he had gotten an age-appropriate lover who was working and self-sufficient. When we met her, we discovered she was blind. We also discovered that Leonard had a new friend who was a bus driver. This friend drove the buses that assisted the disabled. Leonard would ride on the bus with his friend all day. Though neither of these situations was overtly sexual or sexual offending, they fed into Leonard's arousal to vulnerability. Fred was a rapist who loved to have power over his victims. He was abusive in his relationships as well. He came into treatment bragging about his promotion, being a line supervisor in a factory where many non-English speaking women worked. He wielded power over these women all day. This was not an appropriate job for him. Doug, an exhibitionist, brought a photo of himself topless to show my new therapist, a young woman in her internship. Jacob, a man who got off on sexual cruelty, also had his stepson kneel on rice for hours. These are all examples of how deviance is displayed in non-sexual ways. Troy, a psychopathic offender who silently believed everyone was dumber than he was, set up a very disruptive situation during group therapy to humiliate one offender he considered "slow" and cause conflict with the others and staff.

Deviance and Distortions

Offenders engage in what is termed cognitive distortions that enable them to create excuses, justifications, and rationales for their behavior. A cognitive distortion is defined by the American Psychological Association [APA] (n.d.) as "faulty or inaccurate thinking, perception, or belief." All people experience some level of distorted thinking. Cognitive distortions about oneself or others can contribute to depression and anxiety. They are often a focus of treatment.

When driven by deviance, however, the offenders allow the distortions to smooth out anxiety about committing sexual offenses or causing harm to the victim. The distortions assist the offenders in maintaining a positive image of themselves and in blaming the victim. "Then a lot of times I would justify it like that, you know," Jack said, "When I would sexually assault the victims afterwards, you know, and I felt guilty about it, I would just tell myself, you know, I do alot for these people. I really didn't hurt nobody." The distortions allow the offender to interpret reality in a way that suits his demands. "Well, she didn't say no," "she ran around in that towel," or "he was always playing with himself" are types of distortions that blame the victim. Other distortions help the offenders sustain acceptance of their own behavior and positive image of themselves. Jack explained further, "At the same time, it also gives me - it makes me feel good knowing that the parents like me, it makes me feel comfortable on top of them trusting me with their children." Distorted thinking makes offenders feel entitled, special, blameless, and immune to the impact of their behavior to serve the deviance.

Summary

Sexual offenders possess both sexual and characterological deviance that facilitates their ability to commit the most intimate and destructive crimes against others. The power and impact of the deviant urges and desires are profound and hard to fathom for those who do not get gratified by deviance. Do not let the domination of this deviance for the offender be confused with addiction or being unable to make purposeful, instrumental decisions. While the deviant needs may drive the offenders' decision-making and contribute to justifications and rationalizations about getting these desires met, they do not make the offenders unable to make different decisions or appreciate the true nature of their behavior. Remember the offenders' ability to hide their behavior and manipulate the victims into silence and compliance. These instrumental decisions that lead to successful sexual offending prove the offenders' competence.

In conclusion,

- Severe mental illness is not a common explanation for sexual offending. Most mentally ill people are not sexually or otherwise violent.
- Offenders engage in rational decisions to hide, deny, and succeed in their offense behavior.
- Deviance, both sexual and characterological, is a motivating factor in sexual offense.
- Deviant arousal has sexual and non-sexual components. It is complex and powerful.
- Cognitive distortions help the offenders act out on their deviant urges and desires with some level of impunity and immunity to the consequences.

References

American Psychological Association (n.d.). *Cognitive distortion.* APA Dictionary of Psychology. Retrieved from https://dictionary.apa.org/cognitive-distortion

American Psychological Association (2013). *Diagnostic and statistical manual of mental disorders* (5th ed.). https://doi.org/10.1176/appi.books.9780890425596

Doren, D. (2002). *Evaluating sex offenders: A manual for civil commitments and beyond.* Sage.

Eher, R., Rettenberger, M., & Turner, D. (2019). The prevalence of mental disorders in incarcerated contact sexual offenders. *Acta Psychiatrica Scandinavica, 139*(6), 572–581. https://doi.org/10.1111/acps.13024

Ekman, P. (1992). *Telling lies.* Norton & Co.

Felthous, A. R., & Ko, J. (2018). Sexually violent predator law in the United States. *East Asian Archives of Psychiatry, 28*(4), 159–173. https://doi.org/10.12809/eaap1835

Google (n.d.) Deviance.

Hanson, R. K., & Morton-Bourgon, K. (2005). The characteristics of persistent sexual offenders: A meta-analysis of recidivism studies. *Journal of Consulting and Clinical Psychology, 73*(6), 1154–1163. https://doi.org/10.1037/0022-006X.73.6.1154. Retrieved from https://www.icmec.org/wp-content/uploads/2015/10/Characteristics-of-Persistent-Sex-Offenders-Meta-Analysis-of-Recidivism-2005.pdf

Katersky, A., & Kim, S. (2014, November 21). 5 disturbing things we learned today about Sandy Hook Shooter Adam Lanza. *ABC News.* https://abcnews.go.com/US/disturbing-things-learned-today-sandy-hook-shooter-adam/story?id=27087140

Rossa-Roccor, V., Schmid, P., & Steinert, T. (2020, September 8). Victimization of people with severe mental illness outside and within the mental health system: Results on prevalence and risk factors from a multicenter study. *Frontiers in Psychiatry, 8,* 563860. Retrieved from https://www.frontiersin.org/articles/10.3389/fpsyt.2020.563860/full

Salam, M. (2017, October 26). Adam Lanza threatened sandy hook killings years earlier, records show. *New York Times.* https://www.nytimes.com/2017/10/26/us/adam-lanza-sandy-hook.html

Chapter 7

Character Deviance

"He's Not Sick – He's Bad"

"It started to irritate me. She was just down there – fiddle farting around. Pissed me off," said Lonnie, describing his impatience with a girl he was raping at knifepoint. When Otis' victim had their baby while he was using drugs with her, he forced her to leave the baby on the floor. "She just dropped right out," he said, "Onto the floor. I told the bitch, 'don't worry about it.'" "It was only about me. It was always about me," Matt explained, discussing his state of mind when he was assaulting children. All of these offenders revealed aspects of their personality or character that facilitated their offense behavior.

Personality is defined by the American Psychological Association (APA) as the individual differences in patterns of thinking, feeling, and behavior (APA, n.d.). Character is defined as not only the "aggregate of features and traits," but an individual's moral and ethical qualities and ideals (Dictionary.com, n.d.). When trying to understand the motivation and capability of sexual offenders (and other violent individuals) to harm others, it is essential to understand the personality and character elements that contribute to the violent behavior. Too often, the offender's character is overlooked in evaluating, treating, and managing offenders, while other issues become the focus.

Character and personality ultimately determine a person's course of action. What makes one victim become an offender? Why do some people abuse others when challenged? Why do some people commit sex offenses when they drink? All of these answers are "character." Researchers have made many efforts to identify causal relationships between sexual offending and other things – alcohol, a history of abuse, intimacy deficits, social skills problems, and on and on. These factors might all contribute to sexual aggression for a particular person. However, ultimately, there is a constellation of personality and character traits in individuals who commit sex crimes that facilitate and enable the individual to act upon their deviant and harmful urges. The traits that are particularly concerning are traits associated with antisociality and associated with narcissism.

What Is a Personality Disorder?

A personality disorder is defined by the DSM-5 (APA, 2013) as an "enduring pattern of inner experience and behavior that deviates markedly from expectations of the person's culture" (p. 645). A personality disorder is *pervasive*, meaning it impacts all spheres of a person's functioning, like thinking, perceiving, and relating. If a person is a perfectionist at work but is different at home or if a person is suspicious only toward people in a particular context, that person would not necessarily have a personality disorder. Personality disorders are chronic, inflexible, and stable. The disorder is part of the person's *foundation*, the personality and character. It is difficult to change – it is part of the individual's hardwiring.

DOI: 10.4324/9781003156284-10

Personality disorders make up a significant percentage of the mental health diagnoses of violent offenders, including sexual offenders. In fact, when there is a correlation between "mental illness" and violence, it is most often related to a diagnosis of a personality disorder, not another type of acute or severe mental illness. Domestic violence offenders, mass shooters, stalkers, and sexual offenders all demonstrate a significant incidence of personality disorder diagnoses as groups, if they have any diagnosis at all (Bancroft et al., 2012; Eher et al., 2019; Metzi & MacLeish, 2015; Nijdam-Jones et al., 2018; Sorrentino et al., 2018). In particular, personality disorders that are characterized by drama, egocentricity, and externalizing and erratic behaviors, referred to as Cluster B personalities, are diagnosed in violent and criminal individuals. Cluster B includes Antisocial Personality Disorder (APD), Narcissistic Personality Disorder (NPD), Borderline Personality Disorder, and Histrionic Personality Disorder. Antisocial and NPDs are criminal and violent offenders' most frequently diagnosed personality disorders.

While someone with a personality disorder is diagnosed with a mental illness, they are not easily identifiable as someone with a mental illness. A personality disorder diagnosis is a significant and severe diagnosis. However, this disorder is not marked by acute or necessarily obvious symptoms. Individuals with a personality disorder can look very "normal" to others. The symptoms are stable and often do not cause the person distress. Because the personality disordered person perceives the world, themselves, and others in a way consistent with their personality, the person can be quite comfortable with themselves. What agitates the personality disordered person is the rest of the world that does not conform to their view of things. Additionally, the personality disorder impacts the individual's moral and ethical reasoning, affecting how they treat others.

Personality and character traits exist on a continuum. We all have traits that could be considered perfectionistic, controlling, paranoid, egocentric, arrogant, or dramatic. It is when we have numerous traits of the same sort that are powerful and inflexible enough to cause us (and others) problems, then we might have pathological or diagnosable character issues. People may only have several traits that are problematic or chronic. These people may not have continual problems in their perception and functioning, but when a situation arises that challenges the flexibility of the trait, they might find themselves in trouble. For instance, take someone who is generally decent to get along with, but in a crowd always has to be the center of attention. That person might risk making people angry or hurt in a situation where she is not the center of attention, like at her daughter's wedding when she causes a scene. In fact, disordered personality characteristics are more predictive of violent behavior than a full diagnosis of a personality disorder (Dunne et al., 2018; Hepper et al., 2014). Because an offender might only have problematic characteristics as opposed to a full-blown personality disorder, it might be easier to overlook or minimize the impact of these traits.

Some sex offenders can seemingly function pro-socially and effectively, only demonstrating their antisociality or narcissism in the context of their offending, pathologically acting on their egocentric needs. Their ability to seem "so normal" is why examining the individual's character traits is always important. These character elements, including moral and ethical thinking, differentiate those who commit sexual offenses from those who do not. Many people struggle with and effectively control their sexual urges to children, because those people are against harming children and understand the potential consequences and damage. Because those individuals have internal barriers associated with their character, they do not sex offend against children.

Survival of the Fittest: Antisociality as a Character Pathway

I sat across from the man in my program being treated for his violence. He was describing to me the myriad of violent acts he had engaged in since he was a child – burning his grandmother in bed, shooting and stabbing people, his gang activities. I asked him about how he thought treatment was going. He thought he was making some progress, explaining, "I've even caught myself, like, feeling bad like for how people look at me for the things I've done. I don't know if it's really feeling bad or it just kinda bothers me now a little bit. Before it never bothered me – I didn't care." I asked, "Did you have a conscience before?" "No," he said with certainty. "Were there ever things you felt guilty about?" "No," he said again. I asked, "You're pretty certain of that?" "Umm hmm," he said, explaining how "happy and content" with himself he felt after shooting people. "I would just go home and eat cereal after shooting someone," he described. He had APD.

Antisocial Personality Disorder is characterized by pervasive interpersonal and behavioral disregard for the rights of others and the rules of society (APA, 2013). Antisocial individuals do not conform to expectations of lawful behavior, are deceitful and impulsive, and are aggressive to others. They lack remorse, an appreciation or concern for their impact on others, and empathy. They might know the rules and expectations, but have little need to follow them. They can be callous and contemptuous, as expressed by thoughts or statements like, "The bitch was stupid enough to get drunk with me. What did she think was going to happen?" APD is diagnosed in the majority inmates (APA, 2013).

Lonnie, who was quoted at the beginning of this chapter, was very antisocial. He raped two young women. One was 17 and his paramour's younger sister. The night he raped this victim, Lonnie and his girlfriend fought. She left the house. Within 10 minutes of her leaving the house, Lonnie grabbed a knife from the kitchen and went downstairs to rape the victim. He did this to retaliate against his girlfriend. When describing the rape and the victim's terror at being blitz attacked by Lonnie, he got an annoyed tone of voice and expression on his face. I questioned him about this. He explained that he had ordered the girl to put his penis into her vagina, but she was just "fiddle farting around" and hesitating. Her "incompetence" was irritating to him, even describing this horrible crime years later. This was his personality – extremely antisocial and callous. He had absolutely no connection to the victim.

Antisocial traits, like deceptiveness, callousness, lack of empathy, lack of remorse, low conscientiousness, and impulsivity, can exist in offenders without a history of criminality or criminal convictions. Eddie, a man who downloaded and disseminated extremely graphic depictions of child sexual abuse, including children as young as toddlers, was an excellent example of this. He was an EMT, a member of the Fraternal Order of Police, and a volunteer fireman. He presented the judge with a "stack of letters" from community members vouching for his character. "But I lead a double life," he said. He was deceptive to others, lying without feeling to those who supported him. He would sit for hours, masturbating to the images of child sexual abuse with no regard for the victims. He described the meaninglessness of the children's suffering to him. "It was like shopping for fire-rescue equipment. It was the same as, 'I'm hungry now – I'm going to make a sandwich,'" he said, describing how he viewed the images and masturbated with complete disregard for what he saw. He had no qualms about lying to his friends to get their letters of support, confidently approaching them and asking them for the letters while denying and minimizing his offending. His behavior requires antisocial traits.

Lack of Regard for the Rights of Others

One antisocial trait that enables sexual assault and other violent crimes is the disregard for the rights of others or no concern for the impact one has on another person. If you are not worried that others are being harmed because of you or that you will get negative consequences for your behavior, you have no internal crises about yourself. "Worry about only one person – me," Joe wrote, "Only one person matters – me. The worst case scenario doesn't matter, as long as I am taken care of." We can see some support for this idea in our society, with the levels of greed and disregard for others we see. Sometimes it is hard to confront this belief in the offender's character when the community supports it. "Women are there for my pleasure," Art asserted, citing the glorification of the "pimp culture" in his neighborhood. Another offender, when asked what his world view was, responded, "Most of the people are wandering aimlessly, taking up good oxygen and wasting their time."

Even if the offender can generally recognize others' rights, his antisocial values can be activated when another person "deserves" what happens according to the offender's beliefs. This is evident in the how offenders blame victims. A victim has no right to say no if she once said yes. If a victim gets the offender aroused, consent is not required. If a victim comes back or remains in contact with the offender, his rights are abdicated. Again, when the offenders' antisocial beliefs or values are activated in a particular context or certain conditions, it serves to meet their deviant needs. Offenders can project this onto helpers as well. My clinicians have been accused of "not caring" or "just doing this for the paycheck." When the offender can attribute an antisocial lack of concern to others, especially authority figures, it can justify antisocial acts for them. "The world is full of people who take advantage of other people," Mike wrote, "So why not me?" These distortions are why self-pity is destructive for offenders. If he can believe he is not cared for, he can justify disregarding others.

Immunity to Rules or Opinions

Another type of antisocial trait is immunity to other people's opinions, judgment, or evaluation, as well as disregard for the rules or expectations of society. Other people's perspective does not impinge on the view of the offender (Yong, 2018). In a good example, Marcus wrote in an assignment given because he was disruptive in group, "I will force (myself) to pretend as to like and love my neighbors." He goes on, "I will put away my strong intellectual mind, so that I can dumb myself down to the very likes of this class." Not only was he arrogant, but extremely dismissive of anyone's feedback or observations. "That's only your opinion," he would say when confronted.

Bob was a convicted rapist who raped numerous women. He was a short, harmless-looking man, looking a bit like Mr. Magoo when we got him in treatment. He was invulnerable to social pressure, others' opinions, or potential consequences. He had very little anxiety at all. Bob described on offense to exemplify his ability to manage crises. Bob was in the process of raping a woman at gunpoint. A police officer heard the woman's screams. Bob calmly explained to the officer that the woman was a prostitute and was angry he did not have enough money. Bob chuckled as he described how the cop did not believe the woman, all due to Bob's calm demeanor when confronted. I spent some time treating sexually abusive clergy. One Father said he "did not answer to the laws of man." Despite his admission that he had sexually abused multiple young adolescent girls, he stated that he did not hurt anyone, that he was being "nice" to the girls because he was "only nuzzling their genitals with affection." This man was unaffected by anyone else's opinion, invulnerability solidified by his ordainment. He did not even abide by the rules of his profession, though he relied on his profession for his status.

Lack of Conscience, Remorse, or Empathy

Some people do not truly feel sorry for what they have done. These individuals have the trait of callousness or are missing the traits of empathy and compassion. People with antisocial traits can profess guilt. They can feel distressed and feel sorry. But they have a terribly difficult time feeling deep regret for their behavior based on a true understanding of and compassion toward another person they have harmed.

Ken was another very antisocial and frightening rapist. He was extremely cold interpersonally. Ken was flat when he talked about forcibly raping a woman at a community party. She was drunk and sleeping or passed out in her tent. He walked right into her tent and raped her. He then left the tent and sat across from it. He got a beer and watched the woman come to, react, and become hysterical, realizing she had been raped. He drank his beer, feeling completely "empty" toward the woman. Ken was highly antisocial.

Other offenders can use distortions and rationalizations to keep their distress at bay. Others simply deny the impact of their behavior to build a shell of protection. Some hold the victim responsible. Some think that what they did was not that bad. Many offenders are adept at demonstrating the ability to see another's perspective, using that empathy to manipulate the victim. Offenders can weaponize empathy to use it against the victim, then commit harm without the compassion that must accompany empathy for empathy to be meaningful.

We are socialized to feel "guilty" when we have broken the rules. Very often, our guilt and anxiety about what we have done reflect our fear of the consequences or costs to ourselves. Almost all offenders I interview tell me they are sorry, surprised when I do not ask them first whether they are or not. They are further surprised when they offer that they are sorry when I ask them why. I have heard many surprising answers, most often reflecting the offenders' consequences. "I am sorry I went to jail." "I am sorry I lost my family." "I lost everything and paid my time." These statements exemplify the lack of true remorse or sorrow for harming another person. Another clergy offender told a boy that he could be hurting himself severely if he masturbated. He forced the boy to show him his penis, insisting despite the boy's resistance. He abused the boy until the victim felt so much shame and loathing that the boy put lighter fluid on his penis and lit himself on fire. The priest went on to abuse another child, having no regard for the extraordinary impact he had on his other victim.

Sex Offending as Part of the Criminal Repertoire

Antisocial traits or APD alone do not mean an individual will commit a sexual offense. But when someone antisocial commits a sexual offense, the offense might have nothing to do with any deviant sexual interest. The sexual offense becomes another criminal behavior in the person's repertoire, along with other crimes like assault, theft, and drug dealing. Because the sexual offense might have nothing to do with a specific sexual interest, the potential victim pool might be very large. If the individual is extremely antisocial, anyone might be a target. This is the case with offenders who burglarize, rape, and beat the elderly. It is the case with highly antisocial individuals who do not see gender or age as a barrier to sexual gratification.

Al was a criminal with a long rap sheet that included burglary, car theft, assault, and drug dealing. He spent much of his adult life in prison but made time when he was out to impregnate multiple women. Al had a six-year-old daughter he had never met. He was on parole when he and the child's mother decided the girl should meet her father. While she was staying with him that weekend, Al got high and "horny." He raped the child orally, commenting, "A hole is a hole." Al did not have a sexual interest in children. It was just that it did not matter that she was a child. Paulo was another very antisocial offender. He raped a woman and was convicted. He was sent back to jail for sexually abusing his paramour's teenage daughter. While awaiting his violation hearing, he raped his intellectually disabled male cellmate. Paulo always took what he wanted.

Narcissism and Sexual Offending

"I fell in love with the way I looked in her eyes, the way she looked at me," Mark said, explaining why he sexually abused a 12-year-old girl, the daughter of the woman with whom he was having an affair. He was her "first love." She looked up to him, worshipped him, and was completely compliant with him. She met all his narcissistic needs.

Narcissistic Personality Disorder is characterized by a constellation of features and traits related to aggrandized egocentricity. The person with NPD is arrogant, grandiose, exploitive, and entitled. They demand admiration, attention, and special treatment. The person with NPD feels above the rules, lacks empathy, demeans and devalues others, and is envious (APA, 2013). Narcissistic people believe they are superior in all sorts of ways. "You people say I am narcissistic," Damien said, "I'm not narcissistic. You should see me out there. People love me. I'm like Jesus." They expect to be given what they want and need when they demand it. They react very strongly to perceived criticism. One sex offending clergy member I evaluated actualized many traits of narcissism. He was glib and charming, arrogant, and prideful of his profession, even though he had been defrocked for sexually abusing children. "Hold my hand," he said, "I will get you to Heaven." He added that he had not "done anything wrong," though he admitted abusing several children.

Pathological narcissism is significantly correlated with aggression, violence, and sexual offending (Kjærvik & Bushman, 2021; Thornton et al., 2010; Widman & McNulty, 2010), in particular, the traits of entitlement, grandiosity, exploitiveness, and low empathy. While the diagnosis of NPD is significant in offenders who batter their partners, commit mass shootings, and stalk (Bancroft et al., 2012; Eher et al., 2019; Metzi & MacLeish, 2015; Nijdam-Jones et al., 2018; Sorrentino et al., 2018), even the presence of significant narcissistic traits is a predictor for violence and sex offending in an offender. Baumeister et al. (2002) found narcissistic reactions to sexual rejection were an impetus for sexual coercion. When the narcissistic individual is told no, he reacts with aggression and coercion to commit a sexual assault. Other studies have demonstrated that narcissistic traits can predict sexual coercion in both women and men (Blinkhorn et al., 2015)! Sexual narcissism in particular, characterized by sexual coercion, sexual entitlement, and sexual exploitiveness, is associated with sexual aggression (Widman & McNulty, 2010).

Narcissism is not a dichotomous concept. Someone is not either narcissistic or not narcissistic. All traits of narcissism exist on a continuum. Healthy individuals should have a notable level of narcissism – healthy narcissism. Healthy narcissism provides a sense of self and agency in the world. Too little narcissism and a person might feel chronically insecure, unimportant, and without any sense of agency. Too much narcissism and one becomes entitled, arrogant, and egocentric, aggrandizing oneself over others that become devalued. One thing that makes narcissistic traits problematic and pathological is not just how the person sees themselves in an aggrandized, overinflated way; it is how that person sees others as less than, less worthy or valuable. The arrogance of the offender can be unbounded at times. Gus was so arrogant and self-enamored when he would fantasize about sex with his girlfriend, she was just a receptacle for his "super sperm" that he would picture flowing into her, perchance producing another being as significant as he was. Arrogance can make the offender immune to the things that will change his behavior, as can other features of problematic narcissism.

Entitlement

A sense of entitlement is one of the strongest predictors of sexual and physical violence in offenders (Bancroft et al., 2012; Kjærvik & Bushman, 2021; Mann et al., 2010). Entitlement is the belief that one is warranted special treatment, rewards, and privileges without the reciprocity and responsibility that go with those things. The entitled person demands what has not been earned. He wants more than he rightly deserves. Entitled people believe the world should treat them as they expect and that their needs supersede the needs or limitations of others. They have unreasonable expectations that they require to be met. Jake had sex with his wife three hours after she had given birth. "I didn't want that baby to be the last thing that touched her vagina," he said, conveying his belief that his wife's vagina was his. "There were times in my life when I felt the world owed me," Gary said, "I didn't care who I hurt. I felt like my feelings were more important." Entitled men perpetrate most violent offenses, including domestic violence and mass shootings (Bouffard, 2010; Madfis, 2014; Parkinson, 2017; Richardson, et al., 2017).

Entitlement can come from status, wealth, or power, either real or perceived. "I mean, they wouldn't tell on me," said an offender who had been a lawyer, "They would want what I was giving." A former priest said, "I used my position," feeling entitled to abuse the children in his care because he had been nice and gave them things. Offenders feel entitled to sexually abuse others through a sense of ownership ("she was my child"), as a reward ("I did a lot for these people"), or because of their own importance. "I mean, who was she to say no to me? She wasn't even that hot," Charles explained to me, adding, "Look at me" to indicate his attractiveness and irresistibility. Thomas wrote, "I work hard and should get and deserve the respect that is owed me without dealing with reasons why or why not." He believed he had the right to sexually abuse the neighbor's child because he was babysitting.

William abused a number of children, as well as cheated on his wife many times. He felt entitled to abuse others through his distorted expectations of others. His family did not treat him well enough. His attractiveness was irresistible. People wanted him, so he was entitled to provide himself to them. William said that he abused the children to "comfort [him]self and appease [him]self from what [he] was missing" from his own family. During his interview, he became tearful, saying that he "never felt loved enough" by his wife or children. When I asked him what he was attracted to in others, William explained, "Anyone who is going to flatter me or make a fuss out of me, I will be attracted to." "If someone threw themselves at me, I ran to them," he said, "It was my comfort zone." His needs were a result of his insatiable ego and demands, not a result of poor self-worth. He excitedly explained when he worked as a musician, "Sex was so easy. I could have whatever, whenever, with whoever, however many times I wanted." He went on, "Partners waited for me. They took me to the room in cars with champagne."

Exploitiveness

Exploitiveness is the interpersonal ability to take advantage of another person for one's own benefit. It is another hallmark trait of pathological narcissism. Offenders see vulnerability as weakness and opportunity. They are adept at identifying people and situations to exploit and creating situations or states of vulnerability. Trust is a prime example. An offender will work to earn trust from parents or a potential victim, only to exploit that trust for their own gratification. So many situations are ripe for exploitation – a victim's intoxication, dependency, love, disability, loneliness, social isolation. Love and attachment are privileges that come with responsibility for most people. For offenders, love and sympathy are something to exploit. "I saw myself as the ruler, groomer of people," Gregory wrote, "I wanted everybody to want and enjoy me for my benefit." Gregory was "nice." He was a generous tipper. He had parties with very liberal sexual boundaries. He easily deflected allegations for years when he sexually assaulted someone, taking advantage of the intoxication, situation, and his reputation. Until he sexually assaulted a child whose parents he had not groomed.

In shame and confusion, Vince went to his confessor to discuss masturbating to fantasies of boys. His priest told Vince he had a "serious disease," convincing Vince to show the father his penis. The priest told Vince his penis was red, describing the dangers of masturbating because the priest knew of a man with a penis "swollen this big," holding his hands apart. The father stroked Vince's penis; when the boy's penis stayed flaccid, the priest told him he had "passed a test." Vince was relieved. He had felt like "a freak" for masturbating and was grateful to Father for helping him. This priest was extremely exploitive, taking advantage of a boy's trust, shame, and confusion, as well as the boy's affection, to go on abusing him for over a year.

Devaluation of Others and Lack of Empathy

Along with an overinflated sense of self, narcissistic traits can entail the devaluation of others and lack of empathy for others' suffering or pain. James, an extremely narcissistic abuser, said, "I was without a doubt the smartest person I knew and I could prove it." His opinion of himself had changed after being "disappointed" with how he did on the intelligence test I had given him. "I am honestly smarter than most people I know," he clarified, saying he was less smart than he thought. "I blame it on being in jail, hanging around those people," he said disgustedly of the other inmates, people from who he was different. James was in prison for nearly killing his four-year-old stepdaughter after she peed her pants. "I mean that kid, she couldn't do anything right," he said, "Her grandmother just dropped her on the doorstep like trash." James could not begin to identify his impact on the child and her mother by stomping the girl almost to death.

Women are subject to a great deal of devaluation in our treatment groups. It is very hard for new women therapists in our program. The devaluation begins when the therapists confront the offenders or do not respond to their seduction or intimidation. One of my therapists ran group for over a year and a half, only to discover that no one in the group remembered her name, while all of them knew the male co-leader's name. Inmates refer to their victims and lovers alike as a "female." The devaluation of others who do not meet their needs is chronic and salient in these narcissistic offenders. "I had anything I could've desired," William stated, those "things" being women, "They were so readily available." William spoke of others simply as if they were tools for him to use.

"Low Self-Esteem?" The Consequence of Deflated Narcissism

People with pathological narcissism can have very fragile egos. In the face of real or perceived rejection, humiliation, or embarrassment, a person with pathological traits can become highly retaliatory, resulting in a greater propensity to become violent (Baumeister et al., 2002). When the overinflated ego gets pierced, the person can become seriously and inordinately deflated, overwhelmed with a sense of inadequacy that might be perceived as low self-esteem.

However, deflated narcissism is very unlike low self-esteem. An overly narcissistic person never loses the underlying sense of superior value but can become rageful and unduly humiliated by situations that do not support that grandiosity. They can feel unjustly betrayed and, in response, feel provoked, acting out in rage and denigration of the person they blame for their feelings. The narcissistic person demands the world treat them as they expect – if it doesn't, someone pays. The overly narcissistic father will scream at the child for missing a hit at the game. The abusive husband will batter the wife for revealing something "embarrassing." The offender who believes he has been sexually rejected will devalue the victim and sexually assault her out of retaliation or entitlement – who was she to say no to him?

Summary

Character deviance is a primary pathway for violence, both sexual and physical. Identifying the traits of offenders associated with sexual violence and offending is essential to properly understand what differentiates offenders from others and accurately assess their risk and treatment issues. Treating the behavioral issues is incomplete; the character issues of the individual must be addressed. Additionally, recognizing how these traits are expressed in non-sexual ways, causing other types of damage and dysfunction for the offender and others, will give a complete picture of how the offenders' character contributes to their offending.

In conclusion:

- Character deviance is a primary pathway for sexual and violent offending.
- Personality disorders are the most common "mental illness" diagnosed for sexual offenders. Severe acute mental illness is not an impetus for sexual offending.
- A person does not have to have a personality disorder diagnosis to demonstrate a propensity for violence. Antisocial and narcissistic traits are significantly correlated with offending, some traits predicting sexual coercion in both males and females.
- It is character, not only sexual deviance, that needs to be addressed in treatment.
- If we ignore who a person is, and only attend to what they "have" – like an "addiction" or sexual deviance, we will fail in truly understanding and unmasking the offender.

References

American Psychiatric Association (2013). *Diagnostic and statistical manual of mental disorders* (5th ed.). American Psychiatric Publishing.

American Psychological Association (n.d.). *Personality*. APA Dictionary of Psychology. Retrieved from https://dictionary.apa.org/personality

Bancroft, L., Silverman, J., & Ritchie, D. (2012). *The batterer as parent* (2nd ed.). Sage.

Baumeister, R. F., Catanese, K. R., & Wallace, H. M. (2002). Conquest by force: A narcissistic reactance theory of rape and sexual coercion. *Review of General Psychology, 6*(1), 92–135. https://doi.org/10.1037/1089-2680.6.192

Blinkhorn, V., Lyons, M., & Almond, L. (2015). "The ultimate femme fatale? Narcissism predicts serious and aggressive sexually coercive behaviour in females." *Personality and Individual Differences, 87,* 219–23. https://doi.org/10.1016/j.paid.2015.08.001

Bouffard, L. A. (2010). Exploring the utility of entitlement in understanding sexual aggression. *Journal of Criminal Justice, 38*(5), 870–879. https://doi.org/10.1016/j.jcrimjus.2010.06.002

Dictionary.com (n.d.). *Character*. Retrieved from https://www.dictionary.com/browse/character

Dunne, A. L., Gilbert, F., & Daffern, M. (2018). Elucidating the relationship between personality disorder traits and aggression using the new DSM-5 dimensional-categorical model for personality disorder. *Psychology of Violence, 8*(5), 615–629. https://doi.org/10.1037/vio0000144

Eher, R., Rettenberger, M., & Turner, D. (2019). The prevalence of mental disorders in incarcerated contact sexual offenders. *Acta Psychiatrica Scandinavica, 139*(6), 572–581. https://doi.org/10.1111/acps.13024

Hepper, E. G., Hart, C. M., Meek, R., Cisek, S., & Sedikides, C. (2014). Narcissism and empathy in young offenders and non-offenders. *European Journal of Personality, 28*(2), 201–210. https://doi.org/10.1002/per.1939

Kjærvik, S. L., & Bushman, B. J. (2021, May 24). The link between narcissism and aggression: A meta-analytic review. *Psychological Bulletin*. Advance online publication. http://dx.doi.org/10.1037/bul0000323

Madfis, E. (2014). Triple entitlement and homicidal Anger: An exploration of the intersectional identities of American mass murderers. *Men and Masculinities*, *17*(1), 67–86. https://doi.org/10.1177/1097184X14523432

Mann, R. E., Hanson, R. K., & Thornton, D. (2010). Assessing risk for sexual recidivism: Some proposals on the nature of psychologically meaningful risk factors. *Sexual Abuse: Journal of Research and Treatment*, *22*(2), 191–217. https://doi.org/10.1177/1079063210366039

Metzi, J., & MacLeish, K. (2015). Mental illness, mass shootings, and the politics of American firearms. *American Journal of Public Health*, *105*(2), 240–249. https://doi.org/10.2105/AJPH.2014.302242

Nijdam-Jones, A., Rosenfeld, B., Gerbrandij, J., Quick, E., & Galietta, M. (2018). Psychopathology of stalking offenders: The clinical, demographic, and stalking characteristics of a community based sample. *Criminal Justice and Behavior*, *45*(5), 712–731. https://doi.org/10.1177/0093854818760643

Parkinson, D. (2017). Intimate partner sexual violence perpetrators and entitlement. In L. McOrmond-Plummer, J. Y. Levy-Peck, & P. Easteal (Eds.), *Perpetrators of intimate partner sexual violence: A multidisciplinary approach to prevention, recognition, and intervention* (pp. 44–54). Routledge.

Richardson, E. W., Simons, L. G., & Futris, T. G. (2017). Linking family-of-origin experiences and perpetration of sexual coercion: College males' sense of entitlement. *Journal of Child and Family Studies*, *26*(3), 781–791. http://dx.doi.org/10.1007/s10826-016-0592-5

Sorrentino, R., Brown, A., Berard, B., & Peretti, K. (2018). Sex offenders: General information and treatment. *Psychiatric Annals*, *48*(2), 120–128. https://doi.org/10.3928/00485713-20171220-01

Thornton, A. J. V., Graham-Kevan, N., & Archer, J. (2010). Adaptive and maladaptive personality traits as predictors of violent and nonviolent offending behavior in men and women. *Aggressive Behavior*, *36*(3), 177–186. https://doi.org/10.1002/ab.20340

Widman, L., & McNulty, J. (2010). Sexual narcissism and the perpetration of sexual aggression. *Archives of Sexual Behavior*, *39*(4), 926–939. https://doi.org/10.1007/s10508-008-9461-7

Yong, E. (2018, March 12). How psychopaths see the world. *Atlantic*. Retrieved from https://www.theatlantic.com/science/archive/2018/03/a-hidden-problem-at-the-heart-of-psychopathy/555335/

Chapter 8

Sexual Deviance

The Sexual Pathway to Offending

Sexual deviance is a term used to describe sexual interests outside expected behavior or social norms. This is a fluid concept that changes over time. There was a time when age-appropriate homosexual attraction was classified as deviant and disordered. This chapter does not discuss what is "normal" or expected. This chapter will focus on the deviant sexual interests that lead to the victimization of others. People's sexual interests or practices that do not involve victimization are not particularly important to understanding sexual offenders. If the sexual behavior is destructive, abusive, victimizing, or non-consensual, then it is what we are referring to as deviant interest or arousal when it comes to sexual offenders.

Paraphilias and Paraphilic Disorders

Exploring and uncovering the sources of deviant sexual arousal that motivate sexual offenders is often the most disturbing and upsetting aspects of working with offenders. Sometimes the source is incredible, sometimes inconceivable, and sometimes hard to accept. "I licked a guinea pig vagina," Jerry described, along with discussing his fantasies of abusing children. "The only thing she said the whole time was, 'no, please.' I could hear it through the tape. And I kept going," Troy reported, describing how the terror of the victim aroused him when he raped her after taping her face with duct tape. Arnold said of children, "I'm very attracted to their physical features and ... possibly the word innocence or taboo or some combination thereof." All of these offenders are describing sources of their sexual deviance.

Paraphilia is a word meaning, at its roots, love (philia) that goes beyond (para). Diagnostically, the DSM-5 (American Psychological Association [APA], 2013) describes a paraphilia as "any intense and persistent sexual interest other than sexual interest in genital stimulation or preparatory fondling with phenotypically normal, physiologically mature, consenting human partners" (p. 685). Quite a mouthful! What does this mean? Paraphilic arousal encompasses sexual arousal to or interest in anything other than typical sexual behavior with a developmentally mature human. Paraphilia is an umbrella term that covers all types of deviant sexual arousal. Paraphilic interests are not a passing curiosity. The deviant sexual arousal is powerful, more potent than, or at least equal to, the individual's sexual interest in more normative stimuli. Often, individuals with one paraphilic interest have more (Bradford et al., 1992). The intensity of the paraphilic arousal can create a more robust sexual desire and more deviant sexual acts. "I did meet adults on the Internet," the clergy offender said, describing his sexual behavior with men, "but they were all adults over 18. It was the children though." "Did you get the same satisfaction (from adults)," I asked. "Not as intense. Not as intense," he said, looking down, "No, not as intense."

We do not fully understand what makes someone have deviant sexual arousal. The models of etiology are varied and complex (see Healey's (2006) chapter in Hickey). There are

DOI: 10.4324/9781003156284-11

theories related to physiology. A component of behavioral conditioning involves reinforcing deviant interest through masturbation, orgasm, and psychological rewards (arousal, thrill). Some believe traumatic or disordered connections between arousal and deviance are made, like the boy who gets sexually aroused being spanked by his mother and carries that theme into adulthood.

Categories of Paraphilias

There are dozens and dozens of identified paraphilic interests. Likely even hundreds with the material available on the Internet. The DSM-5 includes ten named paraphilic disorders, eight of the most common, and two other categories that enable a clinician to diagnose or identify any other sexual interests not captured by the first eight outlined (APA, 2013). Only some of the paraphilic disorders involve the possible victimization of others. To capture the essential elements of each type of paraphilia, the DSM-5 offers two main categories of paraphilic interests – anomalous activity preferences and anomalous target preferences, anomalous simply meaning deviating from expected norms. The first involves erotic activities, and the second erotic targets.

Anomalous Activity Preferences

Anomalous activity preferences are those deviant sexual interests in which an individual is sexually aroused to and gratified by an activity that is not directly sexual. Getting excited by the idea of having sexual intercourse is not an anomalous activity. However, getting sexually excited by secretly peeping on your neighbor (voyeurism), rubbing up against an unexpecting person (frotteurism), or pretending you are an infant (infantilism) are paraphilic in nature. Many anomalous activities do not harm another person and can be consensual. These include, but are not limited to, getting sexually aroused by bondage, urinating on someone, breastfeeding, getting enemas, or dressing up.

The DSM-5 breaks down these activity preferences even further into disordered courtship behaviors and behaviors involving pain, suffering, and humiliation within the anomalous activity preferences category. Sexual arousal through sexual behaviors aimed at others without their consent, like exhibiting genitals or secretly taping someone going to the bathroom, is in the subcategory of disordered courtship behaviors. Paraphilic arousal in behaviors that include pain and suffering include sexual sadism, strangulation during sex, or receiving sexual suffering (sexual masochism). Voyeurism (peeping), exhibitionism (flashing), frotteurism, and sexual sadism result in the victimization of others, as the non-consensual aspects of sexual arousal are part of the arousal. "I would rub on kids anytime I could," the elderly priest said, "I would do it now if I could." He described how he volunteered at the local fair, standing by the animal cages where the children would crowd around, so he could rub his penis against their buttocks.

Anomalous Target Preferences

This subcategory encompasses the types of sexual arousal that involve a deviant target of arousal. The object of desire might be a child without developed sexual features, called prepubescent (pedophilia). A person might have deviant arousal to other species, like dogs or horses (zoophilia or bestiality). Some people have deviant arousal to a person in a compromised state, like a sleeping, comatose, or unconscious person. Others may become aroused to a victim in a vulnerable state, like someone with dementia, intellectual disabilities, or injured. Joseph, a former Eagle Scout, was convicted after raping a woman he rescued from a car accident. She had a head injury, bleeding with gravel literally in her brain. Before he took her for help, he vaginally penetrated her with his penis, overcome with excitement at her injured state.

Other targets of deviant arousal include objects or non-genital body parts, a paraphilic arousal called fetishism. Someone could have deviant arousal to feet, an amputation site, scars, or blood. People are sexually aroused by panties, shoes, leather, or other objects. Pat, one offender who victimized people over the Internet, had some very unusual deviant sexual interests. He would masturbate to extreme weather events. John, who licked the guinea pig's genitals, also became aroused by wearing children's panties and masturbating in his feces. We have had several offenders who were sexually excited by wearing and soiling diapers.

When Does the Interest Become Disordered?

An individual with paraphilic or deviant sexual interests would not be automatically considered disordered. In fact, DSM-5 specifically changed the name of the diagnostic category from Paraphilias to Paraphilic Disorders (APA, 2013). This change recognizes that for many people, having deviant interests, urges, and fantasies is not a problem for them and do not cause problems for others. Wearing a woman's panties to work may not cause a man any problem in his life, occupation, or relationship. Being sexually aroused by being bound if it is a part of a couple's consensual relationship is not necessarily an issue.

Deviant sexual interests become labeled paraphilic disorders when several conditions are met. First, the deviant interest has to have a level of duration. Someone will not be diagnosed with a disorder because that person experimented, had some fantasies, or engaged in behavior for a short time. The DSM defines the period of thoughts, urges, or behaviors as lasting more than six months. Not only does the interest have to persist, but it also has to cause problems. The deviant interest has to be disruptive or cause harm to the person or others. It has to impair the person in some way. This impairment, disruption, or harm can take several forms. Obviously, if the deviant interest motivates a person to commit a sexual crime, that is a disordered interest. If the deviant interest is so intense that it impairs the person's ability to have sex with a lover or disrupts occupational functioning because the person is up all night masturbating at the computer, it would be at the level of a disorder. If the person with the arousal is distressed, depressed, or ridden with shame about it, the interest would become a diagnosable disorder. Tony was a client who became obsessed with pornography depicting group sex. His partner would not agree to have group sex. He masturbated to the fantasy and images of group sex so much that he could no longer have sex with his girlfriend. His relationship deteriorated and ended. His obsession with pornography and the fantasy of group sex would qualify as a paraphilic disorder.

Paraphilic Interest and Sexual Crimes

No matter how unusual a deviant arousal sounds, just because someone has deviant arousal, especially a paraphilic interest in objects or particular sexual activity, does not mean they will commit a sexual offense or harm anyone. Most people with paraphilic interests would not conceive of victimizing another person. A subset of paraphilic disorders is highly associated with criminal sexual behavior. And combinations of and escalations of paraphilic disorders can also lead to sexually motivated criminal behavior.

Paraphilic Diagnoses Typically Related to Sex Crimes

Inherent in the definition of some paraphilic disorders is the victimization of others (APA, 2013). The definition of Voyeuristic Disorder includes the viewing of an unsuspecting person naked or disrobing. A non-consenting element to this behavior makes it criminal and victimizing. The same is true for Exhibitionistic Disorder, the exhibition of genitals to a non-consenting victim. For both of these disorders, there must be a victim of the acts for sexual gratification.

Sexual Sadism Disorder, the intense sexual arousal from the suffering of another person, can definitely lead to the victimization of another. Sexual sadists comprise the minority of sexual offenders, only about 10% of the civilly committed for sexual crimes (APA, 2013). This is a relief, as sexual sadists are the offenders of our nightmares, comprising horrid stories of serial sexual murder and torture of their victims. Sexual sadists are not the typical participants of "rough sex" or BDSM, who generally are consensual partners with a shared interest. Sexual sadists need their partners' pain, suffering, terror, or humiliation for sexual gratification. One sadistic offender I worked with used to take his four-year-old daughter into the woods at night and abandon her. He would hear her scream and cry in terror, then get aroused by her fear and suffering and sexually assault her. An uninformed family therapist who was working with the victim told the victim's mother to allow contact between the victim and her father in a time of family crisis for "healing." The family crisis was the euthanasia of the family dog. The perpetrator was allowed to experience the victim's grief while they watched their dog die together. It was difficult to make people see how this situation re-enacted the offense for the offender, gratified both by the dog's death and the victim's torment. Charles was a more overt sadist. He broke into his estranged wife's house and raped her for hours with several objects – his penis, keys, a water bottle, a doll, and most terrifying, a serrated knife. He sliced her up very badly inside, so she had numerous reparative surgeries and lost bowel function. She lived only because her alarm went off, and he left, fearing detection. To taunt her, he called 911 to tell them a dead person was in her apartment. Despite being handcuffed to the bed, she managed to pull a comforter to her to stem the blood. He is serving a life sentence.

Pedophilic Disorder is another type of deviant arousal that leads to sexual crimes. Individuals with pedophilia are sexually aroused to children without secondary sex characteristics. While many people do not act on those urges, some individuals do, sexually abusing children. Others seek illegal online material, images depicting child sex acts or sexual abuse. It is vital to understand that most people who sexually abuse children are not "true" or exclusive pedophiles. People who have "exclusive" pedophilic arousal are *only* sexually aroused by children. Exclusive pedophiles represent under 10% of those who sexually abuse children (Hall & Hall, 2007).

Most offenders of children are sexually aroused by adults as well as children. Many offenders who sexually assault children or seek sexual stimuli involving children do not meet the diagnostic criteria for Pedophilic Disorder because their thoughts, urges, or behaviors are brief in duration or are not focused on children as the source of the stimulation. For instance, Frank was an offender who sexually assaulted his six-year-old grandson on one occasion. Frank was not particularly interested in the fact that the boy was a child; he was obsessed with seeing a child's *penis*. Frank had a fetish disorder for the genitals of inappropriate targets – like dogs, roadkill animals, and strangers. He would visit "glory holes," where anonymous strangers would stick their penises through holes in a bathroom wall. Frank was fixated on genitals – the fact that his grandchild was a child was not a deterrent, but it was not his source of interest either. Other offenders who abuse children have other sources of stimulation. Some are sadistic. Some are indiscriminate. Only some people who sexually abuse children meet the diagnostic criteria for Pedophilic Disorder. Also, offenders who prey on post-pubescent adolescents commit many sex crimes. Because their victim choice is not prepubescent, they do not demonstrate pedophilic arousal in their crimes, though they are often referred to as pedophiles.

Offenders reveal arousal to non-content, coercion, violence, or force in diverse and unusual ways. Arousal to rape or force is not a specific diagnosable paraphilic disorder in the DSM-5 (APA, 2013). There is, and has been, significant controversy over the diagnosis of Coercive Paraphilic Disorder, the diagnostic term that attempts to capture the crime of rape and coercion. Scholars argue that rape is a criminal and not paraphilic behavior (Frances, 2011). Rape can stem from many sources of criminogenic need of an offender, reflecting the character issues discussed in the previous chapter along with meeting the non-sexual needs for power, domination, retaliation, and control. As discussed, narcissistic entitlement can fuel sexual coercion without indicating deviant sexual interests or deviant choice of targets.

There are offenders who are very aroused by non-consent, though. Roland was an emergency room nurse we treated. He was convicted of sexually assaulting his 17-year-old daughter. His initial evaluation suggested that he was aroused by adolescent girls. Over the years of treatment, we discovered he was really aroused to non-consensual, violent, and coercive sexual gratification. He assaulted his daughter when she was 17, grabbing her out of the shower and grabbing her breasts. He assaulted her when she was 8, after taking away her glasses and putting her in the dark until she agreed to touch his penis. Roland would sexually abuse his wife by psychologically tormenting her until she "allowed" him to penetrate her anally, something against her religion. He sexually abused his nursing interns, wielding his power to attain sexual favors. Roland sexually abused women with dementia, who he was tasked with caring for as a nurse. These are situations in which true consent was never offered or available to him. The element of non-consent was present in each sexual situation.

The Multiplicity of Paraphilic Interests

It is common to find that an individual with one paraphilic arousal has multiple paraphilic arousal sources. An illuminating study by Gene Abel and colleagues revealed that a significant percentage of sexual offenders who demonstrated interest in one paraphilia had deviant sexual interests in up to ten other paraphilic sources (Abel et al., 1988). Additionally, paraphilic arousal is intense. More sources of deviant sexual arousal contribute to more deviant sexual acts (Bradford et al., 1992).

My experience supports the findings that offenders are highly aroused by their deviance, engaging in more frequent and deviant acts. Offenders routinely discuss masturbating multiple times a day to their deviant fantasies. Some who have access to their victims, like their children, can become obsessed with the pursuit of gratification so much that they can be misdiagnosed when reporting their symptoms without revealing the motivation for the behavior. One stepfather I worked with stayed up all night, peeping on his stepdaughter, masturbating with her underwear he had stolen, and planning new ways to spy on her (including laying in the air ducts with a dental mirror). He was diagnosed with Obsessive-Compulsive Disorder. Others have been inaccurately diagnosed with Bipolar disorder because they demonstrated hypersexual behavior.

It becomes concerning and a greater risk when the offender's sexual offense contains multiple sources of deviant arousal. Paraphilic interests can contribute to offending and reoffending, even if those sources of arousal are not the target victim. It seems that reinforcing one type of deviant arousal leads to the activation of other types. Masturbating to or fantasizing about one disordered interest erodes the barriers and boundaries for different kinds of deviant arousal. This erosion does not just happen with offenders. Decision-making when sexually aroused becomes compromised. Dan Ariely described a study in his book *Predictably Irrational* (2010). The study found that "across the board," male participants were more likely to engage in "odd" or amoral sexual behavior if they were offered that behavior when they were aroused.

Even "harmless" paraphilic arousal can lead to criminal behavior. Richard, a sexual offender convicted of burglary, initially described that his paraphilic arousal was to women's panties. He would touch women's panties hanging on a clothesline to dry. He bought and wore women's panties. All of these behaviors were without consequence. However, as he got older, this was not enough for him. He got "burnt out," and the thrill of the panties was not gratifying. When Richard added the thrill of stealing the panties, it came alive for him again. He stole women's panties from laundromats and off clotheslines, reveling in his ability to get away with the theft as well as the panties. He imagined the women wearing the panties and their reaction to the missing ones. Richard became aroused to his new female neighbor. He combined his attraction to the neighbor with his arousal to panties and thrill from stealing and began stealing her panties. Eventually, this was not exciting enough, so he broke into her house to steal her panties from her bedroom. Imagine her terror and feeling of violation when she caught him in her home "red-handed." Richard was difficult to treat because he felt he had not harmed anyone. His daughter wrote us a letter to protest his treatment, saying a "fetish" was not a reason for sex offender treatment. Unfortunately, Richard's crime was not motivated by his fetish but by his growing excitement and arousal to violation.

Fantasy and Deviance

Fantasy is the primary motivating source for developing and maintaining deviant sexual arousal, motivating offenders to act. An offender's fantasy is powerful, distorted, and self-focused. In an offender's fantasy, he can build up the assault. It can go his way entirely. He can imagine himself as powerful, desired, dominating, or whatever qualities he wants. Like the fantasy of pornography, there is no rejection, no having to deal with another person's needs or feelings, no interruptions, and no threat of arrest.

Sometimes the fantasy is more gratifying than the actual act. Jason was convicted for assaulting his girlfriend's five-year-old son. He recorded himself spanking the boy and putting a pen into the boy's anus. The child's mother found the video. When I questioned him about his behavior, he said he was disappointed. The actual assault was less exciting than his fantasy. The child made "unpleasant" sounds. He preferred to watch the video, transforming it to meet his fantasy. He said he "collected information" to enhance his fantasy from his offense, like how soft the boy's buttocks felt.

Sometimes, very often, the fantasy is not enough. Offenders who use illegal images of children can go further to assault children when the images are not arousing anymore or when they feed the desire to touch a child. Offenders who watch aggressive, distorted images in pornography can become more sexually aggressive or motivated to act out their fantasies. Fantasies allow the offender to sexualize and objectify their victims or potential victims. Juan wrote in his confession after being arrested for raping his stepdaughter this (provided with typos):

J★ and I had sex two times a week ever since after her 17th birthday when I use to come out of work she would run up the stair an ask me if I was finish taking a bath. I would say yes. She'll say I be back. So when she came back she would be naked from the waist down and jump in my bed, spread her legs and tell me to hurry up. Sometimes it use to go a little longer then usual. She'll tell me to hurry up. Other times she'll ask me if I came. I would say no and say well you better hurry up before my mom's come home so she'll like force the issue buy moving and granning til I came and she'll ask me if I was finish. I would say yes. She'll answer damn Juan you took longer then before, ask me for a smoke, go to the bathroom, put her panties back on.

His confession reveals his fantasy – that his stepdaughter was a sexual aggressor. That she moved and groaned to get him off more quickly. And that she was a co-conspirator with him against her mother. An offender's fantasy includes tremendous distortions about himself and the victim and ignores the distasteful, unwanted elements of reality. Remember – the brain is our most powerful sexual organ!!

Ted was a homecare nurse who went into the homes of disabled people to care for them. He had sexual arousal to the rubbery, cloudy plastic that made up shower curtains and caps or rubber pants for incontinence. He spent his vacation touring the factory that made the plastic. Ted's job was arousing to him, as this plastic often surrounded him. When caring for a man severely disabled by cerebral palsy, Ted projected his fetish onto his client, sexualizing him while he changed his rubber pants. After writing out a detailed fantasy of the man that included watching the sun come up together, Ted sexually assaulted the man while the victim wore the incontinence pants. Ted's paraphilic arousal led to more fantasy that facilitated his assault of a patient.

When an offender becomes more and more deviant, adding more and more types of paraphilic arousal to the fantasy, their offending can become more complex. When an offender has to combine multiple sources of deviant arousal to be gratified, it may mean that they have overused a fantasy that has become dull or boring, as Richard did with the panties.

Troy was a repeat rapist who raped a beautician in her shop after closing time. He had a gun and duct-taped the victim's hands and face. He filmed the rape, specifically choosing a beauty shop to commit the crime in so he could watch himself in the mirrors. When interviewing him, I asked about the multiple sources of deviant arousal his crime revealed. "When you acted out, you had rape, the bondage, and the voyeurism – the filming," I said, "Explain how that happened – that you had three (sources of arousal) there." Troy explained the progression of his deviance and how he needed multiple elements in his sex crime to get him off. He began very young, looking at pornography, peeping in strangers' windows, and having fantasies of force. He took surreptitious photos of women, including up-skirting (taking photos up women's skirts without their knowledge). "It happened over the course of a lifetime, all the deviancies building up," he said. He began looking at bondage videos and movies depicting rape. Troy would hire prostitutes to tie up or "force" into sex. However, this was not satisfying. "I've been asked, 'why couldn't you just visit bondage parlors and do that? Or ask a prostitute or even ask your wife,'" he said, "It's the same way with the tapes – it's just not real." Troy needed "real" fear, "real" terror, and the "real" thrill of rape. After raping his first victim, he realized he wanted to watch too, inspiring him to plan to carry his camera and rape in the beauty shop. Troy's perfect offense combined all his deviant sexual interests.

Attraction → Arousal → Action

Fantasy is essential in turning attraction into action. All of us have been attracted to someone or something that could potentially disrupt our lives. Using a conventional example, imagine you are in a monogamous relationship and a new person starts at your job. You find the person attractive. When does this become a problem? The attraction itself is natural, perhaps unpreventable, happening instantly upon meeting the person. If you don't want a problem, you mentally move on, noting that the person is attractive.

However, the attraction becomes problematic when your thoughts linger on the person's attractiveness. You start to wonder if the person is available, if he or she likes sushi, or what car the person drives. You think about something to say to stop by the person's desk. In other words, you begin fantasizing about who, what, where, and how. This fantasy leads to arousal, not necessarily sexual at first, but excitement, anticipation, and stimulation. This arousal can compel action, like waiting in the break room to talk to the person, beginning to send texts and memes. Or prime you to take advantage of an opportunity, even if you do not create it, like quickly volunteering to be on the same committee.

It is the same for deviant arousal and offending. There is a mental and emotional investment in the thoughts and fantasy around the offending. Offenders can look "opportunistic" or impulsive because they act rapidly on unanticipated situations or openings. It is tempting to minimize the offense behavior because the offender did not "plan" what happened, like with an offender who finds himself in the restroom with a child and touches the child's penis or the rapist who finds a college student passed out in her dorm room and rapes her. The offender might lament that he "didn't mean to" and "couldn't help himself." This might be true, but what you have learned about the offender is that the fantasies and urges are active, that his "pump is primed" to offend so that no opportunity is lost. These are very dangerous and difficult to manage people, though we seem to fear the intentional, planful offender more. Remember, both the lion and the spider are predators; they just hunt differently.

The Non-Sexual Sources of Sexual Excitement

As the brain is the more important and influential sex organ, many sources of stimulation feed fantasy and contribute to arousal. As discussed, offenders are aroused by typically sexual things, but also a sense of power, the thrill of being able to manipulate, and props and reminders of their offending. Many people have heard that some serial killers collect "trophies." This is not just a way to count offenses or keep mementos; it is a pathway to the fantasy of the offense.

In treating and managing offenders, it is important to remember that seemingly innocuous and non-sexual things may be very sexually stimulating for the offender. Being mindful and challenging the offender on how he is keeping his fantasy active is an integral part of treatment and risk management. Mike came to the group wearing a logo t-shirt one day. His parole officer was visiting the group. Mike was talking about his new job when suddenly his parole officer cocked his head and asked, "What are you wearing?" Mike's t-shirt logo was of the park where he met his victim the day he assaulted her. It was not only a way he could relive his offense but wearing it to the group was another conquest for him, exhibiting his trophy right in front of the people treating him. Donald was found with a recording of "High School Musical"; he offended teenagers. Al, who was a violent rapist, loved slasher movies. Matt, a voyeur and rapist, got a second job as a limo driver, where he could "peep" on the people he was driving, often intoxicated. All of these are non-sexual examples of sexual stimuli.

Typologies of Offenders: Understanding Preference and Barriers

Over the last few decades, researchers, law enforcement, and clinicians have attempted to establish categories and typologies to sort offenders. Offenders have been described by victim type (adult versus child), relatedness (incest/familial versus non-familial), or the nature of the relationship (stranger versus acquaintance). Offenders get classified as targeting male versus female victims. Or they get classified by how they commit their crime, like angry versus seductive.

Unfortunately, as treatment has become more exploratory, combined with the use of polygraphs, and because we have found tremendous information in untested rape kits, these intuitive categories seem to fall apart. Most offenders admit to "crossover" offenses, crossing lines of age, gender, and relationship (Heil et al., 2003; Simons, 2015). When the backlog of rape kits was tested, researchers found no consistent MO or victim preferences in the rapes identified as belonging to the same rapist (Lovell et al., 2020). The rapists raped children and adults, strangers and acquaintances.

Numerous factors can influence how an offender commits a sexual offense and who the offender picks. While offenders might have *preferences*, that does not mean they will not assault a victim who does not match their preference. An offender who prefers young adolescents but has no access to one might choose an 11- or 12-year-old. Someone who has pedophilic arousal and prefers boys but has the opportunity to include their little sister too, can sexually assault a girl. A coercive offender who prefers not to use physical violence might need to overcome a victim's resistance, so he strangles her. Just because someone prefers something sexually (we all do) does not mean that person will not engage in other types of sexual behavior.

Cliff sexually assaulted multiple little girls. He began abusing his first victim, his wife's niece, when she was six years old, using "a lot of manipulation and bribery" with her. Cliff wanted to perceive himself as nice and gentle, loved and desired by his victim. He would kiss her, put his mouth on her genitals, and ejaculate on her stomach. He never penetrated her because he did not want to hurt her or leave evidence. "I did everything I would envision with a woman," he said. The victim moved away and "left a void" for Cliff. He began abusing his older biological daughter because she was "accessible." Cliff preferred girls who were six to eight years old. He was not thrilled with abusing his own "blood," who also was older than he liked, between 11 and 12. Finally, Cliff had to be "more forceful" with his daughter because she was more resistant. He threatened the child with a knife, something he "had to do" once to an adult woman when he told her she was going to "give [him] some." Cliff's offense behavior aptly demonstrates how someone can diverge from his preferred victim choice, relationship with the victim, and offense behavior to meet his needs.

The victim pool can be vast if the deviant arousal includes a situation, interpersonal dynamic, or anomalous activity or target. Someone aroused to violence or cruelty without regard for victim type can be cruel to anyone. Jeff is an example of this. Jeff was convicted of raping a teenage girl. However, he had also participated in gang rape of an adult woman, raped an animal brutally, and raped his cellmate while incarcerated.

For some offenders, characteristics of the victim or the offense are significant and serve as barriers to sexual arousal and sexual offending. Many very prolific offenders could never get aroused to a prepubescent child. Some could never be aroused to a same sex victim. Other offenders might be deterred by a victim's pain or a bodily function, unable to maintain arousal if the victim cries or bleeds. Some offenders draw a bold line between their children and their sexual arousal.

Deviant sexual arousal and the ability to become or maintain sexual arousal in the face of obstacles or deviant stimuli are highly individualistic, as are our own sexual preferences or sources of arousal. It is critical to fully explore and understand the sexual interests of every offender, as opposed to inaccurately categorizing offenders by the victim characteristics. Defining the offender by the victim can be fraught with assumptions and carry dangerous risks for potential victims and poor supervision.

Summary

Sexual deviance is fascinating, titillating, and sometimes disturbing. It serves as a pathway for sexual crimes, bolstered and impelled by fantasy and distortions. While sexual deviance is not the only pathway to offenses, it is certainly a component. Even offenders with character pathology can maintain their sexual interest and sexual arousal in the face of potential deterrents, like the victim's resistance or rejection.

In conclusion,

- Paraphilic arousal is a pathway to sexual offending. However, most people with deviant sexual arousal do not commit sexual crimes. Many sexual offenders do not have a diagnosable paraphilic disorder.
- Offenders can have multiple sources of deviant arousal. Reinforcing or acting out on one deviant arousal can increase the offender's risk of acting on the arousal related to the sexually criminal behavior.
- The victim's characteristics alone should not define an offender's sexual interest.
- Fantasy and the non-sexual sources of stimulation must be explored and challenged during the treatment and supervision of the offender.
- Deviant arousal is complex and individualistic. It needs to be thoroughly assessed and understood before we can make accurate decisions about the offender's risk and treatment and supervision needs.

References

Abel, G., Becker, J., Cunningham-Rathner, J., Mittelman, M., & Rouleau, J. (1988). Multiple paraphilic diagnoses among sex offenders. *Bulletin of the American Academy of Psychiatry and the Law, 16*(2), 153–168.

American Psychiatric Association. (2013). *Diagnostic and statistical manual of mental disorders* (5th ed.). American Psychiatric Publishing.

Ariely, D. (2010). *Predictably irrational (Revised and expanded ed.): The hidden forces that shape our decisions.* Harper Collins.

Bradford, J., Boulet, J., & Pawlak, A. (1992). The paraphilias: A multiplicity of deviant behaviors. *Canadian Journal of Psychiatry, 37*(2), 104–108. https://doi.org/10.1177/070674379203700026

Frances, A. (2011, May 12). DSM-5 rejects Coercive Paraphilia: Once again confirming that rape is not a mental disorder. *Psychiatric Times.* https://www.psychiatrictimes.com/view/dsm-5-rejects-coercive-paraphilia-once-again-confirming-rape-not-mental-disorder

Hall, R., & Hall, R. (2007). A profile of pedophilia: Definition, characteristics of offenders, recidivism, treatment outcomes, and forensic issues. *Mayo Clinic Proceedings, 82(4),* 457–471. https://doi.org/104065/82.4.457

Healey, J. (2006). The etiology of paraphilia: A dichotomous model. In E. Hickey (Ed.), *Sex crimes and paraphilia* (pp. 57–69). Pearson Prentice Hall.

Heil, P., Ahlmeyer, S., & Simons, D. (2003). Crossover sexual offenses. *Sexual Abuse: A Journal of Research and Treatment, 15*(4), 221–236.

Lovell, R. E., Williamson, A., Dover, T., Keel, T., & Flannery, D. J. (2020). Identifying serial sexual offenders through cold cases. *Law Enforcement Bulletin* (official publication of the U.S. Federal Bureau of Investigation), May. https://leb.fbi.gov/articles/featured-articles/identifying-serial-sexual-offenders-through-cold-cases

Simons, D. (2015, July). Adult sex offender typologies. *SOMALI Research Brief.* Retrieved from https://smart.ojp.gov/somapi/chapter-3-sex-offender-typologies

Chapter 9

Tools of the Trade

The Manipulations of the Offender

Earl was out on bail for raping three children when he committed his last child sexual assault before going to jail. He raped his best friend's 11-year-old daughter, taking her to a hotel to do it. I was astounded that he had access to this child while on bail for other child rapes, especially after he told me the girl's father knew of his charges. Earl patiently explained that he offered his friend a favor, to take the girl Mother's Day shopping for her mom, something the husband/father had not done. "I was being nice," Earl said. He broke into a large, genuine smile. "Doc," he said, "You can never see this coming." Earl succinctly captured how easy it is to manipulate people.

Offenders want to offend. And they want to get away with it as often as they can. They cannot present like someone we would automatically distrust or suspect. They cannot be generally repellent. So they utilize a whole repertoire of manipulations and ways to deceive both the victim and the audience to the offending. Roland understood this. While in treatment, Roland was dirty, sloppy, and unshaven. He would wear inappropriate clothing. He fit the stereotype of a "pedophile." We thought he was making progress when he cleaned up, became more assertive, and got a job – all traditional therapeutic markers of progress and prosociality. He then reoffended. When questioned, Roland said something to the effect of, "Of course I cleaned up! You think anyone is going to come near me lookin' like that!" I am sure that inside, Roland was shaking his head at our stupidity.

This chapter does not address all the specific ways offenders trick and deceive us but describes some overarching techniques and means that allow them to puppeteer the victims and their environment. Society is primed for these manipulations, as co-existing requires a significant level of cooperation, trust, and interdependence. The human condition itself, along with the general good nature of most people, allows offenders to wreak havoc at the most foundational level of community.

Sexual Assault and the "V" Word – Vulnerability

"For me, being an opportunist is looking and waiting for the right time," Jesus explained, "Creating that right moment by convincing people you are not a threat to anyone, by befriending people, gaining their confidence and trust in you until that moment is presented." This offender was eloquently describing the creation and exploitation of vulnerability that offenders are adept at doing.

Sexual assault is about vulnerability. At its very essence. Vulnerability is the state of being open or susceptible to harm or attack. Those vulnerable require care or protection because they are at risk for abuse or harm. Yet, vulnerability is considered weakness, a result of a victim's stupid choices to put herself "in that situation" to be harmed. To be caught vulnerable is to be caught in a shameful state. We attempt to coach potential victims on how to prevent

DOI: 10.4324/9781003156284-12

vulnerability, shifting the responsibility to act "right" onto the victim. In my TEDx Talk, "Sexual Assault and the 'V' Word" (Valliere, 2016), I discuss vulnerability as a moment-to-moment, day-to-day condition of being human, determined not by vulnerability but by those who prey upon it. There is no vulnerability without danger. But in a society that devalues and judges vulnerability, instead of protecting it, an offender can easily succeed.

Identifying and Exploiting Vulnerability – Picking the Victim

"Well, which kid did you have picked out," I asked Ethan, a young offender who could sexually assault a child in church while she sat next to her mother by the time he was 14. Ethan had gone to a bowling alley on a Sunday afternoon, encountering a children's church group. He described the child. "How did you pick him out," I asked. "His socks," said Ethan, going on to explain that mismatched, holey, dirty, or missing socks could indicate a child who was poor or not attended to by an adult. At a very young age, Ethan found signs of vulnerability quickly and in unusual places.

Offenders choose their victims specifically. There are innumerable ways a victim may be vulnerable to perpetration. Common vulnerabilities include poverty, disability, intoxication, social or physical isolation, a prior history of abuse, poor or missing social supports (like a single parent), or a poor reputation. The victim might have a pleasing or submissive personality. The victim might be needy or grateful for attention. Or the victim might be a behavior problem, criminal, or socially stigmatized. Offenders target prostitutes or sex workers because of the vulnerabilities inherent in their work – the time of day they work, the isolated situations, and the social stigma involved. Substance abusing and mentally ill victims face the same barriers to protection from predation. The abusive priest described his victim choice. "You said you could be helpful to them," I said during his interview, "What kind of help did your victims need?" "Some of them were from troubled families, no father image, divorced parents, poor, disadvantaged," he said, "Those were the kind of people I looked for." Offenders choose vulnerable victims because they may also have credibility issues.

Nathan was preyed upon by his Boy Scout Leader, Mr. Moyer. Nathan had pre-existing issues, having been diagnosed with Attention Deficit Hyperactivity Disorder early on and abused by his father. Nathan's peers described him as "annoying" and "pestering." He did not have any friends. Boys Scouts was his mother's effort to get him involved, especially because he had no male role model at home. Mr. Moyer quickly identified Nathan's vulnerabilities and sexually abused him for months. "I definitely made distinctions between different kids," Aiden, an offender of adolescents, explained, "The ones I provided alcohol to were the ones who had less connections to their parents, that got along less with their parents. I knew who the good kids were."

Offenders may test or assess the victim before choosing the victim. "I didn't really like her," Paul said, "I really liked her sister – but she had a mouth on her. Jessy was quiet. I knew she would keep a secret." The offender might float questions to get information about the victim, like Sandusky did to a victim I spoke to, questioning him about how late his father worked and where his mother was. After Sandusky found out that the victim had to walk to school and feed himself, he started showing up to give him rides and take him for fast food. Sarah was a medic who cared about the mental health of her fellow soldiers. Her colleague, a fellow medic, found that if he called her and threatened suicide, she would drop everything to ensure his safety. The third time, he called her at 1:00 a.m. She left her bed and her husband to make sure he was safe. He brutally anally raped her, causing injuries that lasted weeks. She could not go for medical care because the only place to go on the base was where they worked. Not only did Sarah want to avoid the rapist, but she was also familiar with the culture of denigrating and shaming victims that went on in the hospital. The rapist had tested the victim and knew the environmental context that would keep her quiet.

Creating Vulnerability – Crafting a Victim

Not only do offenders know how to identify and exploit someone's pre-existing vulnerabilities, they know how to create vulnerability in their victims. "I lived in a rural area," said Scott, describing how he coerced his girlfriends sexually as a teen, "My girlfriend and I would go for a walk, and I pretty much wouldn't let them leave until, you know, I would get to do what I wanted with them." He knew that physical isolation worked. Other offenders feed victims alcohol, knowing that they can manipulate the victim and her memory and that the victim will be blamed.

Scott did this as well. Scott escalated his offending of one teenage victim after he caught her smoking weed. He used her fear of being caught and her mother finding out to coerce her into exposing her breasts. He penetrated her vagina with his finger after she did so. I asked him when he first learned he could use drugs or alcohol as a tool to manipulate victims. He said,

> Probably when I was 14, 15, when my best friend and I raped the babysitter. At one point in time, my best friend and I got his little brother's babysitter drunk to the point where she passed out, and we took all her clothes off and digitally assaulted her, stole her undergarments and dressed her back up. We hid her underclothes in the park and made a game out of it. When she woke up, she asked where her clothes were. We said we didn't know nothing about that but we saw clothes in the park…. A couple months later we did it to her again. It became a big joke like.

There are overt physical and practical ways to create vulnerability in victims, like isolating or drugging them. But there are more insidious, complicated ways. Offenders are adept at getting the victim attached to them, like them, care for them, protect them, and even love them. Domestic violence offenders are prime examples of how to garner victims' love and attachment, then subject them to terrible acts of abuse. I fully believe that the right offender can victimize anyone. When an offender has intimate knowledge of another person, he can use that knowledge to cause self-doubt, low self-worth, dependency, and fears of abandonment in the victim. When an offender is giving and kind, the victim faces the loss of the good stuff to get the abuse to stop. Offenders know how to build attachment with the victim. "My own personal thoughts on that," explained Ted, "was that I was giving him something he didn't have, something he wanted that I was fulfilling, even though it was wrong, not good for him. I think he saw it as someone caring about him."

When an offender can get a victim to love or become attached to him, it becomes effortless to abuse that victim. Of 50 offenders I surveyed, 67% believed their victim liked or loved them. The percentage is higher when the group excluded those who were convicted of possessing illegal imagery. The offenders who lured minors online almost always built emotional rapport with the victim before requesting naked images or meeting offline. "You are my llama," the offender texted the 14-year-old, "You are the most important person in my life." "Talking to each other literally helps us survive life," he wrote, over time discussing the future children they would have. This is consistent with the findings of a study by Katz and Barnetz (2015) who found that child offenders formed a relationship with their child victims (as well as threatened families). The child victims reported that the emotional connection was the most impactful element of the offending. Very often, when I review the text messages between online offenders and their victims, the texts include promises of love, calling the victim "baby," "babygirl," or "love," and telling the victim he missed her during the day.

Nice Is a Four-Letter Word

As social creatures, we tremendously value positive experiences with one another and strive for affirmative and optimistic states of mind. We like to be nice and have people be nice to us. We want to believe that people are good, believe the best in someone. Being nice is seen as a virtue, a socially important response to others. Given that, the use of niceness by offenders can be a powerful weapon. "I mean, we did a lot of fun things," said Ted, "I took them on trips, social activities so I would gain their liking to me – I would use those opportunities to make them more vulnerable to what I was going to do, what I intended to do."

But ask yourself, what does nice really mean? Does it mean kind, honest, caring, trustworthy? It does not. It means that someone is engaging in socially pleasant behavior. Gavin de Becker (1997) writes, "Niceness is decision, a strategy of social interaction" in his book *The Gift of Fear*. He rightly points out that it is an outcome-oriented behavior that benefits the offender. Being nice does not reveal any character traits. And it always benefits the offender.

Niceness is an effective weapon against the victim. We are highly socialized to respond to niceness in turn. When the victim does not respond to an offender being nice, the victim can experience significant backlash through the offenders or others. How often have you heard a mother reprimand a child who resists an adult's touch? "Hug your uncle! That's not nice!" Jack abused a young boy during and after taking the boy to his football practices. Right before he was caught, Jack called to tell Mikey when he was going to pick him up for practice. Tired of being assaulted, Mikey made a fuss, yelling that he "didn't want to go" with Jack. His mother forced him to go, telling him to stop being rude, that Jack was being "really nice" to take him places. Mikey told about the abuse after Jack assaulted him that very same day.

Women especially are socialized to be nice. When they are not, they are a problem. A clear example of this happened to me while I was traveling. I was eating at the bar, reading, alone because I was traveling. A group of four intoxicated men came in, celebrating one's birthday. When they tried to buy me a drink, I said, "No, thanks." They tried to pressure me into taking it three more times – they were just "being nice." The final time, the bartender even got in on it. I refused again, only to hear, "Don't be like that!" The message was that I was being a bitch. Even though I had my wishes disrespected repeatedly. Another power of "nice" that situation exemplifies is how hard it is to confront someone being nice to you. Imagine what repercussions I would have faced if I had confronted the men on disregarding my "no" three times! How easy is it to set limits with your grandmother when she wants you to take all the leftovers, even if you are on a diet?

Being nice can often contrast the offender with the victim. Often victims are hostile, angry, and traumatized. Through the abuse and manipulation, the offender has created symptoms in the victim, which is then used against the victim. Sexually abuse your stepdaughter for years; she might cut herself, run away, sneak out to see boys, and be defiant. Then you, as the offender, can stand up after the allegations are made and defend yourself. "I have a job! I am good father! Look at her, your honor," the offender can say, "She is a problem! She lies all the time!" The problems the offender created for the victim contrast with the nice, decent, and prosocial offender.

Leonard was a very psychopathic man who had murdered and raped a 12-year-old (among other crimes). During treatment and supervision, he began repairing umbrellas, collecting broken ones from the trash. This concerned us. What we discovered is that Leonard would drive around when it was raining and offer umbrellas to women waiting at bus stops. He gave some of them rides home, after the women accepted his offer from such a nice man. Now a man who murdered and raped someone knew a strange woman's home address. Just like that.

"Grooming" – Preparing the Victim

Once a victim is selected, an offender begins to prepare the victim for the offense. Grooming is a term aptly defined by Tanner and Brake (2013) as "patterned behavior designed to increase opportunities for sexual assault, minimize victim resistance or withdrawal, and reduce disclosure of belief" (p. 1). As most offenders know, gaining the victim's cooperation with offending makes the offending easier, less likely to fail, and easier to blame the victim.

Chris was an offender who identified 96 victims he assaulted. None told on him. He was caught by police assaulting a child in his car. When I questioned him about how this could be true, that he assaulted almost 100 victims who never disclosed, he explained it to me. "I gave them all the choices," he said, "I asked them what they wanted to do or what they wanted me to do to them. If they would meet me or unlock their bedroom window. They were making all the decisions. Who were they going to tell on - themselves?" The more an offender can trick the victim into cooperating, the more the victim can be blamed. Just think of all the choices that a victim who is raped on a date made to put herself in that situation. And this is multiplied if the date included drinking, going to her place, and some consensual activity that she chose. All those choices by the victim leave less work for the offender.

Boundary Violations

One crucial step to grooming is the incremental boundary violations that offenders engage in with children and adult victims. They push through boundary after boundary until the victim is caught in an unmanageable situation. The violations might include sexual comments or jokes, one more drink, insisting on driving her home, or "just a kiss." The offender might become overfamiliar, be overly friendly, or transgress appropriate social expectations, like the sexually harassing boss who asks about his subordinate's sex life. With children, the offender might be permissive, violating parenting expectations. The offender might be physically violating, like walking into the bathroom when the child is showering, leaving his bathrobe open, or letting his son watch pornography with him.

Jack described the slow, progressive steps he took to groom his victims. He said:

> Well, it started out with getting them up in my room, in my bedroom and laying on the bed, playing video games. Video games were a big thing I used, you know, because it's convenience there on my bed and I would wrestle with them. There's a lot of horse playing in my case. You know, young boys, that's, uh, you know, they love to horseplay. So I used that to my advantage to, you know, I got aroused by wrestling with them in the bed, pinning me and, you know, to get them safe or to feel safe or secure with me assaulting them, you know, we would wrestle and I'd say it's getting hot in here and I'll take my shirt off. And most of them follow cue and they would take your shirt off or

I would take their shirt off. I can't … I mean, a lot of time when they got to the point where I was actually to the point where I was naked in bed with my victims, getting their clothes off, took a lot over time. It happened – it wasn't right away you know. It was like one thing at a time.

Jerry Sandusky was excellent at boundary violations, even in public (O'Neill, 2012). While he could be very aggressive and forcible with the boys alone, he incrementally breached the limits of appropriate behavior with his victims and others. He played "tickle monster" with kids and horseplayed with them in public. He showered with them. He put his hand on their thighs in the car, followed by hugs. He gave them presents and perks. He escalated over time to orally and anally penetrating his victims. He was so good at boundary violations, a victim reported that he would appear at the victim's classroom during the school day, take him out of school to abuse him, then return him, no questions asked. People would say, "Jerry Sandusky was a saint."

Socialization to Accept the Abuse

Jack can clearly articulate the slow socialization into accepting the abuse he did to his victims. This socialization to acceptance is a process common to other abusers, who also convince the victims they "asked for" it, provoked it, or deserved it. An offender might socialize the victim by normalizing the abuse or influencing the victim's perception of the abuse. He might tell the victim that this is how people show love. He might say he didn't "mean" it, apologize, and ask for forgiveness. To remain in the relationship with the offender and not suffer loss or consequences, the victim can come to accept the abuse as the toll paid for all the benefits the offender offers.

Progressive boundary violations can be sexual as well. An offender can expose the victim to sexual material or content, like showing the victim how much fun people have when they have sex, using pornography or even cartoons. One offender I worked with spliced pornography into Disney films to show the children. Adolescent boys are highly susceptible to this type of grooming. I worked with several boy victims whose friend had a "cool" dad who gave them beer and weed, leaving his pornography around for the boys. He would encourage them to masturbate, then would watch them masturbate. Eventually, during sleepovers, when the boys were high and drunk, the man would get into bed or their sleeping bags and anally penetrate them. Not only had the boys been socialized to accept the abuse, they felt ashamed and guilty for the other sexual things, as well as for using drugs and alcohol. They felt ashamed for going back to the friend's house after the first assault. The stigma of their choices managed them.

Shifting the Burden to the Victim

"Go ahead! Call the police," the stepfather offender would sob after assaulting the victim. He would hand her the telephone while saying what a bad person he was. He would "beg" her to turn him in; instead, the victim would comfort him. This is one example of how offenders shift the burden of the offending onto the victim.

Missy was a victim I was working with who was in foster care. She was a bright, outgoing child. She was open with her first-grade teacher about why she was in foster care, telling her teacher that her father touched her privates. The teacher told the foster parents, who instructed Missy to keep quiet about her abuse, conveying that she should be ashamed and embarrassed about being abused. This struck me quite hard, making it apparent that the victim carries the burden of the shame, blame, and stain of being abused. It is hard to discuss being a victim. This is in contrast to the many offenders that adopt a righteous, offended presentation about being "accused of such a thing!" Offenders act outraged. They go around telling people about the false accusations they have suffered. They asked for character letters and witnesses to defend them. Jerry Sandusky and others simply acted shocked or explained away their behavior, even after being caught. The victim bears the shame. Jesus, who abused his young sister-in-law starting when she was 10, bragged about the "affair" he was having with her when her allegations came out, saying she was accusing him because he would not leave his wife.

Offenders shift the consequences of their behavior away from them, too. The victim is blamed for telling and "ruining" the offender's career or life. The offender will threaten the victim with the realistic potential consequences for disclosure – daddy will go to jail, mommy will be mad at you, you will go to foster care. When in group therapy, offenders will confront my therapists, saying that we are ruining their family by not letting them return home where their victim lives – as if their sexual offending was not the problem. In trials, the victim's credibility and motive to lie are scrutinized, not the offender's. As if being convicted of a sexual offense is not a motive to lie.

Stimulating the Victim

One powerful manipulation of offenders is to sexually stimulate the victim – putting their mouth on victims' genitals, using sex toys like vibrators on children, or using the victims' natural sexual response against them. Not only does this confuse the message that sexual abuse is "bad touch," it sexualizes the child and shames the adult victim. There is stigma around sexually responding to sexual abuse and assault, so much so that lawmakers continue to publicly comment on how "legitimate rape" will be experienced. I have been involved in numerous trials when the offender was acquitted due to admissions or accusations that the victim moaned, got lubricated, got an erection, or even orgasmed.

In his YouTube video "Why Rape is Sincerely Hilarious," VenerableB (2014) articulates the heartbreak and confusion of having a physical response to being sexually assaulted by his adult female teacher when he was 13. He said,

> I was like "score" because I was a horny 13-year-old boy and I totally wanted to have sex. And now I totally had had sex with an adult I'd trusted … I mean, it was statutory, not real rape. I mean, I wanted it. I must have wanted it because I got an erection from her, stimulating me and the fear. Physically, it felt really good. At the same time, like the worst thing that could possibly happen to me, like I was less than human.

Boys are particularly vulnerable to being sexually stimulated and confused by abusers. Randall, a man who abused over 300 pre- and young adolescent boys, would suck their penises, bragging how he could "get off" any boy, even though he was an "ugly old man." Offenders who are able to stimulate their victims use the victims' response in a distorted manner to prove to themselves that what they are doing is not bad or harmful, to see themselves as giving and unlike a "real" rapist. Offenders use oral rape to supplement their fantasies and keep themselves from blame for "taking" the victims' virginity. Troy, the rapist who bound and duct-taped his victim, put his mouth on her genitals before raping her. When she became lubricated from the stimulation and his saliva, he felt a rush. "There was no better feeling than making her body betray her," he said.

Co-Opted: Preparing the Audience

The first section of this book deals with us as the audience to the offending. As Valenti (2018) writes, "It takes one person to commit a rape, but a village to let them get away with it." Offenders groom the audience as well as the victim, insulating themselves even further by garnering support and minimizing the possibility that the victim will be believed. Offenders set the stage for the offense, creating a cover for their offense behavior. "I put a lot of energy into billing myself as a responsible adult," Josh stated, "Someone who their parents liked and trusted with their kids."

Creating the Public Persona

One of the most important and effective ways to hide in plain sight is to create a public persona that others can believe in and think they can trust. Offenders can present in a highly prosocial and involved way. They make people feel comfortable as if they are known. People around offenders are often shocked and disbelieving when they find out about the offending. "But I know him," they will exclaim, "He wouldn't do a thing like that!" When I hear this, I sometimes question the person on the depth of their knowledge. Do they only know him from work? Have they ever seen him in a conflict? What does he do in his spare time? If I want to be more challenging, I will ask, "Do you know what his search history is on his computer? What he has in his bedside table? What his favorite sexual fantasy is?" These questions can bring to light the difference between the public self we share and the private self we hide.

"I did the same thing to the parents," said the priest convicted of abusing a boy, "I groomed them as well – by visiting the house, making myself available to them, making it look like I was taking care of their son." I asked Allen how he knew his manipulations would work on people. "Well, I knew my wife loved me, we had children together," he explained, "She had invested many years in our marriage." He added, "I knew that she wanted to believe the best in me and did not want to believe that she had been tricked." As we have reviewed, this can be easy for offenders by playing into biases, being nice, and becoming useful and valuable to people. Making people feel important works as well, stroking their narcissism. Jesus said, "The biggest lie was how important they were to me - to get them to think they were really, uh, really a special person to me and a special part of my life and that I needed them to be there was the biggest lie."

Discrediting the Victim

Not only do offenders sometimes choose victims who have credibility issues, but they also put active effort into discrediting the victims, often far ahead of any disclosures. Countless times, in both sexual assault and domestic violence cases, I have seen the offender spend months, if not years, smearing the victim to the outside world, either overtly or subtlety. This discrediting appears in many forms, like telling people the victim is "crazy," portraying the victim as vindictive, or putting himself in a sympathetic light. "I was talking to Scott and Sean," David said to his wife, "I told them I don't feel like Jamie (her) loves me any more, you know, I'm not getting any attention from you, I'm missing your attention." David was sexually abusing their child but telling his friends how his wife was neglecting him far ahead of getting caught. Ed went straight to his commander when he was caught abusing his stepdaughter and daughter. He "reported" himself for adultery, then advised the commander that he should not be surprised if Ed's wife made allegations of abuse in retaliation for Ed's infidelity.

It only takes a Google search on any allegation against a public figure to see how the victims become discredited. Woody Allen held a press conference on the day the investigation began involving the allegations of sexual abuse made by Dylan Farrow, painting Mia Farrow as a vindictive, brainwashing mother at the same time announcing his "affair" with Mia Farrow's young adopted daughter (Kranc, 2021). When Snoop Dogg was recently accused of sexual assault, he immediately tweeted, "gold digger season is here be careful" on his Twitter account @snoopdogg. Discrediting the victim from the outset is very effective when the public weighs in to judge an allegation.

Triangulation and Splitting

Triangulating and splitting are common and valuable manipulations offenders use to control and direct information and relationships to hide their offending. Triangulation is a term from family therapy that characterizes the manipulation of bringing a third person into a conflict to manipulate that person to take sides (American Psychological Association [APA], n.d.). Splitting is defined as a divisive strategy used to pit two people against one another (APA, n.d.)

Offenders use triangulation very effectively, especially given that the sexual assault itself is a natural triangle – the offender, the victim, and the audience. Picture the shape of a triangle pointing up, with the offender at the top. The offender must form and control a relationship between himself and the victim. He can do this in a variety of ways, described in the grooming process – creating a secret attachment or using threats, bribery, shame, and blame against the victim. When that secret relationship is solidified, the offender has to control the information between himself and others. This is when the public persona and discrediting the victim are extremely useful. Imagine a stepfather who lets his victim get out of punishment, sneaks her money, and undermines her mother's authority while he is abusing her. Then to her mother, he complains about her defiance, grades, and interest in boys. Or compares the child favorably against the mother ("I bet you used to be skinny like that"), triggering the mother's competition with and jealousy of her child. Not only has he triangulated the relationships, but he has also caused a split between the mother and daughter, further isolating the victim from a potential resource. When the victim discloses, he can easily lament, "She said she wanted her parents back together since I knew her. Now she goes and accuses me of this – just to get her way."

Triangulation and splitting are effective tools for the offender in many situations. Offenders can pit their group therapist against their individual therapist, their therapist against their parole officer, their spouse against their therapist, or their family against the victim. Treatment providers and supervising agents must remain mindful of this, checking out everything an offender says to ensure he is not setting up a situation of conflict to benefit him. Family members should understand this dynamic and confront it. It is a highly disruptive manipulation that allows the offender to distract and evade accountability.

Use of Power, Position, and Status

"If it was like a regular average Joe, it wouldn't have taken that long," a juror in the first mistrial of Bill Cosby said when asked if the fact that he was Bill Cosby "played large" in the deliberation room (Good Morning America, 2017). Recent times have been replete with examples of how offenders with status, position, and power have gotten away with sexual assault. Jerry Sandusky was first investigated in 1971, then again in 1998 after an 11-year-old boy told his mother that Sandusky hugged him and showered with him (Collegian News Staff, 2021). Jeffrey Epstein was first reported in 2005 (McLaughlin & Frias, 2019). Larry Nassar was first reported in 1997 (Howley, 2018). Chapter 1 discusses our society's glorification of power and status. There is an assumption that people with power are desirable, have more value than victims, and would not risk everything for a cheap thrill or sex crime. Instead, it is because of their position that they can get away with sexual assault with little fear or risk. A former attorney that abused the boys he was appointed to defend assaulted them right in the interview room of the courthouse. Not only did he choose victims with limited credibility and likeability – juvenile delinquents – he had status as an attorney who "cared for those types of kids." If an offender can attain status with or power over the community, the victim, or the victim's family, getting away with a sexual offense is that much easier.

Using Social Beliefs and Misinformation

"Everybody has the image of the sex offender is, as you know, creepy guy who lives on a corner. With his shades drawn and that's not the case," Nathan said, well aware that he did not meet the stereotype. Offenders are as, if not more, aware of the rape myths and misinformation that pervades the public opinion. They use it against us to hide their offense and deflecting the allegations.

When asked how he deflected the allegations against him, Scott said that he attacked the allegations as impossible. "What do you think," he confronted the victim's mother sarcastically, "I work 10, 12, 14 hours a day! And I come home. Yeah, right, I'm up at 2 o'clock in the morning doing this?" Gordon and Fleisher (2002) call this type of deception the truth in a distorted context. An offender can tell the truth, like Scott did, sarcastically, facetiously, or humorously, giving it a context that makes believing it incredulous. Scott <u>was</u> up at all hours when everyone was sleeping to offend the girls! He played on the idea that someone who worked so hard would not have the energy or the time to commit these types of offenses.

Chapters 1 and 2 highlight the persistent myths, social conditions, and constructs that facilitate the offenders' deception. In most cases, offenders rely on our ignorance of sexual offending or mistaken ideas about offenders and victims to deflect and deny the offenses. Offenders who collect illegal images of child sex abuse will say they got the material from websites or pop-ups accidentally, taking advantage of someone's ignorance of technology, peer-to-peer sharing networks, or the dark web. They will exaggerate their drunkenness, making their sexual offending look accidentally or like they were confused. A man who assaults his little stepdaughter who was sleeping in the bed with him and her mother can say he rolled over and did it in his sleep, groggily thinking his six-year-old was his adult wife. Using our misinformation assists the offenders in their deception.

Deception

"If someone is committing sexual offenses, he has been lying since the day it began (p. 40)" writes Anna Salter in *Predators, Pedophiles, Rapists, and Other Sex Offenders* (2003). This is crucial to understand and accept when dealing with offenders. Given that, offenders are very good and practiced at lying. As I like to say, "No is the easiest lie to tell." They are not necessarily nervous. They have a script. And they have gotten away with it over and over and over.

When someone lies repeatedly, they literally undergo physiological changes that make lying easier. As the liar keeps lying, his brain stops reacting, Ariely (Parrish, 2018) explains. Combined with our own "wishful blindness" (Parrish, 2018), especially when faced with a truth that is so costly to believe, it is easy for an offender to deceive us. Offenders offer partial truths because the most effective lies are as close to the truth as possible. They confess to offenses as well, or at least confess to other misdeeds to deflect focus on what they want to protect the most. Riley told his wife about their daughter "touching him in the shower," discussing how highly sexualized the four-year-old was. "She touched your dad, she touched Lisa – she's just a kid," he said, attempting to blame the victim for grabbing his penis and putting it in her mouth. Riley had been abusing the child for over two years; she was highly sexualized. He deflected the attention from himself, telling lies and partial truths to get away with abuse that could have been so evident to an educated audience.

As I said earlier, deception and uncovering deception is a complex subject that I cannot possibly cover in a couple of paragraphs. However, familiarize yourself with how the truth sounds. It is easier to listen for what sounds true than to investigate all of the offenders' claims and stories. The two most important maxims I have for my new clinicians are 1) never stop asking questions until something makes complete sense, and 2) never do the work to make something make sense to you. If an offender is talking and you are filling in blanks, making excuses, doing mental gymnastics to make something fit, then you are helping that offender deceive you. Constantly during group therapy, other offenders will "red cross" someone lying to the group, offering explanations and rationales that the deceptive offender will grab onto and parrot. Make sure you do not accept superficial or non-sensical responses to legitimate inquiries. The truth has a certain ring to it.

Using Social Rules for Control

Immediately upon entering the room, Bill stuck out his hand, grinning. "Call me Bubba," he said. I looked at his hand and told him to put it down. I challenged him about the allegations against him, saying he knew he was accused of digitally anally penetrating numerous young men, right? When he acknowledged this, I asked why he thought offering me his hand was a good idea, given that we were there to talk about where it had been. It got pretty uncomfortable pretty quickly.

Offenders control their victims and others with the social rules they exploit. Social rules or social norms are the generally accepted guidelines for social behavior. They include saying hello in response to a greeting, shaking an offered hand, and being pleasant, helpful, and non-confrontational. There is considerable pressure to conform to these rules; many studies have been done on the power to conform (see, for example, Zimbardo's (2007) book on the Stanford Prison Experiment). What is important to remember is that you are the one being forced to comply with the social rules, all for the offenders' benefit. An offender will break all the social rules in the service of protecting himself. He will become offended by a reasonable question. He will attack your professionalism or affection for him if you "dare" question or challenge him. He will lie straight to your face. He will twist the issues onto you, accuse you of being rude, or threaten to report you. Offenders make reasonable people feel wrong for having concerns, wanting answers, or getting their own needs met. Social rules are the leashes that offenders use to control and manage us.

Playing on Our "Isms" – Racism, Sexism, Ageism, Weightism, and More

It is fascinating how often offenders use our hidden prejudices against us. As we are imbued with biases, we are also saturated with preconceptions, stereotypes, and biases. These include racism, ageism, weightism, and homophobia. And offenders will try to tap into these for their own benefit.

"You don't know what it's like on the streets," a black offender will say. A Middle Eastern offender will claim, "It is like that in our culture." An overweight offender will insist that he "can't get it up" because he is "too fat and has high blood pressure." Chapter 1 deals with the misogyny in our society. Offenders will play on our secret discriminatory and narrow-minded thinking to confuse or mislead us. They will use their religion as a shield. They will insist they are too old to have sexual desire or be a risk to anyone. I was admonished by another professional who thought I was rating an elderly offender's risk as too high. He believed the man could not possibly pose a risk as he was 83 years old. The man was leaving his facility to ride the subway through impoverished areas where kids rode the subway to school. He still carried a photo of his "beloved" dog during these trips. What the other clinician did not know is that he had trained his dog to lick his penis and anus, so this picture was stimulating for the man, as were the children on the train. This was ageism, pure and simple.

Professionals are not immune to being co-opted by their prejudice either. Offenders have presented me with clinical evaluations attributing their sexual offenses against male children as a result of their "confusion" about their sexuality and exploration of their homosexuality. This explanation for child sexual abuse is nothing more than sanitized homophobia. When have we ever explained an offender's abuse of a six-year-old girl as a consequence of his confused heterosexuality? We must be aware of our biases to ensure the offender does not use them against us.

Feigning Harmlessness or Garnering Sympathy

Watching Harvey Weinstein's rapid deterioration during his trial for sexual assault was fascinating. As Harris (2020), "The decrepit looking Mr. Weinstein, body hunched as he slowly rolls forward, contrasts sharply with his former image as a domineering Hollywood power broker." Harris goes on to point out that Weinstein's presentation conveyed an image of weakness that belied the victims' descriptions of rape and coercion, terming this "disability aesthetics," the prejudice against believing that disabled people are capable, competent, or, in this case, dangerous. When dangerous people appear harmless, infirm, or disabled, we are far less likely to believe that they are or were strong, coercive, powerful, or threatening – in other words, capable of rape. The aesthetics of disability leads to harmful prejudices against the disabled that impede their ability to get equal rights or be treated as able community members (Harris, 2019). I have no opinion on whether Weinstein required a walker. I acknowledge the tremendous psychological and physical toll on some defendants facing allegations. I also know that offenders manipulate us by playing on our sympathy, our stereotypes of harmfulness, and our willingness to make decisions on our perceptions of another's helplessness or frailty.

Father Marco lay in his hospital bed as I evaluated him. He was over 80 years old. He chuckled with a raspy, phlegmy voice as he described how he would love "one last chance" to touch a child sexually before he died. Leonard, the murderer and rapist of the 12-year-old, appeared at his parole hearing bent over a cane, with his white bushy eyebrows and mustache. Once he was in treatment with us, he "cured" himself through prayer, throwing aside his cane and striding upright. Offenders repeatedly try to manipulate others through garnering sympathy, feigning illness or frailty, highlighting age or infirmity, or presenting themselves as more intellectually, socially, or physically disabled than they are, all in order to be underestimated. Clayton acted and referred to himself as "slow," resulting in his parents' overprotection and overindulgence while he sexually assaulted his niece. Alonzo acted deaf every time he was confronted – he also lost the ability to speak English. His "language barrier" that appeared and reappeared conveniently allowed him to get out of treatment.

The manipulation that culminates in perceiving the offender as less capable of harm is very meaningful. While we must take an offender's age and infirmity into account with compassion, we must not be deceived into allowing our prejudice to impact our decision-making or ability to hold the offender accountable. My team learned a very sobering lesson about this some years ago. Evan was an offender we treated who had some physical ailments, depression, and cognitive limitations. He became reportedly sicker and sicker, calling out of treatment repeatedly after describing his illness in sad tones and getting sympathy from his counselor, group members, and treatment team. When he showed up for a session, he had lost weight and looked tired. Imagine our shock, intense regret, and distress when Evan got arrested for sexually abusing two little girls he was caring for while their mothers, his "girlfriends," used drugs. Evan also had been using, explaining his weight loss. The entire time he was "sick," he was abusing the children.

Using Fear, Intimidation, Helplessness, and Confusion against Others

Offenders are adept at producing fear and helplessness in other people. With their victims, they can be threatening and abusive. Over half of batterers also sexually and physically abuse their children (Bancroft et al., 2012). Offenders produce fear of abandonment, consequences, and retaliation in their victims. Many of the victims I interviewed who were assaulted by massage therapists were acutely aware that their phone numbers and addresses were in the facility's files. One victim got a text message and phone call from the offender when she left the massage place, underscoring her fear. Victims fear for other victims, their other parent, their pets, not being believed, and innumerable other consequences.

But offenders produce fear in others as well. Parents of Nassar's victims feared the loss of their child's potential. The offender's partner or spouse may fear the truth or the other collateral damage the truth will cause. Therapists can become afraid physically and emotionally of their clients. I broke out in a sweat when treating and challenging a violent rapist who hated women. Simply because I corrected his use of the word "female," he glared at me with rage, leaned forward, and aggressively verbally pushed back, questioning why I "had a problem." Luckily, we were in group therapy at the time. I cannot imagine how therapy would be compromised if I feared my client in an individual session. Offenders are good at filing grievances and lawsuits. They make us afraid and self-protective, personally and professionally.

Offenders are adept at making us tired and helpless. Their victims have already learned that they were helpless against the assaults. Offenders engage in wars of attrition, eroding boundaries and pushing limits until you become exhausted. Offenders will lie so often or for so long, they simply tire us out. They are confusing and take advantage of the disorganization they create, emotionally, psychologically, and interpersonally. They "misunderstand" to their own convenience. Mitchell was accused of sexually abusing his girlfriend's eight-year-old daughter while caring for her when her mom went on a business trip. The girl told her mother when her mother got home on a Thursday night. The mother immediately believed the child, collected the bedsheets for evidence, and called the parole officer. Friday, Mitchell incessantly hounded the mother until she agreed to meet him to hear his "side" of the story. He met with her and talked her into going to a honeymoon resort in the Poconos, where he spent the entire weekend "explaining" what happened and how the child was confused, having sex with the woman, and acting like her dream man. By Monday, the mother called and recanted everything she had reported to the parole officer. When the allegations against Scott came out, he went on a "full blown drinking and drug binge" and "non-stop called" his girlfriend, crying and begging, explaining how the allegations could not be true and how her child was angry at him for grounding her. This worked, but because the child had reported the abuse at school, the mother was not in control of the disclosure.

Confuse with Counterintuitive Behavior

On episode after episode of Chris Hansen's "To Catch a Predator," an offender caught attempting to meet a child victim for sexual contact will sit down and speak to a camera crew at the crime scene. While "counterintuitive" victim behavior becomes the focus of our confusion in a sexual assault case, offenders are the ones truly acting counter to what we would expect. Who would expect a guilty sex offender to sit down and talk on camera to explain how he really wasn't there to abuse the child but to protect her? On a subconscious level, we have expectations of how "real" offenders should act and look. Offenders act in ways to confuse and contradict our assumptions.

One of the most common ways offenders confuse us or their victims is to simply act like nothing happened. The "frat boy" who leaves his victim gagging in the bathroom, bringing attention to himself at the party by yelling and chugging a beer is not perceived as having just orally raped a freshman. The rapist who texted his victim that he loved the "rough sex" the night before and was so happy they tried it, acted confused when the victim confronted him over text, saying, "You physically and mentally hurt me." "Where do you have bruises," he texted back, acting confused and concerned. Another offender, after raping the victim, texted her, "You told me your stomach hurt … not that you didn't want to have sex," adding, "You never told me it was hurting you."

Offenders give gifts, apologize, and thank their victims. They can quickly compose themselves and begin the spin, trying to influence the truth of the victim or the audience. Even before his victim left his home, one offender sat down to write a letter to the victim to tell her how she caused herself to be strangled, battered, and sexually assaulted. He explained in an educative tone how her actions "caused [her] to choke [her]self the more she struggled" and how acting "like a crazy person" required him to restrain her.

Jeffrey Marsalis is an excellent case study on counterintuitive offender behavior (Erdely, 2008). Marsalis was accused of drugging and raping ten women in Philadelphia and convicted of some of the crimes in 2006. He was convicted again in Idaho for drugging and raping a woman in 2009. Marsalis not only misrepresented himself to get dates, exaggerating his status or job, he drugged his victims, so they woke up in the morning groggy and hurting. But when the victims woke up, Marsalis would kiss them, walk them to the car, ask them for another date. He was described as "chivalrous" and fun to go on a date with – at least two victims went back out with him. One victim, Leigh, met with Marsalis to confront him two days after being raped, only to end up drugged and waking in his bed again. When you think of why on earth would this woman go meet with him (to get answers), think of why a rapist who risked being confronted would commit the crime again with the same person! He befriended some of the victims. Jeffrey Marsalis succeeded for so long because he did not act like a rapist. If you google this name, you can find his history outlined online.

Summary

Offenders are expert puppet masters, controlling and engineering their environment to get away with countless crimes. They are interpersonally astute or overwhelmingly frightening, using us against ourselves and us against others to hide, deny, and camouflage their behaviors and intentions. Knowing the ways they manipulate their victims and us can be valuable for identifying and intervening in those manipulations, as well as exposing and unmasking the offender.

In conclusion,

- Offenders strategically and instrumentally engage in the manipulation of their victims and their community to succeed in sexual offending. They are successful more times than they are not.
- Vulnerability is not the fault of the victim. Vulnerability is only meaningful when there is danger. We must focus on the exploitation of vulnerability, not the fact that it exists.
- Offenders exploit basic social rules, mores, and expectations to carry out the preparation, actualization, and camouflage of their offending. We must be aware of this so we are not directed through blind adherence to these things or distracted from seeing the offender for who he is.
- Be fully aware of biases and how they are played upon by the offender. This includes biases about age, infirmity, disability, or limitations. Offenders can create the illusion of harmlessness when they effectively purpose these biases.
- To protect ourselves and prevent being manipulated, we have to be willing to challenge and expose the machinations and intentions of the offender, even when we are uncomfortable.

References

American Psychological Association (n.d.). "Splitting." APA Dictionary of Psychology. Retrieved from https://dictionary.apa.org/splitting

American Psychological Association (n.d.). "Triangulation." APA Dictionary of Psychology. Retrieved from https://dictionary.apa.org/triangulation

Bancroft, L., Silverman, J., & Ritchie, D. (2012). *The batterer as parent* (2nd ed.). Sage.

Collegian News Staff (2021, December 3). Timeline: The child sex abuse case of Jerry Sandusky. *Daily Collegian*. https://www.collegian.psu.edu/sandusky/timeline-the-child-sex-abuse-case-of-jerry-sandusky/article_a0c48260-52e0-11ec-b65e-2bd1a3594e2b.html

De Becker, G. (1997). *The gift of fear: Survival signals that protect us from violence.* Little Brown.

Erdely, S. (2008). The crime against women that no one understands. *Self.* https://www.self.com/story/serial-rapist

Good Morning America (2017, June 26). WATCH: Juror in Bill Cosby sexual assault trial says he hopes another jury has a different outcome "because the mistrial, I don't think it was right." [Video]. https://m.facebook.com/watch/?v=10155955615728812&_rdr

Gordon, N., & Fleisher, W. (2002). *Effective interview and interrogation techniques.* Academic Press.

Hansen, C.(Host). (2004–2007). *To catch a predator [TV series].* Dateline NBC; MSNBC.

Harris, J. (2020, January 30). The truth about Harvey Weinstein's walker. *New York Times.* https://www.nytimes.com/2020/01/30/opinion/harvey-weinstein-walker.html

Harris, J. (2019). The aesthetics of disability. *Columbia Law Review, 119*(4). https://columbialawreview.org/content/the-aesthetics-of-disability/

Howley, K. (2018, November 19). Everyone believed Larry Nassar. The predatory trainer may have just taken down USA Gymnastics. How did he deceive so many for so long? *New York.* https://www.thecut.com/2018/11/how-did-larry-nassar-deceive-so-many-for-so-long.html

Katz, C., & Barnetz, Z. (2015). Children's narratives of alleged child sexual abuse offender behaviors and the manipulation process. *American Psychologist, 6*(2), 223–232. doi: http://dx.doi.org/10.10367/a0039023

Kranc, F. (2021, February 28). The timeline of Dylan Farrow's sexual assault accusations against Woody Allen. *Esquire.* https://www.esquire.com/entertainment/tv/a35634294/dylan-farrow-woody-allen-sexual-assault-timeline/

McLaughlin, K., & Frias, L. (2019, August 29). A timeline of the sexual abuse cases against Jeffrey Epstein. *Insider.* https://www.insider.com/timeline-jeffery-epstein-sexual-abuse-cases-2019-7

O'Neill, A. (2012, June 17). "The Sandusky 8" describe seduction, molestation and betrayal. CNN. https://www.cnn.com/2012/06/17/justice/sandusky-trial-first-week-wrap/index.html

Parrish, S. (Host). (2018, May 25). Dan Ariely: The truth about lies (No. 33) [Audio podcast episode]. In The knowledge project. https://fs.blog/knowledge-project-podcast/dan-ariely/

Tanner, J., & Brake, S. (2013). Exploring sex offender grooming. (Unpublished) http://www.kbsolutions.com/Grooming.pdf

Valenti, J. (2018, September 20). How very bad men get away with rape. Gen. https://gen.medium.com/how-very-bad-men-get-away-with-rape-317e1db7a919

Valliere, V. (2016, October 21). *Sexual Assault and the 'V-word* [Video]. TedxLehigh. https://www.youtube.com/watch?v=QBPgxdCBhYI

VenerableB (2014, March 26). *Why Rape is Sincerely Hilarious* [Video]. YouTube. https://www.youtube.com/watch?v=Ikd0ZYQoDko

Zimbardo, P. (2007). *The Lucifer effect*. Random House.

Prevention, Intervention, and Managing Relationships with Offenders

Chapter 10

How Can I Have a Relationship with an Offender?

Many of us face the decision of whether to have a relationship with someone we know has been convicted of a sexual offense. This may be because the person is a family member, perhaps even our abuser. We may choose to work in the criminal justice or child protective services' field. We may be clinicians who have to establish therapeutic relationships. We may be a friend or a friend to others who have a sex offender in their lives. We might be in a positive to educate or give advice about managing a relationship with a sex offender. We may be in love with one or have to navigate an ex-relationship with an abuser who is a parent to our children.

It is impractical to think we will never have to confront the choice of whether to have a relationship with a sexual offender. An appropriate, educated social support system is critical for the offender to manage their behavior throughout their lifetime effectively. The problem arises when we engage with an offender, personally or professionally. There is little to no advice. Suppose we have not chosen to reject or abandon the offender. In that case, we receive little guidance in dealing in a productive, effective way with the offender that protects us and is ultimately helpful for the offender.

Pressure to Forgive or Deny

When someone chooses to invite or accept an offender into their life, there can be tremendous pressure, internally and externally, to ignore, deny, or otherwise mitigate the reality of the offender and his offending. This includes pressure to forgive, which for many, entails believing that the offender has transformed and should not be held responsible for past transgressions because forgiveness demands letting go.

One of the first red flags in deciding whether to accept an offender into a relationship is whether the offender fully discloses his offense history and takes responsibility for it. You should immediately reject an offender's efforts to blame others, the system, or a misunderstanding for the offense. Offenders will present sanitized versions of the offending or incredible stories of how they were railroaded and wrongly prosecuted, making themselves more loveable and their histories palatable. It is unbelievable how many offenders will offer that they were prosecuted because the victim lied about her age, they accidentally downloaded one illegal image, or they were convicted on a false allegation. Offenders characterize their offenses as "mistakes." Josh quoted to a reporter, "We are not all monsters. We make mistakes," when discussing his relationship with a woman who faced losing her children because of his offense history. Josh was convicted while a Marine of having over 1,500 images and 20 videos of prepubescent children being raped and sexually assaulted. Mistake?? Another offender in the article was convicted as a teen of sexually assaulting two boys, then at 22 of sexually abusing a 15-year-old, then twice again for failing to register. His wife told the reporter that the first conviction was based on false allegations, the second because

DOI: 10.4324/9781003156284-14

he should have "said no" to the willing teen, and the others to the complicated paperwork required with registration (Chung, 2016).

If you have to engage in this type of denial and distortion to care for the offender, you should not get into a relationship with him. If, as a clinician, you must see the offender as a victim first and primarily, you should not be treating the offenders. If you cannot face the fact that the person you care for has the potential for such behavior, you should not choose to have a relationship with the offender. Most 12-step and recovery programs aimed at parents of, partners of, or other family members of people with compulsive behavioral issues, like addiction, gambling, or sex (non-criminal), advise the person not to stick their "head in the sand," make excuses for, or enable the behavior and minimization of the compulsive or addicted individual. This acknowledges that denial and minimization are destructive to the offender and the person in a relationship with him.

Identifying Your Expectations and Your Needs

What are your expectations in a relationship with someone who has violated and exploited another person? Are your expectations unrealistic? Are they too limited? Are they based on a faulty understanding of the offender and the offending? It is essential to examine what you are looking for and what you need/want from the offender, regardless of your role in that offender's life. If you are a loved one, do you need the person to be someone different, like maybe the person who you "knew" before you knew about the offending? If you are a therapist, do you need a sense of security and rapport, trust in the offender, a feeling of safety or effectiveness? As a parole officer or caseworker, do you need less work, less stress, or "just one" offender who gets better?

Offenders are successful because they play on the needs of their victims. "I was amazed," my new clinician recently said, "Literally, the guy started grooming me the minute we met." She was describing the persuasion and grievance he exhibited. She found herself changing her schedule to accommodate his work schedule, only to think it through and realize he had not even secured the job he was describing. She felt the need to be nice, liked, and accommodating so the offender could attend treatment more easily.

Many offenders you will encounter have lifetime disorders that will require ongoing management. They will not be "cured." This means that to be in a relationship with an offender, we must expect regression and the need to recalibrate. We must be realistic about the needs we are getting met in the relationship. The longer the relationship, the more important this becomes. One of the most challenging things to deal with is finding you have been tricked, deceived, or disappointed again. In these cases, explore whether you overlooked something to ensure your needs were getting met. Offenders will become valuable to us and barter that value in exchange for blindness and denial.

Finally, be highly attuned to your own needs on who you need to be as a person, whether personally or professionally. Having a healthy, appropriate relationship with an offender may counter who you need to or want to be. Some of us do not want to live with distrust or be responsible for maintaining boundaries. Some of us feel in opposition to our values to forgive and believe the best in people if we are required to embrace the terrible facts of sexual abuse. Be honest with yourself if a relationship with an offender will cost you too much, especially regarding how you need to be as a person.

Creating and Maintaining Boundaries

One of the clearest indicators that you are being manipulated, or at least that the offender is attempting to manipulate you, is the violation of boundaries. Boundaries are limits that we create for protection. They exist physically, psychologically, emotionally, and sexually. An offender who crosses a boundary has transgressed your limits. There are many examples of boundary violations that occur subtly and quickly in working with offenders. Some examples include:

- Ignoring your "no"
- Pushing time limits, like going over the therapy time
- Coming too close, leaning in, or standing in a doorway
- Commenting on your children, dress, or appearance when in a professional relationship
- Using a name with you that is overly familiar or a nickname, like "Bob" when you go by Robert, or calling his parole agent "Dude."
- Being overly friendly, looking in your things, or pressing an agenda

If an offender breaks or attempts to erode your boundaries, including the rules set in your home, be very aware. An offender who breaks boundaries is engaging in grooming behavior and attempting to establish control in the relationship. It may not seem like anything when someone allows a child to sit on his lap during story time – it is significant to an offender. At its core, sexual offending is the ultimate boundary violation. If an offender is unwilling to adhere to others' boundaries, including legal ones, they are engaged in reoffense dynamics.

Maintaining Vigilance

An author on trauma, Judith Herman (1997) described the efforts of the offender to obscure the truth. She wrote, "In order to escape accountability for his crimes, the perpetrator does everything in his power to promote forgetting. If secrecy fails, the perpetrator attacks the credibility of his victim. If he cannot silence her absolutely, he tries to make sure no one listens."

One of the most exhausting things in having a relationship with an offender is the vigilance it requires from us. We must be on guard for deception and manipulation. We have to take nothing for granted. There is no such thing as a mistake or accident that are not worth asking about, and inconsistency is an issue. It is not as if these issues do not arise in other relationships. If you are in a relationship with someone with a drug addiction or if someone has been unfaithful, this vigilance is part of the relationship. Support groups for families of those with addiction problems (like Al-Anon) stress the importance of attention and willingness to face the constant possibility that the person has relapsed.

Vigilance for Manipulation

"My ability to paint a picture with only the colors I want you to see," Tim wrote when explaining the things about him that helped him offend criminally and sexually. He went on, "Telling you only the least little bit as possible … this meaning I have the capabilities to keep a lot of very important facts of the situation out of the conversation." As we have discussed throughout, offenders are keenly aware of how to manipulate us. Our ability to identify and confront the manipulations when they begin is crucial to managing a relationship with an offender.

An Example of the Misuse of Social Rules

The victim's child made a 911 call and then ran to the neighbor's house, crying hysterically. The ambulance and police arrived. Body cams captured the battered, bloody crying victim. The perpetrator was arrested. The offender alleged that the victim's injuries came from his attempts to "calm her down," portraying her as out of control during a conflict. In the days after the offense, this is the text exchange between the perpetrator and victim.

PERP: [Send the victim an article entitled "What are the signs & symptoms of Borderline Personality Disorder"]
VICTIM: It is abusive to tell someone they have a disorder. Glad you know your ex-wife's disorder. You probably pushed her to that point. Do not text or bother me. I will get a restraining order and I do not want to be beaten anymore. Stop texting me. I am blocking you.
PERP: I wouldn't be here if I didn't want us.
VICTIM: You want me to help you get out of trouble. You don't care about us.
PERP: I want to figure out what the problem is. I know it's not just me.
VICTIM: Wow. Goodbye.
PERP: I have problems, but I know I'm not the only problem.
VICTIM: Stop harassing me.
PERP: Let me know when you want to talk then. Love you.
VICTIM: I don't want to talk anymore. We can't save us. I am done. I'm not going to stay around and be blamed for this shit and I am not going to be told I have something your ex-wife has. You are beyond abusive and I am afraid of you. I am scared what you are going to do to me. I cannot continue to live this way. Please leave me alone.
PERP: I was having a conversation with you and you walked away from me. You won't talk about issues with me and that I feel are important. I am trying to communicate with you but I can't when you walk away from me.

What can you identify in this exchange between a perpetrator and victim? The offender attempts to "diagnose" the victim with a disorder marked by emotional instability and volatility to prove to her he did not beat her but restrained her, attempting to influence the victim's reality. He tries to use social rules and love to control and manipulate her. He ignores her boundaries and her efforts to end the exchange. This brief interaction shows how quickly and relentlessly an offender will engage in manipulation. Imagine the work the victim had to do to defend herself from these tactics every day, all the time when the offender was challenged. He portrays her as the problem, as unwilling to share the responsibility for the abuse and unwilling to talk to save the relationship. He ends a text with "love you" which she does not respond to – yet.

Other Clever Manipulations

Gavin de Becker (1997) identifies other types of manipulations as well. Remember, social rules or expectations are powerful tools for the offender to use against us. Against the backdrop of us having to be "nice," cooperative, forgiving, and professional, offenders engage in perceptive and clever ways to co-opt us into their agenda. One example is *forced teaming* (De Becker, 1997). The offender presents an issue as if it was a "we" problem, like when the offender cannot travel for work and says, "Doc! Doc! We got a problem. My boss will be pissed if I can't go!" WE do not have a problem; the offender does because he did not request travel permission. When an offender attempts to equalize your relationship or share the responsibilities of their woes with you, enlisting your help inappropriately, this is a problem.

Other manipulations include *typecasting* and *loan sharking* (De Becker, 1997). They are insidious ways the offender begins to get us to do the work for him. In typecasting, the offender will compare us negatively to others, seducing us into proving we are "not like that." They will describe their "crazy ex-wife" who cheated on them, so their new love interest remains calm, reliable, and faithful, vying for the offender's trust and love. The offender will describe how awful and abusive his last therapist was, so his new therapist will bend backward to support him. In the same vein, loan sharking is when an offender presents himself as doing extra, implying we should appreciate something, so we owe them something. "Doc! I always pay my bill! I always come to group! Now you're going to question me like this," an offender will lament. The offender who "graciously" comes to the parole office to submit the urine screen in an attempt to extract leniency, a favor, or an exception for "all he does" and how cooperative he is. While prosocial behavior should be acknowledged, there are two points to remember: (1) it is likely that the offender's prosocial behavior was part of his offense behavior, and (2) people should not be congratulated or rewarded to doing what they need to or living up to basic expectations. "Well at least I didn't hit her," an offender will say, expecting to be congratulated.

Vigilance for Deception

In her book *Lie Spotting,* Pam Meyer (2010) says that lies are cooperative. They require decisions and action from both the liar and the target of the lie. She points out that we are highly ambivalent about the truth. This is why lies work.

Lies work because sometimes we want to be lied to; face it. Do you really want to know how someone is doing when you ask passing in the hallway at work? When we are invested in the liar and when the truth can be damaging, we especially want to believe a lie. In general, people mostly tell the truth. That's why the truth has a certain ring to it. You don't need to think everything is a lie, but you must be vigilant for deception.

Too Little, Too Much

When an offender provides too little or too much information, it is important to examine what he is saying. As Tim said above, giving too little information is highly effective. As a rule, lying by omission is an easier way to lie than fabricating a lie (Ekman, 1992). Lying by concealing is easier and more passive. It is less shameful, easily excused ("I forgot"), and very easy to blame on the listener. Every supervising agent or parent has heard, "Well you didn't ask me!" If you hear this from an offender, reject it. It is the offender's responsibility to provide the whole truth, especially if they seek a relationship with you, whether personal or professional.

Too many details can be as deceptive as too few, especially when the details are irrelevant to the question asked (De Becker, 1997; Hall & Poirier, 2000; Rudacille, 1994). Too many irrelevant details hide the missing relevant details. It gives the impression that someone is being thorough. It wears us out because we get tired of the bullshit. Recently in group, Noah spent 15 minutes answering my yes-or-no question. When I finally stopped him and confronted the fact that he gave no information, he said he was trying to "explain." However, he had not said one word about his offending or answered my question. Purely manipulative. Deceptive people will give many details to "set up" their story, like an elaborate prologue, and give you bare-bones information about the important things.

Pay attention to the information you get and don't get. After you are done talking to the offender, review what he told you. If it is confusing, vague, or contradictory, or if you find the information you want is entirely missing, go back and get the information. Very often, professionally, we see this has happened to us when we go to write a treatment note or evaluation and realize we are missing a lot of information. If this occurs with an offender, do not just write it off.

Using Anger or Aggression, Being Affronted by Questions

Offenders use anger, intimidation, and being offended to deflect questions. They will attack the question to make us uncomfortable, like saying, "Why are you asking me that" or "What do you mean by that?" It is designed to turn the spotlight on us and gain control of the conversation. The focus goes off the offender when we are reacting and defending ourselves. Questioning our motives or information by acting as if a question is an accusation is another technique. A question is a question. An offender should not be refusing to answer a question. Most of us simply answer what we are asked without issue. We may wonder why we are being asked something and question the person, but an offender's immediate attack, rebuttal, or affront is a sign that something is wrong. A question to someone who has broken the law and everyone's trust is not entitled to be offended when their behavior is questioned.

Our Own Arrogance

One way liars succeed is that we presume to know what they are lying about or why they would lie. "He is just lying to himself," "he is embarrassed/ashamed," "he is confused," are all excuses for lying that reflect the listener's assumptions. It is dangerous to presuppose what an offender is lying about or what is motivating the lie. The use of the polygraph is common in sexual offender treatment. It detects distress around particular topics. Time and time again, my team and I have made assumptions about what is hidden, only to find out we were asking the wrong questions and missing the critical issues. The offender needs to answer the question, "Why are you lying," not us.

Attend to the Non-Sexual Displays of Offense Dynamics

One of the most difficult things in managing a relationship with an offender is identifying and intervening in the non-sexual displays of offense dynamics. I have reviewed these throughout the book, but offenders will bring these into their relationships. You need to know how the offender succeeded in offending and how they groomed others to watch if he is grooming you.

"I lied my way out of everything by playing the victim, complementing people," Clarence described, "I was a war veteran and wore my hat everywhere. I said I couldn't read or write. I played confused." Clarence went to the VA for treatment for his "confusion" and alleged brain injury. Clarence was a client who had raped his adoptive daughter and exploited his wife, an Asian woman he married while serving in Vietnam. He would come into treatment, smiling and goofy, wearing his hat, and befriending everyone in group. A different Clarence appeared when these offense dynamics were challenged and he was not allowed to wear his hat and complement people. The Clarence who was not grooming people and trying to appear harmless was a resentful, sullen Clarence who violated his parole because he was trying to lure a woman to his car to abduct and rape her.

Make sure that you have an authentic relationship with the offender. Pay attention to efforts to control you, make you submit, or give you too much stimulating information. Sometimes offenders disclose their offenses to loved ones inappropriately, with too much graphic and erotic detail, acting out their interests in shocking people. We are treating an offender who was acting out the thrill of getting over on people – he downloaded pornography using his prior therapist's wifi signal before his session.

Summary

Because we see the concepts of evil and bad as extreme and all-encompassing, we cannot conceptualize that the good guy is also the bad guy. We are not dichotomous beings. As the old fable goes, there are two dogs inside us – one good and one evil. The dogs fight all the time. The one that wins is the one we feed the most. Having a relationship with an offender requires that that we acknowledge that not only does the offender has problems in their personality and behavior, he has allowed those problems and deviant desires to overwhelm and conquer everything else – his love for his family, his need for freedom, his regard for others. In a truly caring relationship with an offender, we will help him never let this happen again, or we will get out to protect ourselves.

In conclusion,

- Having a relationship with the offender requires us to be uncomfortable, challenge the status quo, and remain vigilant to deception and manipulations.
- If we are not careful, we can be co-opted into the offender's world or protect him by denying, minimizing, and sanitizing his offense behavior.
- By loving, valuing, or caring for an offender for who he truly is, not what we want him to be, we can offer one of the most potent deterrents to reoffense – an educated support system that can be part of the offender's arsenal to resist the pull of deviance.
- Offenders are not rare, nor can they be relegated to isolation, away from the rest of us. They are individuals with strengths and talents that can and should be incorporated into our community with the *right* kind of support and accountability. But we must never forget their potential for harm.

Stopitnow.org has a tip sheet online for some signs to look for regarding signs that an adult is at risk of abusing a child. It can be found at https://www.stopitnow.org/sites/default/files//documents/files/signs_an_adult_is_at_risk_to_harm_child_0.pdf

References

Chung, M. (2016, December 13). Women reveal what it's like to be in a relationship with a sex offender and why they stay. *Inside Edition.* https://www.insideedition.com/20454-women-reveal-what-its-like-to-be-in-a-relationship-with-a-sex-offender-and

De Becker, G. (1997). *The gift of fear: Survival signals that protect us from violence.* Little Brown.

Ekman, P. (1992). *Telling lies: Clues to deception in the workplace, politics, and marriage.* Norton.

Hall, H., & Poirier, J. (2000). *Detecting malingering and deception: Forensic distortion analysis* (2nd ed.). CRC Press.

Herman, J. (1997). *Trauma and recovery.* Basic Books.

Meyer, P. (2010). *Liespotting.* St. Martin's Griffin.

Rudacille, W. (1994). *Identifying lies in disguise.* Kendall/Hunt Publishing.

Chapter 11

Assessing Promises

What Does Real Change Look Like?

"Change begins at the end of your comfort zone," said Roy Bennett. He was not wrong. Change is hard. It is even harder to change something you have invested in, taken risks for, and been deeply gratified by, sacrificing nearly everything. It is especially difficult to change enduring personality traits and entrenched patterns of sexual arousal and deviance. Assessing change in sexual offenders is difficult. It challenges our notion of change – what changes, how quickly, and how permanently. We have to adjust our idea of change, deepening and widening it.

There are instruments designed to measure change in sexual offenders, geared toward clinicians or supervising agents, like probation officers. The instruments focus on assessing the risk levels of offenders and evaluating the presence or absence of stable and dynamic/changeable factors related to the risk of recidivism. The Stable-2007 and Acute-2007 (Hanson et al., 2007) are designed to capture the presence of fluctuations in risk factors in an offender. However, true change is not just the assessment of risk factors. And the ability to assess change should be available to others in the offenders' support system.

What Doesn't Matter

In general, people change when they are uncomfortable with themselves. Either they risk meaningful consequences or find themselves in conflict with their ideas, self-image, or needs/desires. For the vast majority of offenders, the demand for change comes externally – their motivation is extrinsic. All the offenders I have treated have come for treatment because someone or something outside of themselves has required treatment. The external sources include parole, a spouse, an employer, family or custody court, or a pending hearing date for sentencing. The offender is distressed, not necessarily about his behavior, but about the potential consequences of not being in treatment. This makes treatment very difficult, as everyone knows the adage "you have to want to change."

Compliance

Given that someone has to want to change, many offenders are willing to be compliant, as opposed to change. As I said very early in this book, treating sexual offenders is the easiest job in the world – if you do it wrong. Offenders are, for the most part, extremely compliant. There is a striking contrast in our treatment groups between the violence intervention group and the sexual offender treatment group. While some members belong to both groups, the violence intervention group members are blatantly combative, defiant, and non-compliant. They struggle and complain. They resist changing, their change coming slowly after they protest and justify. Sexual offenders (before they are invested in treatment)

DOI: 10.4324/9781003156284-15

are compliant, sit quietly, pay their bills, do their homework assignments, and pleasantly chat with one another, reluctant to challenge the other members. *Their group behavior is like their offense behavior – pleasant, prosocial, and accommodating on the surface while protecting their deviance inside.* A therapist, parole officer, or family member satisfied with this behavior and introspection level will be pleased. Some will be convinced that the offender is addressing what needs to be addressed.

It is crucial to remember that compliance is the offender's pre-offense behavior. Sex offenses are secret crimes. It behooves the offender to avoid attention, not be a problem, and evade scrutiny. That is how they succeeded when they offended. Compliance needs to be the most basic starting place for change because non-compliance is very meaningful. While the absence of compliance is important, the presence should not be overvalued.

Feeling Guilty/Distress

The same should be true if the offender expresses guilt, distress, or remorse about his behavior. These things are not particularly meaningful. It is basic and should not be overvalued. You might not even understand the source of the distress. Offenders feel distress related to the unknown, being exposed, giving up their secret behaviors, looking bad to others, or consequences. Just because an offender "feels bad" for his actions does not mean those feelings reveal genuine remorse, empathy, compassion, or sorrow. "I felt guilty every time I did it," said James. His guilt was not a deterrent to future sexual offenses. We overvalue the meaning and impact of guilt. "They didn't know anything about the bad things I was doing and when they did find out about it, it's not that they excused it," Ted said about his friends who overlooked his offending, "I think they saw it as a flaw, a great flaw, certainly a bad thing, an evil thing, but they saw I had remorse for what I had done." His remorse did not stop him.

As with compliance, if the offender is completely without distress about his offending or consequences, that is very telling. That may mean that the individual is narcissistic, antisocial, or even psychopathic. Here is one example of an offender we ultimately deemed unamenable to treatment. As an assignment, we asked him to write about why he refused to discuss his offenses and history. He wrote,

> I want to protect everything that I stood for all my life … honor, code, and the ability to keep secrets. These are long lost character traits that have no meaning to the youth today and in the 21ˢᵗ century. These qualities are deteriorating in our society and that is why the American people are falling apart … I could of given up this information in trade for my freedom but I chose to stand strong in my beliefs. So, why would I be willing to share this information today with anyone, let alone a stranger. Can this hurt me? Yes, not only would it destroy my fine qualities that I possess … In conclusion, instead of being condemned or persecuted for my honest[y], my values and discipline, I should be respected and admiration should be directed towards me!

I do not need to point out the lack of willingness to change with this offender. But even this offender reiterated my previous point. He showed up for treatment. He paid his bill. And he was livid when we discharged him for not being involved in treatment because he was complying with all our requests, even doing his assignments (like the one above)!

It does not matter if the offender complains that treatment, parole, or changing is making them uncomfortable. He needs to be uncomfortable. Change is hard. And examining and untangling the justifications, motivations, distortions, and desires that motivated such a profound set of choices should be arduous and challenging. Offenders can be incredibly resistant. They need dedication and commitment to change. They need patience as actual change takes a long time, not just showing up to a 12-week course on anger management or decision making. True change includes alterations in thinking, modifications of the belief and value system, and the adoption of sophisticated skills to manage deep-rooted, well-established patterns, traits, and fantasies that will enable the offender to thrive without reoffending.

Being Cured

There is no "cure" for a paraphilic disorder, a personality disorder, or the attraction to deviance. Being cured is not the goal – it is not the change necessary. When we assess change, it does not matter if the person is cured. I would argue in fact, that if any offender says they are cured or any treatment professional says that an offender is no longer or will never be a risk, this is a very serious problem. Adjusting our idea of change must incorporate the belief that the offender will be responsible for monitoring and managing their deviance for the rest of their life. It is the same as people with addiction must recognize the possibility of relapse and return to addiction for the rest of their lives.

Good "Self-Esteem"

Self-esteem is an amorphous concept that has been around in the psychological literature for decades. It is a term used interchangeably with self-worth, self-value, or self-confidence. Self-esteem is a catch-all term to characterize how good you feel about yourself. But it is discussed without context or reference to things like conscience, empathy, and regret. It is also addressed in offender treatment outside of the concepts of narcissism, faulty expectations of the world, and self-pity.

Often offenders and their support systems are overly focused on the offenders' self-esteem. They believe that low self-esteem can lead an offender to seek solace in sexual abuse of children or underlies the decision to batter his spouse. Some believe that being uncomfortable with oneself hampers change. The problem with this way of thinking is twofold. First, people with narcissistic traits believe that they should not just feel good; they should feel great about themselves. They think they should feel good without the coexisting requirement of having earned a good sense of self. Offenders want to avoid any negative feelings about their behavior. This is how they continue to offend sexually or commit other forms of maltreatment. An active conscience will make us feel bad about what we did and what that means about us. It is important. Second, offenders often have problematic expectations of how they should feel about themselves and the world; they believe they have to feel good about themselves all the time to maintain productivity and prosocial behavior. If they do not feel good, they can become self-indulgent, justifying poor or abusive behavior. They can become full of self-pity and resentment. This can lead to their increased risk of offending.

Offenders need to learn that negative feelings about ourselves is normal. They must tolerate periods of distress or upsetting self-reflection and examination that lead to change. They need to learn to make decisions to make these negative emotional states transient and manageable, improved by positive choices and behaviors that enhance self-worth rather than indulging them by withdrawing and acting out irresponsibly.

Most important for offenders and all of us is an accurate perception and assessment of ourselves. Our sense of self-worth should not be over- or underinflated. It is fluid, changing based on how we behave in the world. All of us feel poorly about ourselves at times and in different contexts. I may have good "self-esteem" as a therapist, but my self-esteem as a professional athlete sucks. I am not an athlete and should not measure myself against professionals in this context. The value of self-esteem as a general concept is not helpful in treating offenders. While no one should live overwhelmed by shame and humiliation, we must look squarely at who we are and what we have done to begin to change. As Lincoln said, "When I do good, I feel good. When I do bad, I feel bad. That is my religion."

What Matters When Assessing Change

If we must judge if someone is "really" changing, there are some fundamental principles to remember. Change takes time. The more complicated the change needed, the more time it takes. Change is not sudden or easy. Change concerning long-standing habits, thinking, or behaviors requires change in the foundational pillars and values that allowed the offense to happen. As an additional complication is that the offense behavior and its rewards can be more potent than the consequences, as most offenders have succeeded in offending more than they have been caught or punished.

"Anything After 'But' Is Bullshit" – Taking Responsibility for the Offending

In his book about batterers, Lundy Bancroft (2002) does an exceptional job of outlining all the steps it takes to take true responsibility for abuse. Admission is essential, but not enough. To truly take responsibility for the offending, an offender not only has to admit fully without blaming anyone or anything but must admit that he made choices and decisions to pursue his goal. He cannot say, "I did it, but I was drinking" or "I did it, but it was an accident." There can be no excuses or deflection from his instrumental choices to gratify his deviance.

An offender has to accept the wrongness of his behavior. It does not matter if the 14-year-old girl "consented." It does not matter if "no one knew" that he was secretly recording them in the bathroom. It does not matter if "they were only pictures." Sexual offenses are wrong. The offender has to understand and accept this. There was not a good enough reason to violate another person in any way. When we do something wrong, there are ramifications. The offenders must deal with people's feelings about their offending and the consequences. This is without self-pity or the expectation that others should "get over it" or stop making them "pay" for their actions. Offenders must recognize that what they did had an enormous impact on others. They are not entitled to make others feel bad about being angry or traumatized. Offenders should not demand forgiveness or absolution. If they can do these things and take true responsibility, they should be willing to do what is necessary to prevent a reoffense and begin the reparative work that is needed. Complaining about treatment, supervision, or any consequence of their behavior shows they have not taken full responsibility.

There is very reliable way we have found to test whether the offender has truly internalized the concepts of responsibility in our program. We do introductions when a new person enters group as well as listen closely to an offender when an intern starts or there is a new clinician. The clients that have been parroting what they think we want to hear will immediately revert to their old language and explanations of their offending, fraught with minimization and denial. Suddenly, someone who has said that he assaulted his daughter will tell the new group member that they "made love."

to dealing with someone, judge if they are honest, and evaluate changes in their behavior or presentation. This does not work with offenders. As discussed throughout this book, offenders are adept at hiding in plain sight.

In his book *Evaluating Sex Offenders,* Doren (2002) explains this succinctly. He states that "too strong a reliance on our impressions" leaves us vulnerable to being influenced and manipulated by clients whose goal is to convince us of their harmlessness, sincerity, and honesty when they do not exist (p. 38). Research shows that an interview with a sexual offender can detract from an accurate assessment of risk and that the interview is the weakest link in understanding the offender (Doren, 2002). Actuarial instruments to assess static risk factors are designed to be scored on historical and offense information, excluding the need for an interview.

In a relationship with an offender, the interview should be the last thing you rely upon for information. During therapy, during a visit with a supervisee, you should not leave doubting the factual material you have at your disposal. If the facts outline an offense that seems so unlike the offender, you have not learned that the offender did not do it or is not "that bad"; what you have learned is there is a big gap between the offender's public self and his private and secret self.

Do not forget or underestimate the impact of your own narcissism as well. We like to believe we are a good judge of character, that we are able to read the person before us. Some of us like to believe that we are good at detecting lies or seeing through another person. Even if you are skilled, you should not rely solely on yourself to identify and understand the offender. Use all of your available resources, remembering that the last thing you should rely on is the interview.

Challenge and Confrontation

Working with offenders requires us to challenge and confront their thinking and behavior. Persuading, cajoling, or passively expecting to receive information does not work with the offending population, who by nature are invested and rewarded by the deviance they are trying to protect (Bancroft, 2002). You must be willing to question the offender, press them to dig deeper, and not tolerate superficial responses and reports about their life.

Challenge and confrontation should not be confused with yelling, degrading, or humiliating an offender. Aggression is not effective. Unfortunately, some treatment professionals have retreated from the idea of confrontation because they are afraid that it is an aggressive technique, do not want to make the clients uncomfortable, or even more, are fearful of them. Challenging should trigger thought, reflection, or a dismantling of distortions and fantasy. It is unrealistic to think a client can find his own way to changing the complex thoughts, fantasies, and urges that motivated him to offend. Additionally, role modeling appropriate confrontation teaches the group to challenge and give feedback effectively and provides an opportunity for the offender to internalize the challenges he should begin giving himself.

Accountability and Agency

The American Psychological Association [APA] (n.d.) defines accountability as the "extent to which an individual is answerable to another" for their actions, decisions, and judgments. Agency (American Psychological Association, n.d.) is the power or ability to effect change or influence. Both concepts are critical in the treatment of offenders. But it is difficult to hold people accountable. What makes it more difficult is when we are unclear about what

Walking the Walk

It is incredibly easy for offenders to parrot treatment concepts, give apologies, and make promises. This is especially true in structured treatment and interviews; their skills are amplified if the therapy is manualized. "They were more interested in just the right answers – the clinical book answers which made it a little bit easier to be honest," Juan said, "Once you figured out that, that's what they wanted, it made it easier to get through." Juan got recommendations for parole and, once he got into outpatient treatment, though he would be there only a "couple of weeks."

An offender must consistently demonstrate the insights they are professing in treatment over time. It is not enough to say and regurgitate. They must show that they can see and intervene in their problematic behavior and thinking. It should not be an external source, whether a spouse, a therapist, a group member, or a supervising agent, who says, "Is that a good idea? What are the risks in that?" The offender should be able to identify and challenge others on thinking distortions, justifications, and problem behaviors. But they should also be able to identify their own. You should be able to see examples of this in their interactions with you and their choices at work and home. They should be reporting their struggles, as change is hard and sporadic.

For example, it is meaningful when an offender comes into treatment and says something to the effect of, "My wife and I were really looking forward to that movie, but when we got there, it seemed to be full of teenagers, so we left." It is important that they report when they have not made the appropriate decisions, too. Offenders should bring to the table what they are struggling with, even if they have failed in the struggle. My treatment team was out together for dinner after an event. One of the offenders in treatment with us showed up at the restaurant with his parents, sitting outside near us. Shortly after, we saw him get up with his mother and move inside. He told his therapist later that he believed that was the right thing to do. He understood his voyeuristic urges, recognized how he wanted to eaves-drop, and intervened. This is a sign of change. Another sign of change is not announcing how much he has changed to insist on some special treatment.

Identification of and Intervention in Risk Situations

The previous example highlights how this offender understood his deviance, understood the non-sexual means he could reinforce it, and decided to intervene. He could have jus-tified staying – it was a public place, he had his parents with him, he could not really hear us anyway – but he did not. He recognized his urge, knew how one thing could lead to another, and did not want to feed his deviance. He did this for himself, intrinsically moti-vated, not because he would have "gotten in trouble."

This is an example of real-life identification and intervention in a risky situation. He did not simply avoid the situation by leaving. He took into account his parents' needs but asserted himself. He did not get angry or resentful. He did not test himself. This is how an offender who is changing or has changed responds to risk. If an offender insists he has changed so he can handle it or will "never do it again," he is likely failing to protect himself and others.

Almost always, an offender's risk situation is not characterized by an immediate oppor-tunity to commit a sexual assault. Reoffending is a process, not an event. A risk situation is a situation that can contribute to stimulating the offender, reactivating the deviant urges. It can be a situation where the offender passes a "test," and becomes overconfident, prov-ing to himself and others he is "fine." A risk situation may provide the offender tools or information to carry out a future offense. A risk situation may be a situation that poses a risk to others. For example, an offender wanted to attend his son's Little League game. He was going to be accompanied by his paramour, who knew the rules he had to follow. He set a time limit and had identified a place to sit that limited his access to children. He had no history of arousal or attraction to boys. So what was the risk he failed to identify? He forgot that his son's teammates' parents knew he was a registered sex offender; his arrest was publicized. The risk was that there would be a confrontation, or he would embarrass or distract his son. The idea of risk and risk management has to be broader than just the risk of committing a sexual assault in the immediate situation.

Full Accountability for Self-Management

An offender who is truly changing should expect to be fully accountable to those in his life. He cannot get offended by distrust, even if it is frustrating. He should answer questions when asked. He should seek help if he begins struggling or backsliding. He should make the decisions and sacrifices his offense history requires to keep himself safe.

This means that an offender should not expect or rely on others to manage himself. He should not only obey his parole restrictions or therapy rules; he should understand the rationale behind the limitations. He should be able to adhere to the principles of managing himself regardless of circumstances. An offender who has changed will not make his parents leave their home to go see his victim, their grandchild. He will leave home without a hassle. The changed offender will not blame others for his decisions, like a pedophile handing live chicks to children and playing with them for hours at work because his boss asked him to do it. He will understand his need to be fully accountable for managing himself and protecting others.

No Re-creation of the Victim/Perp Relationship

Manipulation and grooming come so readily to the offender that it is vital to assess at all times whether the offender is attempting to recreate the victim/perpetrator relationship in other relationships, including the one they have with you. When asked how he groomed his former therapist, Tony said, "I play it off like I have it all together, I have all the answers and that I'm Mr. Nice guy. I fell back into that role of trying to be seen as Mr. Nice guy and not capable of doing all these things." Be aware of these dynamics and the role the offender might try to put you into in the relationship. The offender might put you in a parental role to manage him or to be an authoritarian inappropriately. He might be oversolicitous and get you involved in rescuing or working hard to help him. He might try to garner your sympathy or protection. The offender might triangulate you with others so you take his side. These are all things offenders do to their victims. Recreating unhealthy roles and dynamics in relationships shows that things have not changed.

Fully Educated Support System

Appropriate social support is critical for maintaining change and decreasing risk. An offender working toward change in his life will be willing to establish a support system that understands his offenses and risks and is ready to challenge him. What we see so often instead is the offender who surrounds himself with people who "don't want to hear it," have a "hard time believing it," or offer absolution and forgiveness so the offender "can move on" in life. A healthy support system cares for the offender without whitewashing or denying the issues.

A healthy support system does not try to put the offender at risk or make excuses for problematic behavior. It does not reinforce antisocial thinking or narcissistic self-pity.

In our program, we ask offenders to include members of their support team in some aspects of their treatment. When they leave the program, we have them make a recovery contract in which they describe their behaviors before offending or when deceiving others. The contract solicits a commitment from the supports to challenge and confront the offender if they are concerned, the offender is isolating, or the offender begins acting in a concerning way. Developing a knowledgeable and caring support system provides a great deal to the offender potentially throughout the offender's lifetime.

Summary

Change is hard. It takes a long time. It is uncomfortable. True change is stable over time and situations. Offenders have a significant responsibility to change. They must change things about themselves that have led to sometimes catastrophic consequences to others. Asking them to go through the laborious process of change is not too much to ask.

In conclusion,

- Several things do not matter in a typical manner when it comes to assessing change in offenders. These include compliance, guilt or distress, being cured, or self-esteem.
- If an offender demonstrates a lack of distress or compliance, or professes to be cured, it is improbable that he has significantly changed.
- Truly taking responsibility goes far beyond admitting. It includes a lack of excuses, admission of intentionality and purposefulness, and acceptance of the consequences of their choices.
- The offender's insight should actualize an offender's insight into behavior and life choices.
- An educated, caring support system can be highly beneficial to an offender's adjustment and risk management.

References

Bancroft, L. (2002). *Why does he do that? Inside the minds of angry and controlling men.* Berkley Books.

Hanson, R. K., Harris, A. J. R., Scott, T.-L., & Helmus, L. (2007). *Assessing the risk of sexual offenders on community supervision: The dynamic supervision project (User report, corrections research).* Public Safety Canada. http://www.publicsafety.gc.ca/cnt/rsrcs/pblctns/ssssng-rsk-sxl-ffndrs/index-eng.aspx

Chapter 12

"But I Am Telling the Truth!"

Suggestions for Investigation, Supervision, and Treatment of Offenders

Investigating, treating, and supervising sexual offenders are very difficult. You must agree to absorb terrible information accompanied by vivid imagery. You have to maintain vigilance, be on the receiving end of hostility, and expect your clients to deceive you about things that can result in harm to others. It takes a particular kind of willingness and dedication to do the work. It impacts us and our sense of safety in the world. Sometimes it affects our parenting, sex lives, and decisions about where to go. Sometimes, being what the offender requires taxes our sense of self.

Because of the significant challenges a sex offender bring to supervision and treatment, our requirements are different from what is necessary in more traditional roles. A treatment provider unwilling to challenge and address the offender's denial, manipulations, and deception will be weakened in efforts to help the offender change (Flora, 2001). An overburdened parole officer or caseworker who is relieved that the offender is polite and compliant may cooperate with the offender's superficiality and subterfuge. Whether you are treating or supervising an offender, you have to negotiate the protection of the community with the offender's needs. You will also have to learn how to manage authority, something we clinicians are not typically taught. The roles and demands of working with sexual offenders require us to go outside a traditional therapeutic or social work role and deal with concurrent issues like risk, safety, judgment, and decision-making that may go against rapport or the conventional tasks of the clinician. Involvement with the court can be daunting as well.

In the decision to be a thorough, dedicated investigator, supervisor, or treatment provider to sexual offenders, you are promising to go above and beyond your traditional roles. You are making a commitment to keep the community safe, to gain skills at dealing with manipulation and deception, and to forge ahead in spite of numerous disappointments and failings. John Connolly (2007) wrote, "It has always seemed to me that there are two types of people in this world: those rendered impotent by the sheer weight of evil it contains, and who refuse to act because they see no point, and those who choose their battles and fight them to the end as they understand that to do nothing is infinitely worse than to do something and fail." This is one job where this quote aptly applies, as there is hardship in our willingness to truly see the damage from and deviance in sexual offending.

This chapter is not meant to offer or outline a treatment program. It does not provide supervisory or investigative protocols. I offer below information and principles to keep in mind when establishing a helping relationship with the offender.

The Overvalued Interview

We rely on our judgments and impressions of others to guide our understanding of who that person is. This works generally. We use our impressions of others as reasonable guides

DOI: 10.4324/9781003156284-16

we expect. It is important in working with offenders to follow the principles of good leadership – have clear expectations, communicate these expectations assertively, provide tools and means to achieve the goals, and have consequences for failure to be accountable or meet expectations.

Accountability leads to a sense of agency. You cannot change what you do not take responsibility for. The ability to influence your own outcome, do what is expected, and achieve an appropriate result are empowering. Allowing someone to complain, hide, and feign helplessness does nothing to achieve therapeutic goals. Ultimately, too, in working with someone who has the potential to be incredibly harmful, we are obligated to the community. Keeping the community safe will provide safety to the offender as well.

The Team Approach

When an offender is released into the community, he is usually released into a team – his treatment, his supervising agency, and his support system, with the potential inclusion of child protective services and the victim's treatment team. It is beneficial for all the team members to work together. We will all have different pieces of information and different roles that will assist in providing a comprehensive picture of the offender's functioning.

Agent Anthony Mondello is a sex-offender parole agent who has worked with our agency for over 20 years. He attends groups at times with all the agencies where his offenders go to treatment. Mr. A. Mondello (2022, March 6, personal communication), in communication with me about this book, talked about the importance of visiting the programs and being a part of the treatment team. His goal is not only to assess the quality and functioning of the programs in terms of supervision needs, but this:

> Another reason is that this is quite possibly the most manipulative caseload and the offender must know that treatment and supervision are on the same team. They will try and manipulate both. You must be aware of that and present a united front in order to prevent that. Just seeing his agent in treatment group, sitting with treatment staff, will give an observable confirmation that is much more powerful than simply telling the offender during a home or office visit, "I am part of the treatment team and work together with treatment."… There are those professionals who will ask, "Do your offenders talk in group with their agent there"? The answer is yes, they do. The reasons may be that they observe other, more experienced group members presenting information in group and giving feedback with the agent present, they observe the agent, who also has an understanding of treatment, asking relevant questions and participating in the group along with the counselors. The offender gets to see firsthand that the agent is willing to sit in the group with the offender, taking a personal interest in his success and not simply issuing an instruction to attend and then waiting for reports.

Triangulation

Triangulation is the manipulation described in Chapter 9 when the offender pits one against the other. Triangulation occurs often when working with offenders involved with other agencies. The offender will complain about treatment to the parole agent. The offender will tell their mental health provider about how mistreated they are by parole. They will tell their wife how "those people" want to keep us apart. Triangulation is easy for offenders when those involved with them do not communicate. It is vital that all people involved in the investigation, treatment, and management of offenders communicate. This includes the offender's family, caseworker, employer, church leader, therapist, psychiatrist, and supervising agent.

Confidentiality

That being said, the offender can manipulate through confidentiality. It is the perfect tool to prevent communication. I strongly recommend that you require confidentiality waivers between professionals who are working with offenders. This does not mean each session is reported to the clients' probation officer with all the details. What it means is that we can and will talk to one another for management and transparency. The clinician needs to know what is found on a home visit and what medications the client is receiving or what is changing. The probation officer needs to know the therapeutic polygraph results, while reporting the offender's drug screen results. All parties need to communicate with whoever the offender is living or working with to ensure that the offender is being truthful and accountable.

Maintaining Boundaries and Knowing Your Role

When you are working in a team with an offender, understand your role. If you are investigating, do not try to counsel. If you are a therapist, do not try to do the parole agent's job. If you are a supervising agent, do not think you understand the particular therapeutic or risk issues that the clinician does. I once worked with a client who had seduced his probation officer into doing his therapeutic homework assignments with him. When we confronted this, she pulled him from treatment and allowed him to return to live with his girlfriend, who had a child victimized by her ex-husband. It was a disaster.

Your personal boundaries are important to protect as well. Anything you disclose or reveal that is personal will be used against you in some way. A pedophile will comment on the picture of your children on your desk. Your bumper stickers will become a discussion point. The information on your website will be scrutinized. The offender might use this information to groom you and get you to be more familiar than you should or to "prove" your bias against them. Dropping your professional veneer should never be accidental with an offender. An intern of mine who is now on staff as a licensed psychologist learned this the hard way. An offender had seen his Mets sticker. After a game when the Mets won, the offender yelled to him, "How 'bout those Mets?" He found himself high fiving the offender and being led into a conversation while the offender's therapy time was going by. Another staff member was told, "Well, I know you don't do this for the money. I saw your car." With any criminal offender, it is important to protect your personal information.

Dynamic Risk Factors

Dynamic risk factors are risk factors that are changeable and fluid. They will rise and fall depending on the offender's internal and external situation. Hanson et al. (2007) identify numerous dynamic factors associated with risk. It pays to familiarize yourself with these factors, which include (but are not limited to): antisocial behavior; victim seeking; deterioration in treatment; hostility and resentment; poor problem solving; distorted attitudes; degradation of women, children, or victims; sexual and emotional dysregulation; and sexual entitlement.

One sign that I do not see discussed thoroughly in the literature is when denial reappears in an offender who has previously been making progress. Or even worse, when his fantasies become salient again and very stimulating. When either one happens, it usually means that the offender has someone around who is supporting the denial or that the offender has to deny for, like a new paramour. In my program, a reappearance of denial has meant the offender has had contact with the victim or someone in his family that believes in his innocence. It has meant that the offender is approaching a situation with another potential victim. It has meant that he has re-engaged with an antisocial peer group. Something has happened to require a regression into denial. Something important and destructive.

Another issue is when the offender suddenly has access to more salient aspects of his offense fantasy. Memories tend to fade in intensity unless they are being reactivated and reinforced. We might intellectually know that our past lover smelled like the cologne he wore, but we will not be able to access that smell easily over time. Visual memories and thoughts stay relatively available, but other sensory experiences tend to diminish. When an offender suddenly has a resurgence of intense sexual fantasy, something is stimulating him.

Chris taught me this. Chris was in treatment for quite a while when he started looking physically run down and tired. We explored and confronted this for some time. We made Chris meet with the staff to explain what was happening, why he was regressing. He told us he had become depressed because his best friend had moved away. He said to cope with this, he was masturbating to fantasies of his victim. When I asked what he was fantasizing about and the content of his fantasy, he said, "Well, the way she looked, the way she smelled." "What? What do you mean the way she smelled," I asked, surprised. Chris had not seen his victim for over ten years. I could not believe he could remember the way she smelled. She was a small child when he offended her. He offered some explanation, but it did not make sense. I called his probation officer and asked if he would go to Chris' house. There, they found a baby that Chris had fathered unbeknownst to his probation officer or the treatment team. The baby and her mother were living with Chris. Chris was masturbating to fantasies of the baby.

Change Is Meaningful, But What Does It Mean?

When something changes with an offender, it means something. It may not mean anything nefarious, but it is still meaningful. When change comes quickly or unexpectedly, it is more likely to indicate a problem than progress. A sudden change in demeanor toward you or treatment indicates a shift in the offender. If a compliant offender is suddenly non-compliant or vice versa, find out what is happening. Why did he suddenly shave his face? What is that new ring on his finger? How come he got a brand new car when he said he lost his job? All of these things need exploration and need to make sense. In my experience, rapid weight gain or loss, a change in appearance, new expensive shoes, repetitive illnesses, and job change have all meant that the offender was involved in dangerous, illegal, or victim-seeking behavior.

The Myth of the Supervised Visit

If you are in a position to supervise visitation between an offender and a victim or a potential victim, please understand that it cannot be done. Supervision of an offender *might* prevent a sexual offense from occurring, but it does not prevent the offender from communicating or influencing the victim.

I have worked with offenders who have offended during a visit. They have tickled and stimulated the victim. One offender gave his victim a vibrating spirograph pen which she put in her crotch because he had used a vibrator on her when offending her. One with a foot fetish tickled his daughter's feet during a visit. But more importantly, the visits give the offender stimulation and reinforcement of his fantasy. When the victim is glad to see him, he can tell himself that she still loves him and he didn't hurt her. He can smell her hair. One offender had the child's mother bring her blanket for him to sniff during visits. Playing with the victim can reinforce the offender's belief that the victim was not harmed and enjoyed the offending.

These visits give information to the child as well. The offender can communicate threats or promises. The offender can show the child that he is in control and that the caseworker likes and trusts him, not the child. He can engage in inappropriate behavior in front of the supervisor that the supervisor cannot or will not manage, like one offender who withheld food from his victim because she would not kiss him. No one did anything. No one did anything about the offender who whispered in his victim's ear that he better "take it back" so he could return home. The visits allow the perpetrator to remain in an influential relationship with the victim. Supervised visits remind the child that returning to the offender is the goal. Two separate victims told me this about their supervised visits:

> I want people to believe me and I'm telling the truth…I just want to be away from him…I'm not going to live much longer if I have to be around him. I can't handle this stress and fear any longer…no one should have to be afraid like this every day.
>
> If I have to visit them, I won't go and if they send me home, I'll run away again and if I keep being sent home, I'll kill myself. I'm not suicidal, I'm fighting for myself and my little sister, but death is better than living in that house with them and that abuse.

Children and victims understand the maintenance of the offender's public persona. "My dad's a good actor," one victim said, "he pretends to care when people are around and when they leave, he will slap me in the face." Another said, "That mean look my mom gives during the visit … I know that look." Other children in our practice have identified other problems with the supervised visits. The physical touching, when parents bring food ("food that the kids use to eat before the abuse"), the smells that remind the children of the abuse, and when parents are "two-faced." Sexual abuse is intimate and private. Offenders send signals to children, trigger them, and communicate messages that someone not in that family or dyad can understand. "He told me during my visit that he couldn't wait till we went camping," the girl told me. The abuser assaulted her the first time when they were camping.

Perhaps most poignantly, supervised visits might provide the child with the "best" daddy or mommy she can have. Offenders are often on their best behavior, attentive and calm. The child is at minimal risk of being abused during the visit, so he can be free to play and be loved, getting all the things wanted from the offender with none of the danger. The child does not act afraid because there is no danger. Then the child's behavior is used to "prove" that the offender is not a risk and is not feared by the child.

Dynamics Define the Offender, Not the Victim

I will reiterate this. It is the sexual offense dynamics that are of critical importance in the treatment and management of the offender. These dynamics appear pervasively and repeatedly. They are what make the offender cross age and gender barriers. They are why an offender can be a risk to someone other than his one or two identified victims. An offender's victim pool is more extensive than his convictions show. Supervising him and managing based only on the information known from his conviction is a mistake. Making rules or restrictions based only on the victim we know of is a mistake. It is tempting to rely on the polygraph to tell us about the offender. Still, it is more important to identify and address the dynamics that the offender is exhibiting throughout his treatment.

Summary

That is why I refused to say no. When a boy looks my way and I say, you let me love you as even your father never loved you. I kiss him. He kisses me back. We strip make love. So happy, he tells his best buddy, his best buddy, says that's dirty! and calls the cops.

And now I'm the bad guy, the molester. I'm 50 years old. 6' 6", 195 pounds. Black. Boys see me and know they can love me and I will never harm a hair of their heads except the head of their cocks and the pubescent nectar of their loins down my throat. I live in Allentown, P.A. I am here in Lehigh County Prison a few more months. Surely I will get parole. Summer is just around the corner. Lots of parks and rivers, woods, nudist camps. They can only keep the leash on so long – they can't watch me 24/7.

This is a letter from a convicted pedophile awaiting his release onto probation. We are not sure who he was writing to when this was confiscated. I only know he is right – we "can only keep the leash on so long." But we are out there to try to keep the community safe.

It takes a special type of professional who wants to work with the sexual offender. I am grateful whenever I find one or meet one who is interested in genuinely doing the hard work it takes. It is important to remember that you are working with people who have a level of deviance that changed their relationship with the world so that they risked everything to hurt someone, in pursuit of their gratification. Working with people who have done this requires the ability to see the world and others for what it is, to recognize danger and face the realities these offenders present boldly. If you can do this and do it properly, you are doing something important that helps not only the offender, but your community.

In conclusion,

- You have to be willing to go outside your comfort zone to ensure the offender goes outside his and cannot control you. You have to challenge and confront and view the offender's presentation with you in the proper perspective.
- Accountability and agency are important pillars to change and improvement. Getting an offender motivated to change and be accountable requires challenging him.
- A team approach is critical for the prevention of triangulation and manipulation. Each player on the offender's team has vital information to share.
- It is imperative to be aware of the dynamic or changeable factors related to risk in offenders. Being mindful of these factors will allow you to assess the offender in real-time, all the time.
- An offender's changes should be understood and make sense. You should scrutinize sudden or random changes in the offender's presentation or lifestyle as they may be related to risk situations.
- Contact between an offender and victim or potential victim is fraught with hazards for the offender and the victim. Carefully consider any decision to allow contact between an offender and a potential victim.

References

American Psychological Association (n.d.). *Accountability*. APA Dictionary of Psychology. Retrieved from https://dictionary.apa.org/accountability

American Psychological Association (n.d.). *Agency*. APA Dictionary of Psychology. Retrieved from https://dictionary.apa.org/agency

Bancroft, L. (2002). *Why does he do that? Inside the minds of angry and controlling men*. Berkley Books.

Connolly, J. (2007). *The unquiet*. Emily Bestler Books.

Doren, D. (2002). *Evaluating sex offenders: A manual for civil commitment and beyond*. Sage.

Flora, R. (2001). *How to work with sex offenders: A handbook for criminal justice, human service, and mental health professionals*. Haworth Press.

Hanson, R. K., Harris, A. J. R., Scott, T.-L., & Helmus, L. (2007). *Assessing the risk of sexual offenders on community supervision: The dynamic supervision project (User report, corrections research)*. Public Safety Canada. http://www.publicsafety.gc.ca/cnt/rsrcs/pblctns/ssssng-rsk-sxl-ffndrs/index-eng.aspx

Chapter 13

Prevention Tips and Strategies

Preventing damage before it occurs is the ultimate goal for most of us. To that effort, there are many resources with prevention tips on protecting your children from being sexually abused. Simply Google sexual abuse prevention; you will find thousands of valuable tips, including being involved with your children, trusting your gut feelings, and respecting children's boundaries. For adult women, there are tips about not leaving your drink alone, not being alone in risky situations, and setting up safety plans. I will not reiterate the readily available strategies. I want to discuss additional issues to consider when attempting to prevent sexual violence.

I want to highlight that almost all strategies for prevention focus on the victim's choices and behaviors, contributing to the backlash and blaming victims receive when they do not follow prevention tips as if they asked to be assaulted because they did not follow the rules. The burden for prevention should not be on the victim alone. As discussed in the early chapters of this book, we have a society that supports beliefs and values that facilitate sexual maltreatment and abdicate the offender's responsibility.

Unfortunately, I believe our good intentions in providing prevention tips that focus on victims' choices contribute to the problem, even while offering some sound advice. We cannot expect children to protect themselves and tell when we ask children to be obedient, keep our secrets, and follow social rules. We keep children ignorant of sexual knowledge, impairing their ability to understand and identify what is happening to them. We teach them about "stranger danger" when very few children are harmed by someone strange to them. We make them feel ashamed, blamed, and wrong when they are abused. Our reaction to any victim risks conveying criticism and judgment, or worse the disbelief that can be more traumatic than the assault itself. And do not rely on legislation or laws to prevent sexual violence. There is little evidence that community notification, registries, or housing ordinances prevent sexual assault (Zgoda & Mitchell, 2021). What they do, however, is give us a false sense of security.

So what are some ways we can do better? Below are additional ideas and tools to add to your prevention repertoire.

Be Aware of Your Biases – Confront Your Subtle Blaming

Hopefully, after reading this book, you have become aware of some of your biases or reliance on misinformation in understanding offenders and how they work. Questioning your biases in how you see offenders and victims or how you perceive stories or situations will be beneficial in allowing you to educate others and how you communicate to victims. Having an open mind for all possibilities when faced with an offender's behavior will allow you to make more accurate assessments of what is happening to prevent his reoffense or harm to someone else.

DOI: 10.4324/9781003156284-17

We also have to address our more insidious and understated biases and judgments. When we say, "Well, no one deserves to get hurt, but …" or "It's terrible what happened, but what was she thinking," we are still victim-blaming. Even though we try to coat it with compassion, we are still judging.

Another very judgmental thing we do is ask victims the question "why?" Why didn't you tell? Why did you go back? Why didn't you listen? Dread of the question "why" and the judgment it implies keeps many victims from help-seeking. If the victims who were not prevented cannot come forward, we cannot help prevent future victims.

Educating Our Children

Children learn about sexual abuse prevention through ideas like "stranger danger," "good touch/bad touch," or through simple edicts, like "don't let anyone touch your privates and if they do, tell me." This is not enough. This type of education ignores all the things we know about sexual abuse and sexual offenders. Current trends that prohibit sexual education for children disable us from protecting our children even more. The idea that sexual knowledge destroys sexual "purity" or will contaminate children in some evil way allows offenders to further exploit their ignorance and naivete. Remember, in this context, the term children applies not only to small children but also to older children and adolescents. Adolescents are a population that is very vulnerable to abuse. Obviously, all education about abuse should be done in an age-appropriate manner.

Education About Sexual Abuse

Here are some things children should be taught about sexual abuse to increase their likelihood of and ability to tell:

- The vocabulary – children need to know what body parts are called, so they can tell without shame. I know a case against a perpetrator failed because a victim could only talk about "giggle berries and tickle sticks." She did not have the words to report it. *A Very Touching Book* by Jan Hindman (1983) is an excellent, thorough, direct book for educating children without the shame and titillation that secrecy conveys.
- That sexual abuse is about "secret" touching or touching trouble, not "good" or "bad." It should not be a secret who is touching the child.
- That sexual abuse can sometimes feel good, "weird," or "tickly."
- That sometimes people who are liked by the child or parents will sexually touch them and ask them to keep secrets. Sometimes it could be a parent or a family member.
- That the child should never worry about getting anyone else in trouble – it is not their job. The child should know that when someone older touches you in any way, it should not be a secret. If the child does not want it or likes the touch, they can say no.
- That even if the child promised to keep a secret or took money or candy to keep a secret about touching, it is not wrong to break the promise. This is never the kind of secret they have to keep, no matter what.
- That even if the child was curious or somehow "did stuff too," they will not get in trouble.
- That if the child cannot tell their parents, they should tell someone. Generate a list of people the child might be able to tell – like a doctor, teacher, or aunt.
- That it is never, ever their fault. No matter what. It is always a grown-up who is responsible. Tell them that you will never be mad at them and that kids can't go to jail.

Teach children the truth about sexual abuse and sexual offenders, not the myths. Help them understand that sometimes nice people are dangerous. Teach them that sex is good, but it is for grown-ups. Sex is not scary and secret but is private and complicated. Sexual abuse is scary, secret, and something grown-ups know better about.

Education About Consent, Respect, and Intimacy

We fear talking to kids about sex so much that we forget to talk to them about healthy sexual boundaries, consent, intimacy, and respect. We forget that the "sex talk" is a continuous discussion that changes with the child's emotional, social, and sexual maturity. A young girl who is very physical with her uncle throughout her childhood has to understand how the interaction needs to change when she starts getting older, getting breasts. Privacy changes over time. What are some basic concepts children need to know and then learn again as their interests and needs change? Here are a few which we should teach at the appropriate time and age of the child:

- Consent – children must learn that "permission" applies to bodies, too. They would not take their friend's cell phone without permission. They cannot touch people without permission either. Consent is a concept that children need to understand for themselves and others. Using examples, we can teach children what consent is and isn't. We can teach them about the wrong ways to get what you want. Children learn that lying is not okay to get something, but we have to connect this to sexual consent. It is not okay to use manipulation, drugs, alcohol, money, isolation, or pressure to extract "consent." We must educate children and teens that this is not consent or respect. Silence is not consent.
- Respect for boundaries – children need to learn to respect the word no. They need to understand that it is okay if someone does not want to be friends. They need to be able to tolerate loss and limits. It is easy to immediately take your child's side, especially when the child is hurt. But it is important to help them process the grief and frustration related to hitting a boundary or experiencing a loss rather than feeding into a feeling of victimization or persecution that justifies boundary violations. When someone says they are not interested, it is not okay to incessantly text to find out why or ask for another chance. It is not okay to retaliate when someone hurts your feelings. It is not okay to touch someone when you don't have permission, even if you are "joking."
- Intimacy – children need to learn how to be intimate emotionally and the respect it requires. They need to learn about healthy conflict, managing emotions and sexual feelings, and getting good advice. Defining what a genuine relationship is and what it entails will guide the child through love relationships and friendships.
- Danger and technology – children should be taught about the risks and realities of what can happen online. You should discuss how a stranger can feel like a friend, how images stay online forever, and how people may not be who they seem to be.

Role Modeling: Violence Is Learned, So Is Respect

Part of prevention is role modeling. Especially for men, being a proper role model for sexual respect is critical (Katz, 2006). Boys must learn to respect and honor others, including themselves. If boys learn to beat women because they are exposed to this growing up, they can learn how to respect women from male role models that show respect and constraint. It is not enough for men to role model non-violence; men must communicate values and beliefs about men, women, and sexual respect in their behavior, language, and attitudes.

Some values that can contribute to sexual disrespect are formed in unexpected ways. When we coach children to hit it into left field because "the kid out there is slow," we teach children the value of exploiting vulnerability. When we allow an older child to humiliate his adoring younger sibling, we teach the child that love is something to be abused. When we roll our eyes because we have to feed our tween's hamster again, but do it anyway, we teach a child you can disregard something that depends on you for care. Role modeling not only comes from confronting, educating about, and adhering to principles that promote respect; it comes from being and expecting others to be accountable for how they are acting and what message they are sending.

"Don't Be That Guy" (STV News, 2021) is a powerful anti-sexual violence campaign in Scotland, targeting the sexist and sexually harassing behavior that precedes sexual violence. It is a video of men telling men, "Don't be that guy," after confronting them on various problematic behaviors. This is the type of role-modeling and challenging norms we need.

Make Conflict Your Friend

Offenders count on us to observe the social rules that dictate our expected behavior. They expect us to avoid conflict and accountability. They manipulate us, make us feel guilty and defensive, or wield the discomfort and stigma of facing sexual abuse as a shield for their behavior. You can do several things to deter an offender in your environment, simply by demonstrating that you are not afraid to face abuse and will not tolerate it.

Say Hello to a Sex Offender

One of the reasons registries do not work is that people are overwhelmed with the information. They do not understand what the information means and do not use them. And, when they do find out someone is a sexual offender, the information is not used productively. The most productive use of a registry is to allow you to introduce yourself to an offender to let them know you are aware of them. This should be done respectfully, without threat or animosity. Fear, avoidance, and anonymity give the offender the space to do what they need to do. When they have eyes on them in a way that is not threatening or making them feel like victims, they can be deterred from behavior others might detect. You can also tell your children to let you know if that particular neighbor approaches them or tries to befriend them. Making yourself known establishes a boundary and demonstrates your willingness to address the issue of risk.

Set the Boundaries Immediately

When placing your child or loved one in a potentially vulnerable situation, make your expectations clear, even if it seems awkward. I do not mean come to the door with a shotgun when your daughter brings home a boyfriend. In fact, if your loved one fears an aggressive or overreaction from you, that person is less likely to come to you for help. But you can tell a person calmly that you expect your child or loved one to be treated appropriately. You can question the daycare worker about what safeguards are in place to prevent sexual abuse. You can let the Boy Scout leader that you expect him to follow the no one-on-one protocols and will be checking in on that. You can set boundaries assertively, calmly, and clearly to inform the person in charge of your loved one that you are paying attention and will not hesitate to question what does not seem protective. You will establish yourself as different for all the offenders that rely on a parent's inattention or lack of involvement. A former sex crimes officer would always intentionally, but casually, tell new people in her daughter's life her prior occupation. She felt this politely established a set of expectancies that contributed to protecting her daughter.

Acting Upon the First Red Flags

If your child is acting uncomfortable, getting isolated, or bringing things home (like money) you do not expect them to have, don't just write it off. If your gut tells you something is off, act upon that. Say something if the person is a little too close, touchy, or goofy with your kid. If your daughter starts calling you less, withdraws, or does not bring her boyfriend to family functions, do not withdraw or get resentful. Get closer to her. When something feels wrong, address it. If you are wrong, so what? If you are appropriate, calm, and respectful, someone without an agenda will respond in kind. Remember, acting offended is a weapon offenders use to deflect attention.

Challenging Social Rules that Control Us

All the tips I provide require that we push against the social rules and norms that control us. It can be uncomfortable, but it does not make you wrong. You might get some reaction to your decisions. "Oh god, don't make those kind of jokes around her," you might hear if you say that rape or sexist jokes make you uncomfortable. If you are respectful and not combatting abuse with abuse, your behavior is not inappropriate. It will speak volumes to those searching others for vulnerability, fear, or inexperience to exploit. If you say no, point out when that limit is being violated. Do not go along to get along.

Being a Proactive Bystander

A significant movement in sexual assault prevention is training bystanders to intervene in situations where there is or is a risk of maltreatment of another. Being a proactive bystander can include many, many choices to intervene when it appears that someone is at risk of being assaulted or at risk of assaulting someone. When done appropriately, bystander intervention can be invaluable in preventing abuse or addressing community or societal norms that facilitate and support abuse. A proactive bystander can confront bullying or scapegoating. A bystander can protect a drunk potential victim from being led away from her friends. A bystander can redirect his friend who is pressuring a love interest.

There are scientifically grounded ways to effectively intervene in even volatile situations without escalating the problem (Miller, 2017; Novak, 2022). Learning the tools to intervene can arm you to be active and intentional in preventing or stopping a situation in real life. Being a good bystander can be highly preventative. If you do not feel you have the skills, learn them.

Learning to Say Yes – Healthy Sexuality

Sex and sexuality in our society continue to be very difficult to discuss openly and appropriately. When it comes to sex, we need to understand that sex is fun, healthy, safe, and fulfilling. We fail to tell kids how good sex can be, especially when love and respect are involved. Instead, we allow pornography, media portrayals of frequent, indiscriminate sex, or stories of fantastical or deviant sexuality to define their understanding of sex.

We continue to have gender role expectations of sexuality. Women are expected to use birth control and manage the sexual arousal of men. But how can we identify when to and be able to say no to sex when we still have trouble saying yes? Especially with adolescents, we do not teach them how to choose sex. It is easier to identify what feels bad and when you do not want sex when you are clear on what feels good and what you do want. Confusion about identifying sexual assault would decrease if there was an open discussion about sexual decision-making and sexual enjoyment. Victims would not be confused about whether they were raped when they were clear about saying no because they have the option to say yes. They will know that just because it is not violent does not mean it is not violating.

We need to be open about how to handle strong sexual urges as well, for both men and women. If young boys could be taught about their early and potent sexual feelings, to expect them and how to manage them, perhaps we could prevent some juvenile sex offenses. Sexuality and sexual behavior appear in humans at a very early age. If we could treat sexuality as natural and manageable part of the human condition, perhaps we would develop better skills at preventing sexual offending.

Accepting No Excuses for Abuse

Finally, and most importantly, we must not accept any excuses for sexual assault. While this will not stop all sexual assaults, it will combat the ease at which offenders offer and we accept excuses and justifications. If, as a society, there is never a good enough reason to rape someone, juries will not struggle as much. We will not be manipulated as much. The offender will have more barriers to overcome, internally and externally, to succeed in sexual offending.

Summary

We have a long way to go in terms of preventing sexual assault. As a society that superficially expresses horror about sexual assault and derision for the sexual offender, we continue to fail in adequate efforts at prevention. But we can do it. Supplement your protective efforts with more information and broader strategies that enhance prevention in our society and contribute to the prevention of people *becoming sexual offenders,* not just victims.

In conclusion,

- Children and adolescents need a different or more comprehensive education on sexuality that includes consent, respect, and intimacy.
- We can take specific steps to fortify our boundaries and address issues in our society that excuse and facilitate sexual assault.
- There needs to be more focus on preventing people from becoming sexual offenders, not just victims.
- We can deter sexual assault when potential targets are educated, and bystanders intervene.

References

Hindman, J. (1983). *A very touching book.* Alexandria Association.

Katz, J. (2006). *The macho paradox.* Sourcebooks.

Miller, C. (2017, December 12). The #MeToo moment: How to be a (Good) bystander. *The New York Times.* https://www.nytimes.com/2017/12/12/us/the-metoo-moment-how-to-be-a-good-bystander.html

Novak, S. (2022, May 10). How to be a good bystander. *Discover.* https://www.discovermagazine.com/mind/how-to-be-a-good-bystander-according-to-science

STV News (2021, October 21). "Don't be that guy" [Video]. YouTube. https://www.youtube.com/watch?v=wf-rOrOXoRI

Zgoda, K., & Mitchell, M. (2021). The effectiveness of sex offender registration and notification: A meta-analysis of 25 years of findings. *Journal of Experimental Criminology.* https://doi.org/10.1007/s11292-021-09480-z

Chapter 14

"No Victims, No Excuses"
Conclusion

Sexual offenders are particularly challenging – in our work, our lives, our community. These challenges seem insurmountable at times. They are skilled. They are successful. They operate with the backdrop of a society replete with misogyny, unhealthy sexuality, and disregard for victims. Offenders hide in the shadows cast by the images they produce, the shields they use, and barriers we face to confronting them. We are not helpless, but it does take courage to confront sexual abuse and assault in our society. "Courage," said Maya Angelou, "is the most important of all the virtues. Because without courage, you cannot practice any other virtue consistently."

There is significant hope in the work we do, whether it is treatment, supervision, investigation, or prosecution. We have hope when we choose to accept an offender into our lives. Hope is crucial to the work we do, crucial for our resilience. However, hope, too, is a four-letter word. It should help us, not blind us. When we are hoping, we are doubting. Sometimes hope motivates us to change our perceptions and our understanding so we can maintain our hope. How do we sustain hope without the blinders?

- *We need to see what is, not what if?* We need to see offenders and ourselves clearly and accurately, accepting all of it. We need to accept the dark reality of sexual abuse and the motivations of those who abuse. We must accept as reality the satisfaction in cruelty. Then we can make change happen, because we will know where to begin.
- *Offenders need to intend not to* – it is not enough to not intend to. When an offender says "I didn't mean to" when it comes to sex offending or other problematic behaviors, it is not good enough. An offender has to make active choices to avoid being destructive, they have to "mean not to." They need to make the same intentional, instrumental choices to be safe as they did to be harmful.
- *We need to keep aware that offenders know us and know their victims.* They are successful because they pay attention. They know our biases, our blind spots, and our assumptions. We need to challenge these things in ourselves so they are not exploited. We need to pay as close attention to them as they pay to us.
- *Offenders are not surprised by the victim's behavior.* They know how victims will respond and put effort into directing the victims' response. They also know that victims will be blamed and will confuse us with their "counterintuitive" behavior.
- *We need the truth about sexual abuse.* We need the truth from offenders. We need to use language that conveys the truth. We need to educate ourselves. We need to educate our children. We must not let our discomfort with the truth dissuade us from seeking it.
- *We must stand up victims, safety, and respect.* We can do this, protect the community, and give sexual offenders the opportunity to be part of our community with accountability

DOI: 10.4324/9781003156284-18

and care. We need to choose the side of safety, protection, and freedom from abuse – not the side of the offender versus the victim.

- *We need to truly believe that being part of a community is an awesome privilege with the responsibility to do no harm.*

It is easy to set the bar low for offenders, to not expect much from them. Yet time and time again, an offender will rise to the standards my treatment team and I set. He will look in his mirror with courage and face the things he needs to face, while maintaining his positive qualities, using his strengths to modulate his flaws. This can be the result, written by an offender named Bill, completing his treatment:

> Dear deviance,
>
> It is time for you to leave. We have been together for quite some time. You even waited patiently while my personality flaws developed. Things like an inflated ego, a selfish heart, my need to be held in high regard – even worshipped, were slowly growing in my personality. You knew about my attraction to young girls but I wasn't quite ready yet to take the big step. You saw me cross boundaries but never really take the plunge into the depths of deviance.
>
> The genesis of it all was when I became a person of authority, a teacher. I was the master of my classroom filled with young girls and boys who wanted to please me. I held their fates in my hands. What an awesome responsibility; my own little kingdom with obedient attention seeking subjects...

At the end of therapy, we have our clients do a number of things, one of which is to write a goodbye letter to their deviance, outlining what the deviance has cost them, how they see their deviance, and what values and beliefs they have adopted to combat the return of the deviance. The clients produce amazing letters, showing insight and change in their perspectives and language about their offending. In these letters, they address the consequences and sorrow of their decisions, as well as acknowledge the positive changes that accountability and transparency have made in their lives.

> I could blame you solely for my collapse but we both know that's not true. We worked as a team leaving a path of deceit, heartbreak, anger, mistrust, sadness, guilt, and betrayal. We both have to go. My former self is becoming a better person so I have no need for you. Even more important I know myself now and how I let you get in.
>
> I am going to lock you out. With this knowledge of me and becoming accountable for my actions you will not return. Be warned because I have weapons to assure that you don't. I have a loving family and new friends that will help me. I have tools to remind me that you were once here. Now I can keep my pathways to enjoyment, love, empathy and discovery open without your influence. I can give all of myself to those I love.

"I can give all of myself to those I love." This is the gift that we can give the offender when we unmask him. When we strip away the facade, he can be seen. Then, and only then, can we offer change. Then and only then can we protect ourselves.

Appendix A

Important Concepts to Remember –
If You Are a Victim

Tackling your trauma is difficult. Some of it will heal. Some of it will not. Perhaps some of it should not as being sexually assaulted is a violation of such magnitude, its seriousness should be forever notable. This does not mean you have to suffer. What it means is that you may develop tools to better love and protect yourself and others. I hope the tips below are ideas that make sense to you, that are helpful to you in understanding yourself and the abuse with clarity, and help address some of the thoughts and feelings that hurt you.

- It was never your fault. No matter what. You did not ask for, provoke, or deserve to be sexually assaulted or abused. No matter what. Nothing you tell yourself or that the offender told you will ever make that true. There is no offense that demands rape as a punishment.
- Don't deal with your abuse by idealizing it. It did not make you stronger. It did not make you wiser. It did not make you kinder. You did those things for yourself. In the face of something you did not ask for, an extra burden you carry, YOU did those things. YOU.
- Love is not weakness. Vulnerability is not the problem. The exploitation of it is. Being loved is an honor and a privilege that deserves protection and responsibility. It is not that you were unlovable or undeserving. It is that the person who hurt you did not deserve your love and was incapable of loving you the way you deserve.
- If maintaining attachment to someone harmful means not loving yourself, don't do it. Adopt the belief, "If loving you means not loving me, it is not love."
- Your abuse is only part of you. It does not define you. When you are feeling terrible because of what happened or feeling like it makes you who you are, look in another mirror. We are surrounded by mirrors telling us who we are. Some of those mirrors are distorted, like fun house mirrors, because the people who created them only showed us images of ourselves to meet their needs. Look in the mirror of the people who love you, respect you, and look forward to your company. The mirror of your creativity, your talent, or what gives you peace. Turn away from the mirror of your abuser.
- If you were little or younger or caught in the moments of your relationship when you were abused, reflect back with accuracy and fairness. What I mean is do not engage in hindsight bias. When you look back, ask yourself if you made decisions based on what you knew in that moment, not what you know now. When you went on that date, you did not decide to go knowing you would be raped. When you were a little boy, you did not choose to keep the secret because you enjoyed being abused. Remember precisely who you were then. Did you believe in Santa at the same time you were supposed to manage abuse? You must have faith that you made the best choices you could with what you knew at the time because you did.

- Do not focus on what it was about you that made him/her hurt you. Focus on the abuser and what it was about them – self-centeredness, callousness, and justifying the need to be abusive. Don't tell yourself they did the best they could. If they did, they would not have made you keep it secret. If you want to blame drinking, think of this – if you sexually abused someone after you had been drinking, would you ever drink again? If someone is having urges to sexually assault another person, his failure to get help or do something to protect someone else is only the offender's responsibility. Offenders do what they do because they want to. In many ways, that makes you pretty much meaningless in the face of that.

- The abuse felt terribly personal. The offender, by blaming you or twisting the information, made it about you. But do not make the mistake of thinking it was personal in the sense that it was *only* between and because of you. Almost all offenders have other victims, the vast majority of them. You are not special in that way. If you believe it was only because of and about you, you will make mistakes, sometimes terrible ones. One of the most terrible mistakes is when you allow your children around a perpetrator believing that he would "never do that" to your children. This happens often in families when the perpetrator abuses the grandchildren, facilitated by the abused mom's or dad's belief that the offending was so personal, the perpetrator would not do it to someone else. *Offending is always about the perpetrator.*

- Being sexually assaulted can make you feel damaged, unlovable, and unattractive. Sometimes after being assaulted, giving away sex or using it gives a sense of power or control over it, because having it taken can make you feel owned. Victims sometimes go to either extreme – making themselves unattractive and unlovable or trying to make themselves attractive and pleasing to everyone and anyone. Instead of trying to get rid of the need to be attractive and lovable or allow it to be indiscriminate, focus on being lovable and attractive to someone you like too, someone who values you and is attracted to your spirit as well as you physically. Instead of asking if the person likes you, ask yourself if you like the person.

- When you are being harsh to yourself or you do not trust your perspective, think of what you would say to someone you love, like your best friend. Would you blame your best friend for getting raped? If you would not say it to your best friend, don't say it to yourself. And, when you don't trust your self-perception or your internal monologue, ask yourself what your best friend would say to you. Or even better, reach out and hear what someone who loves you would say – and believe it. Do not rely on your trauma to tell you who you are.

- You will not see yourself clearly if you do not see the perpetrator clearly. Do not compromise because you need that perpetrator's love. Holding others accountable is critical to defining ourselves.

- Be very, very careful about what you look for from the perpetrator if you choose to have an ongoing relationship. You might get an apology, but that does not mean you will not be hurt again. You will forever need to be vigilant. Someone capable of sexual violation will be capable of other violations that hurt you.

- If your gut tells you something is wrong, act on it. Simple as that. You know the secret, covert signs, and behaviors of the perpetrator. Protect yourself and others. If you are wrong and "overreact" in the moment – who cares? I am not advising that you make an allegation when you are unsure if anything happened; I am just saying do not ignore your feelings.

- Finally, understand that healing and trauma involve a great deal of loss and grief. This aspect of trauma is often overlooked. You must lose and grieve the ideals, hopes, and dreams involving the person who hurt you. If it is a parent who sexually abused you,

you must face that you will never have the parent you wanted or deserved. You have to grieve the future, because you have to make different decisions now. You have to grieve the losses that involve you and the world – that idea you are invulnerable, that if you make good choices you will be safe, and that people are always basically good. Sexual assault alters your sense of self, others, and the world. Honor and care for your grief.

I want to offer you hope and empowerment in dealing with the impact of the sexual abuse. He is not "your" rapist, he is a rapist. You are bigger than your assault, not defined by it, but modified. When you are feeling overwhelmed, remember to words of *Superheroes* by The Script (2014) – "*When you've been fighting for it all your life, when you've been struggling to make it right, that's how a superhero learns to fly. Every day every hour, turn that pain into power.*" Appreciate yourself.

Note: If you are currently in a relationship with a violent, sexually assaultive perpetrator, be honest about the risk he poses to you. Safety should be your primary concern. Confronting or leaving a perpetrator should be done strategically and cautiously.

References

The Script (2014). *Superheroes* [Song]. No sound without silence.

Appendix B

Important Concepts for Family Members/Spouse of the Offender

You may be in the unenviable position of navigating the complex landscape of having a family member or spouse who is a sexual offender. You may face societal backlash and rejection. You may have to live with modifications in your life that impinge on your freedom and impact your decision-making. You may be tempted to resent and lash out at others who do not know your loved one like you do, feeling persecuted or unfairly judged. You may feel caught in a Sophie's Choice type of situation – choosing between two loved ones in an untenable, unbearable situation. There is little guidance for the profoundly complex situation you are in, so I hope these tips will bring some clarity and guidance for the situation you have to master.

- You may be mistaken about the choices you think you may have to make. It is reasonable, initially, to believe you must choose between the victim and the perpetrator. This is true in terms of **believing** and **protecting**. Remember what you have learned through this book. The true choice is not choosing who to love – do not mistake this. You will likely continue to love both the victim and the perpetrator family member. But having feelings for the offender should not dictate how you think and the decisions you make to provide safety for others. Love and accountability are not exclusive. Love and truth are not exclusive. Loving someone for <u>exactly</u> who they are is the biggest gift we can ever give.
- Though it is unusual for people to see this, you are a victim of the offender as well. Through no fault or choice of your own, the offender has blown up your life. You are collateral damage and have to face the loss, grief, and responsibilities that the offender has burdened you with through his actions.
- If you are invited to be part of the therapy with the offender, do it. Do not buy into any self-pity or allegations that the offender is being persecuted. Keep in mind that he committed an egregious offense that changed someone's life. The victim will have to contend with the impact of the offender's behavior forever. The offender cannot assert that he paid his time, or whatever. It is the offender's life-long responsibility to ensure he will never hurt someone again. Good treatment will attempt to help the offender establish a knowledgeable support system that will protect the offender and others. Remember, too, that all it takes is one important person in the offender's life that supports lies or denial to undo all the therapeutic work.
- Along with the offender's therapist, consider their supervising agent an ally. It is important that the agent can count on you for accurate, objective information that helps the offender stay compliant to supervision and safe from reincarceration and reoffending.
- You may struggle with extreme or distorted thinking about you and your responsibility for the offender or the offending, especially if you are the offender's parent. It

is important to take an honest inventory of yourself. If you did excuse, overlook, or disbelieve things that facilitated the offending, examine these things. Get education. Commit to not allowing yourself to do these things again. If you can honestly say you did not contribute to the offender's behavior because you were deceived as well, then don't suffer with inappropriate guilt or shame. Sometimes we deny because the feelings associated with admitting are very painful. Denial is your enemy.

- Truly caring for an offender means taking steps to make sure he does not commit another crime. When an offender is doing well, this is never an issue for you. It becomes an issue when you begin to worry things are not going well, or when your questions get deflected. An offender engages in behaviors that will put you off balance, keep you out of his business, and make you feel bad for asking questions. These are all signs that things are going awry.

- If you are hoping, you are doubting. What I mean is that if you find yourself "hoping" that the offender is okay, "hoping" that he is telling the truth, "hoping" that he is getting better, then you are actually doubting these things. We do not hope for things we are certain about. When we know things are true, we don't have to hope. If you are hoping, you are doubting. If you need someone to promise you something, you are also mistrustful. You have reservations about whether someone will come through for you or is committed when you ask for a promise. We never ask for promises when we are sure of something.

- You cannot control the offender. You can participate in supporting them in the right way. You can educate yourself. You can hold the offender accountable. But you cannot be the control agent. You can never truly supervise the offender. You can hold the offender responsible for their choices.

- Sometimes responsibility requires consequences. The offender in your life made numerous choices to be selfishly gratified. At the time, the offender made the choice to risk all the things he might be complaining about – no time with his children, no ability to go to a water park, or the distrust of others. Do not take on the burden to alleviate those consequences, whether through advocacy or your own decisions.

- Grief and loss are going to be part of your process. You have lost a lot because of the offender's decisions. You have lost your ideas of the past and future. You have lost a sense of certainty. You must grieve the fact that the offender's love for you or the family was not bigger than his deviance. Give yourself time and space to grieve. Feel the associated anger, sadness, and betrayal. Remember that acceptance means accepting it all, not just the parts that make it easy.

- Become educated and aware of how trauma can impact the victim. Trauma is confusing and disorienting. It can impact thinking, behavior, and perceptions. Also, do not always rely on the victim to know what they need. A younger sibling will want to see their big brother, regardless of the damage caused. A child will want to see their parent. Children also want ice cream all day. Do not let yourself be seduced into easier decisions because the victim "wants it." It is a shortcut. Sometimes it will be up to you to make the more difficult, more protective decision.

- Take care of yourself, always.

Appendix C
Questions to Understand the Offender and His Deviance

Below are questions I find useful in examining offense information and offender behavior to gain insight and understanding of the offender's motivations and fantasies. Examining the behavior of the offender can often reveal elements that he will hide or protect, strengthening your understanding of his deviance, experience, and risk issues.

What Does the Offense Behavior Demonstrate in Terms of the Perpetrator's:

- Sexual arousal?
- Crossing of boundaries?
- Comfort and confidence in crime?
- Special, personal, or unique elements?
- Violence or acts that exceed their utility?
- Ability to take risks?
- Pattern or practice?
- Escalation?
- The complexity of the fantasy?
- Grooming techniques? With the victim? With the audience?
- Public persona?

What Does the Victim Selection Demonstrate in Terms of the Offender's:

- Experience?
- Ability to identify and exploit vulnerability?
- Ability to and means of creating vulnerability?
- Ability to gain access to the victim?
- Predatory behavior?
- Interpersonal needs?
- Sexual arousal needs?

What Does the Preparation for the Crime Indicate About the Offender's:

- Time, energy, investment in the crime?
- Creativity and experience?
- Ability to influence the victim?
- Skill in preparation of the victim?
- Skill in preparation of the community?
- Interpersonal needs met by the crime?

- The depth of the criminal fantasy?
- The interpersonal, social, or environmental risk issues?
- The use of substances, props, lures, or other instruments?
- The combination or multiplicity of paraphilias?

What Does the Offender's General Persona Tell You About:

- How same or different the crime seems from him/her?
- How they groom authority?
- How they camouflage themselves?
- What arousal needs are met daily? Have they surrounded themselves with stimuli?

Case Examples

Tony abused two 8- to 10-year-old females. He was 26 and the children were grandchildren of his 62-year-old wife. In treatment, Tony revealed that he had first abused his victims as infants. He stated that he would change their diaper and become aroused. He would then digitally penetrate them and masturbate.

What do we need to ask? What might we look for? What are the covert dynamics that may not appear directly in his sexual act? What does the behavior tell us about who he is?

There are several important aspects of Tony's offending that need exploration. These include: the age of his wife and what the nature of the relationship is; how he navigated the significant age difference; what he was aroused to when changing the children's diapers; what aroused him to the children when he assaulted them; and what his interpersonal behavior was.

Tony was abusive to his wife. He was aroused by the smell of the babies' dirty diapers and sexualized that. He was controlling and domineering, aroused not only to the physical elements of the prepubescent girls, but his ability to dominate them. Tony was the primary caretaker of the girls when they would stay with their grandmother. She worked while he babysat. He had isolated the children from their grandmother as well.

Frank was a 72-year-old man in treatment for assaulting his 6-year-old granddaughter. During treatment, he revealed he had had numerous encounters with men by sucking their penises. He had anonymous sex in bathrooms and rest stops. He masturbated the company watchdog each morning. He picked up a dead deer from the road and put his finger in its vagina. He used pornography extensively.

Frank was sexually preoccupied and had an obsession with genitals, as well as a paraphilic arousal to children and animals. Age was not a protective factor for him. His deviance pervaded his entire life and his occupational choices. He had other victims. He had no sex life with his wife as this was too "normal" for him. He was not aroused to her, but this was not an issue in their marriage because he had chosen a fairly asexual partner.

Ralph was a 45-year-old man in treatment for the sexual abuse of his three stepdaughters, ages 8, 10, and 12. He abused them in a variety of ways, including pinning the 10-year-old to the wall in the bathroom and forcefully penetrating her vagina with his finger. He would walk around the house with his bathrobe open. He would come into the bathroom while the girls were urinating. He would blare pornography from the television while they were on the phones with friends. He would read from the Bible while sitting naked or barely clothed in the bathroom while the girls tried to bathe.

In this example, see the voyeurism, exhibitionism, and pedophilic arousal. Ralph was also very cruel and controlling. This came out in his therapy as well, when he was extremely demeaning to the female therapists. The multiplicity of his paraphilic arousal demonstrates how deviant he was because he needed multiple sources of deviant arousal for stimulation. He was also very bold with his offense behavior, revealing the confidence he had in his ability to control the children and control the environment. Playing pornography when other children were present reveals a high degree of risk-taking as well.

Index

Abel, Gene 80
adolescent victims 62
ageism 96–97
anchoring bias 22
anomalous target preferences 77–78
antisocial traits 68, 70–71
Ariely, Dan 81
arrogance 110
attraction toarousal toaction 82–83
atypical sexual interest 61–63
audience 19–22, 24–28, 45, 99; discrediting the
    victim 93–94; offender grooming 45; preparing
    93–96; public persona, creating 93; to a sexual
    offense 7–17; in sexual violence facilitation 7–9;
    victim/audience preparation 50–51

Bancroft, Lundy 115
Barnetz, Z. 88
Baumeister, R. F. 71
bias 9, 47, 61, 93, 96–97, 100, 127–128, 134;
    anchoring bias 22; confirmation bias 21–22;
    constructs of complacency 20–23; denial bias/
    normalcy bias/status quo bias 20–21; halo bias
    22–23; hindsight bias 21, 136; loss aversion 20
boundaries 106–107; violations 90–91
Brake, S. 90

Campbell, R. 10
Carter, L. 44
change 112–118; being cured 114; compliance
    112–113; feeling guilty/distress 113–114; fully
    educated support system 117–118; meaning-
    fulness of 123; risk situations, identification
    of and intervention in 116–117; self-esteem
    114–115; self-management, full accountability
    for 117; taking responsibility for the offending
    115; victim/perp relationship, no re-creation of
    117; walking the walk 116; what matters when
    assessing change 115–118
character 2, 20–21, 25, 33, 52, 59–63; antisocial
    character 61; antisociality as a character pathway
    68–71; definition 66; deviance 66–74; disorders
    60; elements of 2, 67; judging 120; personality
    and 66–67; problematic character traits 59, 61, 67

character deviance 66–74; antisociality as a char-
    acter pathway 68–71; definition 66; elements of
    2, 67; immunity to rules or opinions 69; lack of
    conscience, remorse, or empathy 69–70; lack of
    regard for the rights of others 68–69; personal-
    ity disorder 66–67; sex offending as part of the
    criminal repertoire 70–71
co-defendants 7–17; audience role 7–9; power,
    status, position, glorification of 15–16; societal
    building blocks for good offense construction
    9–16; see also audience
coercive paraphilic disorder 80
community 9, 23, 45, 119, 125, 134–135;
    perpetrator status and 15–16, 69, 95, 121
compliance 47, 65, 112–113
confirmation bias 21–22
confrontation 22, 53, 117, 120
confusion 98–99
Connolly, John 119
consent 129
counterintuitive behavior 27–28, 99–100, 134
Courage to Heal 38

de Becker, Gavin 25, 89, 108
deception 25–27, 63, 95–96, 107; "deception
    detection" techniques 26; vigilance for 109–110
denial 19–29, 106, 119, 123; bias 20–21; relation-
    ship impact on 45–46
deviance 66–74, 114–116, 119–120, 141–143;
    criminogenic or sexual needs 49; denial of
    46; distortions and 64–65; fantasy and 81–83;
    non-sexual displays of 64; offender's investment
    in 44; power of 63–64; sexual deviance 59–63;
    sources of 37–38; see also character deviance;
    sexual deviance
Doren, D. 120

educating children 128–129; about consent 129;
    about intimacy 129; about respect 129; about
    sexual abuse 128–129
Ekman, Paul 63
entitlement 11–13, 35, 60, 71–72, 80, 122
Evaluating Sex Offenders 120
exhibitionism (flashing) 77

For Product Safety Concerns and Information please contact our EU
representative GPSR@taylorandfrancis.com
Taylor & Francis Verlag GmbH, Kaufingerstraße 24, 80331 München, Germany

www.ingramcontent.com/pod-product-compliance
Lightning Source LLC
Chambersburg PA
CBHW080134270326
41926CB00021B/4472

persons changed significantly nor has there been visible change in conditions in which they live in most countries. India is a case in point.

The shift in approach to disability care from segregation to integration or inclusion is the first step to the recognition of their basic human right to participate in all social and political activities as citizens. Resultantly, more and more children with a handicap, in theory, have the right to attend regular schools and participate fully and without restraints in community life, and have a visible rightful place in society. Full citizenship implies the understanding that disability is not so much a consequence of injury or defect, but rather a consequence of social norms and values (Boertjes and Lever 2007).

In many ways the notion of self-hood or person-hood is interconnected with the notion of citizenship. It is citizenship that gives an individual identity and nationality, which is the basis of all state interventions for its citizenry. Affirmative action for the disabled that enables them to exercise their citizenship rights is part of this same continuum. This is necessary because the recognition of the right of the disabled must be translated into action through programmes that enable them to exercise their rights, and this is only possible with a paradigm shift in the approach of the state and society. This has not happened. Under normal circumstances, images of children connect their inferior position with emotional dimensions in two ways that do not entitle children to say who they are themselves. On the one hand, overriding images of children are created on the basis of adult experiences of their own childhood, this becoming a means by which to compensate real contact with children. On the other hand, compelling images of children appear to be embedded within societal discourse whereby children prove that the world and the environment in which they live needs to be changed. However, in the case of disabled children the sense of self is not only constructed by society but the fact that the child's disability is a fundamental factor in the construction of his or her very person, that is 'me' (de Lauwe 1984).

In an attempt to describe the development of the sense of self, a psychoanalyst says,

> Children who are frustrated in their efforts to develop a positive and healthy sense of self will make their mark in some, often disturbing, ways. It may be necessary for the child to terrorise, bully or see people frightened, worried, crying, at their wits' end. Such a child may have to be first, to be captain all the time. The child may have to rebel against coercion, refuse to do anything expected of him or her, or insist on doing everything that is forbidden. (Bonime 1989: 136)

The implication is that every child, disabled or non-disabled, needs to feel significant in one way or another. If they cannot make their mark in some positive way, they will express themselves in a deviant or distorted way.

The binary of disabled/non-disabled reflects at a deeper level a paradigm of 'normality' that has become accepted by society. 'The disabled students are relegated to a silent and silenced world where they become what they are perceived as being: incapable, illiterate, dysfunctional and non-productive members of school and society' (Peters 1999: 104). Even within the disabled, if the child is not mentally disabled, he/she will fall into the category of mentally 'normal'.

Priestly (2001) highlighted some of the negative assumptions that underlie the constructions of disabled children in the contemporary society. They include (i) a pre-occupation with impairment, (ii) a pre-occupation with vulnerability, (iii) a pre-occupation with services, (iv) exclusion and discipline, (v) denial of complex identities. Children constantly have to encounter notions of 'normality' and 'difference' in the response of society and the state.

Because of this internalisation of impairment, vulnerability, exclusion and negation of identity, and treatment as different and abnormal, many disabled persons feel more comfortable holding on to their identity of 'disability' for negotiating with society and state. A disabled person said, 'My disability is a fundamental factor in the person that is "me". I do not want to deny this by calling myself "a person with special needs" nor any other euphemism, nor do I want to deny the collective identity we (disabled people) have achieved for ourselves. Therefore I am a disabled person and proud of it' (Russell 1996: 186).

Disabled children too do not want to be constructed as 'different'. For instance, Fara, a 10-year-old, one of the children who was invited to the UNICEF 's International Day of Peace in 2006, who gave her message with the assistance of an interpreter, declared, 'I was born unable to hear or to speak. So I wish that people would not treat me differently because I cannot hear them. I wish that children like me are not discriminated against and that everyone accepts everybody with whatever differences they might have.'

Disability and Education

For many decades, education as a human right has evolved through global initiatives such as Education for All (EFA) and the Salamanca Statement. However, UNESCO cautions that reaching the goals of EFA is one of the most daunting challenges facing the global community. Despite the Millennium Development Goals (MDGs) representing a global partnership, calling civil society to promote primary education by 2015, it is clear that millions of the world's disabled children cannot obtain a basic childhood education, particularly in developing countries.

Even in the wealthiest countries, many disabled children and youth are educationally segregated from the non-disabled, particularly if they are labelled with significant cognitive impairment. International agencies such as the United Nations and the World Bank have generated funds for educational development, but these funds are administered with the assumption that the 'west is best', thereby urging developing countries to mimic educational policies in the United States and the United Kingdom in order to prove their aid-worthiness. This 'McDonaldisation' of education reproduces the labelling, resource allocation and social dynamics long criticised in disability studies (Gabel and Danforth 2008).

In fact, Anne Bishop (2002), writing on child-rearing practices in western countries in her book *Becoming an Ally: Breaking the Cycle of Oppression*, describes how abusive child-rearing practices in countries such as Canada are. Though she discusses children in general, it is not difficult to perceive that disabled children more than the non-disabled children are abused in subtle ways by their parents. For instance, if a child is crying, say, on a bus, parents will scold him/her and try to hush him/her up, because they don't want others to think they are not caring for their child. Vanmala Hiranandani, in a personal communication with the author said, 'According to my experience of living, working and researching for the past ten years in US and Canada, the answer is that the so-called "developed" countries do not involve disabled children in decision making'.[2]

There have been instances when the government's department of child welfare staffed by social workers has been called in if a neighbour perceives that a parent is neglecting his/her child. So, parents try to exercise a lot of control over their children, in a culture that my students astutely describe as one of 'social control'.

Although theory and practice in developed countries has largely moved towards inclusive education, there has been some critique in these countries as inclusive/integrated education is not really the best in these countries, because of the lack of resources for inclusive education, and because teachers have yet to develop their knowledge and skills on inclusive education, etc. So, that is a debate in itself.

The other pressing subject of concern in developing countries is the forcible use of the pharmaceutical drug Ritalin that is given to children who are perceived by teachers as being hyperactive—a condition labelled as Attention Deficit Disorder. The use of Ritalin has been condemned by parents and researchers alike; however, since the pharmaceutical industry is a powerful lobby in the US/Canada/UK, these practices continue. The purpose of giving this drug to children is to keep them under control, so teachers don't have to expend their energy to deal with children who are perceived to be overactive. However, it is often the case that these so-called 'hyperactive' children are just naturally curious and physically energetic that may not necessarily be in tune with the social expectations of being in a controlled or authoritarian classroom. It is the pedagogy, the classroom atmosphere, what is taught in schools and how, and the attitude of teachers that must change, rather than forcing drugs on children. There is very little mainstream discussion on Ritalin these days, but a postgraduate student in Canada remarks, 'It is the same old mentality of keeping people in their place'. There is a more widespread social control in developed countries than meets the eye, although there is not much mainstream literature about it.

An Indian Case Study

Negotiation with the education system has always been a serious concern of disabled children. The system to deal with the education of disabled children in India typifies the system of governance with respect to the disabled citizens.

Although the policy documents related to education in India say that the objective is to ensure that the physically and mentally handicapped should be integrated with the general community as equal partners to prepare them to face life with courage and confidence, barely 7 per cent children receive some kind of education in special or regular schools (Ghai 2006). In the hierarchy of social disability and physical and mental disability, with such high rates of uneducated children (almost half of all children are out of school, two-thirds of whom are girls), the chances for disabled children to acquire an education are practically non-existent, thereby they are denied educational opportunities to develop the knowledge and skills required for survival in a changing world (Sadgopal 2006).

The Government of India has perpetuated the discrimination in the way it delivers programmes for disabled children. Whereas the general educational needs come under the purview of the Ministry of Human Resource Development, the responsibility for *special education* is discharged by the Ministry of Social Justice and Empowerment, thereby sandwiching the education issues of disabled children between the two ministries. The result is that though various schemes were launched in the country to promote the education of children with special needs, the vision of true inclusion seems to be lacking. For example, in principle the Integrated Education of Disabled Children (IEDC) launched in 1974 and revised in 1992, several of the government programmes such as District Primary Education Programme (DPEP), Janshala, the joint programme of the Government of India and five UN agencies, and the newly launched scheme of Sarva Shiksha Abhiyan (SSA), reiterate the need for a just inclusion of disabled children in regular schools. Further, by virtue of the Persons with Disabilities Act (Equal Opportunities, Protection of Rights and Full Participation), 1995, better known as the PWD Act, as well as the UN Treaty for the Rights of the People with Disabilities, 2006 ratified by India, disabled children should be in inclusive school settings. However, even a cursory glance at suggestions in the act such as part-time classes, non-formal education, open schools and open universities for children with special needs belie the thrust on inclusion.

Prior to 2002, Articles 41, 45, 46, all directive principles of the Constitution of India, were the only articles pertaining directly to the right of education. In 1992 two Supreme Court rulings (viz., Mohini Jain v. State of Karnataka and Unni Krishnan v. State of AP) declared that the right of education was directly connected to the fundamental right to life (viz., Article 21). Citing both the universal declaration of human rights as well as the international covenant on economic social and cultural rights in support of the judgement, education was considered a fundamental right. One of the measures for achieving the goal of education for all (EFA) was the Eighty-sixth amendment of the Constitution passed in the Lok Sabha on November 28, 2001, to make the right to free and compulsory education for children of 6–14 years of age a Fundamental Right; parents were named as the agents responsible for providing opportunities for education to children in the age group of 6–14 years. Notwithstanding the fact that this is an impossible task for most parents, the government continues to encourage privatisation efforts that require a considerable investment on the part of people who are also fighting the stigma of disability. The suggested alternatives of non-formal education, minimum levels of learning and multi-grade teaching do not spell hope for the disabled. It is worthwhile to take note that whereas the disability act seeks to provide education till 18 years of age, most of the educational policy documents stop at 14. Also, the issue of early childhood care so essential for every child has been overlooked. Disabled children do not find representation in the Integrated Child Development Services (ICDS) reinforcing exclusion (Ghai 2001). The observation of the National Policy on Education Review Committee, 1990, that ICDS had come to acquire rigidity, bureaucratisation, low performance, lack of community participation and insensitivity to local needs, patterns and sociocultural conditions, is worth remembering. The Committee lamented that the ICDS policy of non-inclusion of disabled children into their programmes was symptomatic of the wider malaise in Indian society, indicating an overall policy of exclusion. It kept 4 to 5 million children with special needs in dire need of services at the critical age of 0–5 without services. Although ICDS was mandated to include all children with special needs, the implementation of the programme got disrupted as no financial allocation was made and it appears that no fiscal allocation has been done in the budget (Alur 2006).

My contention is that under a globalised economy such commitments will remain more an exercise in rhetoric rather than real change. This becomes even more significant when one realises that the Government of India had re-constituted the Central Advisory Board of Education (CABE) vide Resolution dated July 6, 2004. Though initially not considered within its frame of reference, the government did include inclusive education at the behest of the Public Study Group (formed in 2004 with funding from the Council for Social Development) and further, based on the disability rights movement's slogan 'Nothing for us without us', two rights disability activists were nominated to the Central Advisory Board of Education (CABE). The fact that the government had not opened the issue for a more serious discourse by including persons from the disability sector from the very beginning clearly shows the need to adopt a critical attitude towards such gestures for their token value. An assessment of the educational programmes also reflects the serious educational realities for the disabled as they still have not been negotiated. For example, while on one hand there is a directive that as far as possible, every child with special needs should be placed in regular schools with support services, a little later the same policy document talks about the need to strengthen special schools *as far as possible* and *wherever necessary* to obtain their resource support in convergence with departments and agencies working in that area. Similarly, support services that are listed include only physical access to resource rooms at cluster level, special equipment, reading material, special educational techniques, remedial teaching, curricular adaptation or adapted teaching strategies. It is clear that there is no holistic understanding of disability and its obvious medical connotations. The miniscule grant of ₹ 1,200 ($25) per disabled child to be incurred in a financial year makes the programme a mockery. Similarly, during the drafting of the Draft Action Plan the minister in charge declared that, 'It should and will be our objective to make mainstream education not just available but accessible, affordable and appropriate for students with disabilities', following which the government seems to have forgotten the commitment made by their minister in parliament and did not provide the funds needed.

Health Issues

The International Conference on Primary Health Care held on September 12, 1978 expressed an urgent need to prioritise health for the world community. The conference affirmed that health, which is a state of complete physical, mental and social well-being, and not merely the absence of disease or infirmity, is a fundamental human right and that the attainment of the highest possible level of health is a most important world-wide social goal whose realisation requires the action of many other social and economic sectors in addition to the health sector. As part of society, disabled children were obviously seen to be the recipients of accessible health care. However, access to early intervention services, including early detection and identification, support and training to children and their families is still a dream in a number of countries in the world. In fact, disabilities result from malnutrition, from causes such as low birth weight and premature birth, or neural tube defects (NTD). The latter is a condition that leads to considerable and irreversible disabilities which are linked to maternal health and can be prevented by including folic acid supplements in pregnant women's diet. Further, research indicates that mean weight and hemoglobin levels of disabled children is significantly lower than their 'abled' siblings at the same age (Yousafzai et al. 2003). Unless basic medical support systems are provided, disabled children cannot be part of society and achieve their full potential. For instance, of almost 0.6 million visually impaired children, the government provided canes and glasses to barely 68 and 4,959 children respectively. Similarly, only 6,212 children have undergone eye surgery at state expense. Although these figures only relate to the visually impaired, they speak volumes about the state's concern for the welfare of disabled children (Disability India, July 2007).[3]

Provision for equal access to comprehensive health services is not available to disabled children. Systems are not in place in terms of laws and policies for the disabled in general. Whether it is disabled children living in situations of violence and its immediate aftermath, or children living in disaster areas or street children and children in illegal colonies, these are children who, because of systemic neglect, are denied their human rights.

Another right that is withheld by societies such as in India, is providing sex education to children. The difficulty heightens if the children are disabled. Dr Achal Bhagat, a psychiatrist with Saarthak, an NGO, says, 'There is enough research from outside of India for example people who have psychiatric disability are at the risk of HIV aids. Disabled children are at times more prone to HIV AIDS. The protection system that exists for other children does not exist for disabled children'.[4] Priti Prabhughate, an activist with The Humsafar Trust says, 'A child's sex education is gathered from a range of sources, such as their parents, school and friends. Difficulties for the disabled child include misconceptions that disabled people are non-sexual (or should be) and don't need sex education. The myth is that that intellectually disabled people are potential sexual deviants, and should be denied sex education in case it "gives them ideas". As a result children with intellectual disabilities may be confused by sex education unless the information is presented to them in ways they can understand.'[5]

Gender Issues

Disabled girls are doubly disadvantaged in most societies; being a girl and being disabled are both considered a curse. Thus, penetrating the veneer of resistance that disabled women confront in a society where the dominant norm that operates is that of a perfect/unimpaired body, is a very difficult task. One father in a remote village of Bihar lamented, 'Wasn't it enough that we are poor. Why did *kismet* (fate) have to add to our burden further by giving us a *pagal* (term used for developmental disability) daughter?' (Ghai 2001). When the birth is an unwelcome event, the life course is a denial against humanity itself. Disabled women and girls face the same human rights abuses that non-disabled women suffer, but their social seclusion amplifies the abuses.

Even in the case of advocacy the concern for male disability overrides the concerns for disabled women. Any index, whether it is education, employment, marriage, etc., shows that disabled men feature more than the disabled women. What is significant is that despite the same legal stipulations, disabled girls still experience marginalisation in both familial spaces as well as social spaces such as education, employment, recreation and intimacy. Although disabled girls are more exposed to violence the support systems are inadequate to protect them. In an NDTV report (September 18, 2007), a two-and-a-half-year-old girl with cerebral palsy was abandoned by her family. In 42-degrees heat, the girl was lying under the bushes. Workers at the metro construction site in Noida's Sector 14, near Delhi, found her and took her to the police, who asked an NGO to help.

There are other types of discrimination too. Disabled girls experience forced sterilisation and the reason is the fear of pregnancy. Research on sexual assault in the west indicates that violence faced by disabled girls may be more chronic and severe, and takes forms such as withholding of essential care and medication. In USA, Ashley, a six-and-a-half-year-old diagnosed with static encephalopathy, a condition in which her brain is in a permanent and unchanging state has been cared for by the parents. As she grows she would eventually become too large for her parents to take care of her, including feeding, changing, bathing, and positioning her during the night. They were also concerned at the prospects of her sexual development, including menstruation, breast development, and her fertility. Consequently her parents decided to have a hysterectomy, removal of her breast buds, which would eliminate the development of breasts altogether, and medical treatment to limit her final adult height (known as *height attenuation*) and weight through hormone therapy. The reason given was that her breasts would cause discomfort with the straps used to hold her in her chair.

Disabled girls and boys are far more vulnerable to abuse and exploitation than normal boys and girls. A child who is physically challenged may understand what is happening and is aware of the consequences of the abuse, but lack of mobility would render her completely helpless. In the case of the mentally challenged children, they are unaware of the consequences of the act and may even submit 'voluntarily'.

Recognising the special situation of such children, in legal systems an intellectually impaired girl cannot legally give consent to be a party to a physical act, as she does not understand the consequences. What is worse, the legal mechanism is often inadequate to deal with such cases. There is no provision in the judicial system that requires special assistance to the mentally challenged victim to be able to give their statement in court. Thus it is left to the sensitivity of the presiding judge to decide.

Accessibility Problems

Disability can stop children from going out and having fun with their friends and peers, described as 'barriers to doing', that are restrictions of activity arising from social or physical factors (Thomas 1999). Although research findings identifying physical barriers in school playgrounds are not available, experience is that there are barriers to inclusion in playgrounds. Disabled children want resources, equipment and support so they can access everyday things, which most children take for granted, such as interacting with friends and playing in the sports fields. Even for disabled adults a simple pleasure such as going to watch a movie is unattainable. Adding ramps to schools, for instance, which are not usable is of no use as it is a mere token. Endorsing the shift towards inclusion in built and social environment is the concept of Universal Design. Disability activists have advocated 'Universal Design' to create a model of inclusions.

Societal Attitudes

Societal attitudes are a critical factor in defining life experiences, opportunities, and facilitate interactions with peers and teachers of disabled children (Chubon 1992). Negative societal attitudes towards people with disabilities could be viewed as 'invisible barriers' to successful rehabilitation. For instance, 12-year-old Ushna says, 'I wish I did not have to go to school as I hate teachers. They always think that disabled children are useless. I wish I did not have to go.'

For disabled children school is a contested terrain. They are either deprived from school because their families do not realise and accept their need for it, or because the schools are not equipped to take them in. Visually impaired sisters Bindu and Bina from India, who are two of Vaishali-based Mandal Paswan's four blind daughters, have never been to school. Their father has been made to live with the dictum that if you are blind and belong to a backward caste, your destiny is written by the society. 'These girls run errands like washing dishes, helping in fields, etc. It's only then that their mother feeds them', says Paswan.[6] Poonam, a child with cerebral palsy, could not attend classes beyond the sixth class as the school was not accessible. She stayed on the second floor and the parents found it difficult to carry her and there was no support either for her or the parents. She asks, 'How can I manage to attend school? But I wish so much . . .' Not many decisions about their everyday experiences can be negotiated.

Clearly, as Isabel Guerrero (2007), World Bank country director for India says,

> India has an impressive set of policy commitments to its citizens with disabilities. The challenge facing Indian society now is to translate those commitments into better lives for disabled people. This includes identifying disabilities in young children, getting more disabled children into school and preparing them for the workplace and family life, and most importantly working to reduce the social stigma which disabled people face.

Can Disabled Children Be Their Own Agents?

Whether children can be their own agents, whether they have the right and capacity to participate in decisions concerning themselves, has been a subject of discussion for sometime now. Children, both disabled and non-disabled are dependent on the positioning and vision of adults as well as society in determining how much they can participate in decisions concerning themselves. Though terms such as 'traffic danger' and 'stranger danger' show adult concern for children, there is a desire also to manage children. The realisation that adults are very powerful is to be understood in context of citizenship. For children as well as adults, power is defined here as 'the complex and intersecting systems of regulation that operate to show up frames of relevance for children's everyday participation and active engagement in school, home and the community' (Danby and Farrell 2002). Forgacs (1988) reminds us of Gramsci who, when writing on power relations in society, argued that there are two ways that the elites of society maintain power: the first is brute force and second is by shaping their beliefs at a subconscious level, so that the majority of the oppressed buy into the status quo. This leads to formation of a hegemony, which works as a unifying system of ideas that are so widespread that individuals in society accept these beliefs without even realising it. In this sense, disability is a marker and signifier of identity. Its negative rendering becomes the basis for social exclusion from citizenship.

Citizenship simply implies an indispensable connection between individuals and the state. Exclusion of disabled children from full political status needs to be investigated because despite the discourse on child rights as well as the rights of the disabled, an understanding of disabled children as active agents remains hazy (Forgacs 1988).

Citizenship rights include civil, social, economic and political rights. Citizenship practice is the active exercise of rights through democratic action and civic responsibility. Citizenship is a complex theoretical concept and a set of practices that order the dynamic relationships between individuals and the state, and among individuals. It has three dimensions:

- *Rights and responsibilities*—which go hand in hand
- *Access*—to resources, as well as to opportunities to participate in society, and
- *Feeling of belonging*—in the broad sense of national identity, and in the everyday sense of identifying with the local neighbourhood and the community as a whole (Valentine 2001: 3).

For disabled children, all three dimensions are problematic. To begin with it is important to understand children in context of disability because children's lives are not homogeneous and need to be studied in all their diversity (Brannen and O'Brien 1995).

Jill Swart-Kruger (2002) points out that there is a vast difference between 'hearing' children speak and 'listening' to what they say. Especially for disabled children, the difference between listening and responding is important. As Sheridan Bartlett says, 'It is an oversimplification to suggest that merely giving young people a voice will lead to age-sensitive policies and practices in the absence of follow-through and attention to many other more mundane factors such as regulatory frameworks, impact assessments, budgets, training and monitoring' (Bartlett 2005). Unless we develop platforms for advocacy and legal redress for disabled children, we cannot succeed.

As with all other children, 'governance for disabled children' and 'governance with disabled children' are significantly different. Sometimes giving young children an opportunity to be heard suffices. However, this is not enough. As Roger Hart explained years ago, there are many levels of participation through his 'Ladder of Participation', which describes different stages of adult–child interaction (Hart 1992). What would apply to all children, would apply to disabled children as well, except that some additional support systems must be created to ensure that they can move from one level to another.

Mitu's story

Disability is a very misused term, my personal feeling is that it is not as serious as it is made out to be. . . . I look at disability as a slight incapacity to function and this little difference does not give anybody the authority or the right to discriminate. . . . I refuse to be segregated on the basis of this slight disability. . . . In the pre-inclusion years we were given excuses for being segregated, excuses like they can't cope with the studies, they cannot sit or stand like the others, etc. My school had selected me as an inclusive candidate but it was turned down because of visual difficulties and the fact that I could not walk. I was upset but today I have overcome these small rejections of life and grown in my mind. Moreover, today, with inclusion, the teachers from the special schools are themselves approaching regular schools and advocating mainstreaming. This is really heartening . . .

I am on the verge of a major transition in my life. I am about to leave my school and join the outside world, a different world, a real world. . . . Right now I am going through mixed feelings. I feel concerned that my new environment may not be accepting, that I will be made to feel different and segregated. . . . Given that the overall aim of the government's policy is education for all, I would like to say that All includes Me, and I am as excited as any other 16-year-old to begin my college life. I will work harder than I ever have, I will be stronger than I ever have and I will be a success story. This is my aim, this is my ambition.

Personal communication with the author

Giving opportunity to children to be their own agents must begin at home. However, parents sometimes given to pressures of living are not able to help a child, particularly a disabled child, to become productive and autonomous. They have to make a choice between employment and caring for their children because affordable child care and other services are not available. For instance, in Jehangirpuri, a slum in Delhi, India, Smita and Arjun, who are rag-pickers, could not send their seventh girl child, afflicted with polio, to school because the school agreed to admit the disabled child provided the parents picked and dropped off the child to school. Given their economic compulsions, Smita and Arjun were unable to ensure that their child had the opportunity to exercise her own agency. It is the state that must be responsible to ensure that all children, including the disabled children are able to realise their rights, which includes making services accessible to them. However, even the more articulate disabled have to fight for income tax deductions, hand driven cars, motorised chairs, concessions in air travel, etc. Notwithstanding the fact that these issues are important, the child or adult who is poor and disabled and not vocal cannot claim the rights and equal opportunities that might have been given by the state.

In the absence of state mechanisms for support within families, shouldn't residential care institutions become an option? But how many such institutions are there? Even where they are available, most institutions are not concerned with physical, cognitive, social and emotional needs in any way comparable to family settings. For instance, there are many schools for the blind, especially in metropolitan cities like Delhi, Chennai, Mumbai, etc. Many of these institutions provide basic education, but little else. The quality of care is inadequate and the disabled students are open to physical and sexual abuse. What is also painful is that disabled children are submitted to collective routines and are powerless to make use of adequate spaces to allow the distinctive personality of each individual to grow.

As Penny Nicholls, strategy director at The Children's Society, UK says:

> There are simple things in life most of us take for granted such as choosing the food we eat, when we go to the toilet and speaking out when we feel threatened. Disabled children placed away from home are often denied these very basic rights and are more at risk of harm than other children. Every child

deserves a good childhood and disabled children placed away from home should have access to an independent advocate to safeguard this entitlement. (Nicholls 2007)[7]

However, we cannot assume that disabled children cannot become active agents as there is the possibility of resisting the hegemony. Most of the narratives of disabled children, such as visually impaired children, seem to tell us more about society than about blindness. For instance, initially Sakshi was denied experiencing the feeling of being different. But, on probing further she blamed the schools for such experiences, 'It often happens in government schools when we have to go somewhere and we don't get any help.' Priya also talks about a similar experience, 'Usually I don't feel that I am blind. I only feel so when some child in school refuses to help me with work, or doesn't listen when I call out to them. Then I don't feel good.'

Though facing insurmountable barriers, there are children who voice their concerns. Some of the ways in which they cope with the given harsh reality is worth noting. Jahoda and Cattermole (1988) reported that the active agency of disabled children is critical. When asked about disabled teenagers' identities and aspirations, they seem to express hopes and fears about their 'future selves' that are shaped less by their disability and more by other social influences (Jahoda and Cattermole 1988). This situation is not essentially Indian. A visually impaired boy in the two-year education programme for blind children in north Ethiopia states,

> My life was full of fear . . . my mother would not allow me out of the house; because I was blind she said that if I went out I would fall down and get a second disability. I was lonely because all the other children went to school. . . . Since I have been in this programme (non-formal education classes for blind children), I have learnt not to have fear—now I go

anywhere, I have many friends because I am learning like other children. . . . My uncle did not believe I could learn so he asked me to write a word and I wrote it. Now I am confident I can attend my local school, if I have any problem I will ask my friends. . . . When I grow up I want to be a teacher.

There are ways in which children negotiate the experience of disability in their everyday lives. Findings on the basis of two research projects at the undergraduate level indicated that though they are concerned about a number of barriers, disabled children identified at least one thing they were good at which could be either a school subject or painting that was considered as their competence. Thus their agency was linked to a sense of achievement, good relationships with peers and favourite activities. As one of the students said, 'That's it, I'm in a wheelchair so big deal. I do whatever I can do and I have no time to feel sad' (Singh and Ghai 2009: 130).

What is interesting is that all children do make some choices for themselves. Some of the older children were found taking on more responsibility for themselves or trying to persuade their parents to allow them to take charge.

There are some disabled people who reject their disability identity by proclaiming, 'I'm not disabled, they are'. To them, to admit to being disabled would seem to admit defeat, and the person who rejects disability identity may be labelled 'heroic' or 'inspirational'. However, there are other disabled people who embrace their disability and thereby their identity.

What is perhaps more important is the fact that many of them do not see themselves as disabled in all situations, which challenges the notion of 'global categorisation' proposed by Shevlin. Kenny and McNeela as this implies addressing only one facet of the person. It appears that though the identity of being disabled is sometimes seen as a ground for difference, it does not necessarily become an essential character. However, disabled children do speak out freely about their concerns, recognise the fact that children's rights are important, and participate in decision making related to their lives (Shevlin et al. 2002).

One of the ways of ensuring children's participation is by having children's own associations. Such associations are often established by, but certainly organised and administered by children themselves. For instance, Making Ourselves Heard, a project in the United Kingdom, aims to ensure active participation of disabled children and young people in all decisions directly affecting them; in the development of their local communities; in the strategic planning of services; and in all aspects of the work of the Council for Disabled Children, an organisation that works to influence national policy that impacts upon disabled children and children with special educational needs and their families.[8] Participation Works is another organisation in the UK that aims to promote the active participation of disabled children and young people, making sure their voices and success stories are heard.[9] Yet another example is Kids As Self Advocates (KASA), in the United States of America, which is a national, grassroots project created by youth with disabilities. KASA believes that children and youth can make choices and advocate for themselves if they have the information and support they need. It believes young people with disabilities will have control over their own lives and futures. This can happen by teaching youth about their rights, giving peer support and training, and changing the systems that affect our lives to include society. Muskan, an NGO in India, was envisioned by intellectually impaired young adults and works on self-governance. The trainees conducted surveys and made appropriate arrangements to conduct the sessions. The young adults set up the auditions for events such as the annual day celebrations. Following the 5W's (what, where, when, which, why) all were encouraged to think and plan. The young adults are responsible for taking the visitors around; they give preliminary information regarding the services being provided by Muskan. They also make presentations to visitors during awareness campaigns. They are panel members for the question–answer sessions and anchoring programmes—important steps in the direction of self awareness and advocacy. A special effort is made to empower each to exert whatever level of control is possible on their environment.

Conclusion

The UN ratification of various acts such as The United Nations Convention on the Rights of the Child and the UN Treaty for the Rights of People with Disabilities is a first step in the recognition that all children are citizens-in-becoming and, therefore, have rights and entitlements that must be made available to them. However, full implementation of this Convention and others like it requires more than formal equality of treatment. It may necessitate differential treatment in order to allow children with disabilities to achieve their full potential in the realisation of all their rights. The instances discussed here do not comprise the whole range of possibilities. The cultural context, socioeconomic and political circumstances require different methods and tactics. What is critical is the need for the creation of governance systems that are sensitive to the needs and rights of disabled children and those that recognise the right of both non-disabled as well as disabled children to be able to participate in decisions concerning them.

∅

Notes

1 Personal communication with the author.
2 Personal communication with the author.

3 See http://www.disabilityindia.com/html/newsjuly.html, accessed on March 17, 2011.
4 See karmayog.org/publichealth news/publichealth news3213. htm., accessed on March 17, 2011.
5 See http://www.humsafar.org, accessed on March 17, 2011.
6 Published on Thursday, October 26, 2006 at 7:51, updated on Wednesday, April 16, 2008 at 2:58 in India section http:// ibnlive.in.com/news/born-blind-disabled-by-their- community/ 24734-3.html, accessed on March 17, 2011.
7 http://www.childrenssociety.org.uk/whats_happening/ media_office/latest_news/Disabled_Children_Denied_ Their_Voice_3834_news.html, accessed on September 4, 2007.
8 See http://www.ncb.org.uk, accessed on March 17, 2011.
9 See www.participationworks.org.uk, accessed on March 17, 2011.

ℒ

References

Alur, Mithu. 2006. 'Education for the Disabled: Wither Budgetary Support', in *India Infolinne News Service*, February 24.
Bartlett, Sheridan. 2005. 'Good Governance: Making Age Part of the Equation—An Introduction', *Children, Youth and Environments*, 15(2): 1–17, available at http://www.colorado. edu/journals/cye, accessed on March 17, 2011.
Bishop, Anne. 2002. *Becoming an Ally: Breaking the Cycle of Oppression*, Fernwood, Halifax, *Canada*.
Boertjes, Marajan and Marcia Lever. 2007. 'Parents and Children with Disabilities within the Youth Care System—A Dutch Perspective', in Stan Meuwese, Sharon Detrick and Sjaak Jaansen (eds), *100 Years of Child Protection*, Wolf Legal Publishers, Netherlands.
Bonime, W. 1989. *Collaborative Psychoanalysis*, Associated Universities Press, Cranbury, NJ.
Brannen, J. and M. O'Brien. 1995. 'Childhood and the Sociological Gaze: Paradigms and Paradoxes', *Sociology*, 29(4): 729–37.
Brown, H. 1994. 'An Ordinary Sexual Life? A Review of the "Normalization Principal" as it Applies to the Sexual Options

of People with Learning Difficulties', *Disability & Society*, 9(2): 123–44.

Burns, J. 1992. 'Normalisation Through the Looking Glass', *Clinical Psychology Forum*, 39: 22–4.

Chubon, R. A. 1992. 'Attitudes toward Disability: Addressing Fundamentals of Attitude Theory and Research in Rehabilitation Education', *Rehabilitation Education*, 6: 30112.

Corsaro, W. 1997. *The Sociology of Childhood*, Pine Forge Press, Thousand Oaks, California.

Dalal, A. K. 2002. 'Disability Rehabilitation in a Traditional Indian Society', in M. Thomas and M. J. Thomas,. (eds), 'Selected Readings in Community Based Rehabilitation', Series 2, *Asia Pacific Disability Rehabilitation Journal*, 1: 17–26, 2001.

Dalal, A. K. and N. Pande. 1999. 'Cultural Beliefs and Family of the Children with Disability', *Psychology and Developing Societies*, 11(1): 55–75.

Danby, S. and A. Farrell. 2002. 'Children's Accounts of Adult-determined Regulation in Their Everyday Experiences'. Paper presented to the Australian Association for Education Research Conference, Brisbane, December 1–5.

———. 2004. 'Accounting for Young Children's Competence in Educational Research: New Perspectives on Research Ethics', *Australian Educational Researcher*, 31(3): 35–49.

Davis, J. and N. Watson 2001. 'Where are the Children's Experiences? Analysing Social and Cultural Exclusion in "Special" and "Mainstream" Schools', *Disability & Society*, 16(5): 671–87.

Forgacs, David. 1988. *An Antonio Gramsci Reader, Selected Writings, 1916–1935*, Schocken Books, New York.

Gabel, Susan Lynn and Scot Danforth. 2008. *Disability and the Politics of Education: An International Reader*, Peter Lang Publishing, INC, New York.

Ghai, Anita. 2001. 'Marginalisation and Disability: Experiences from the Third World', in M. Priestly (ed.), *Disability and the Life Course: Global Perspectives*, Cambridge University Press, Cambridge.

———. 2003. *(Dis)embodied Form, Issues of Disabled Women*, Shakti Books, New Delhi.

———. 2006. 'Education in a Globalising Era: Implications for "Disabled" Girls', *Social Change*, 36(3): 161–76.

Goodley, Dan. 2007. 'Towards Socially Just Pedagogies: Deleuzoguattarian Critical Disability Studies'. Revised paper submitted for Special Number of *International Journal of Inclusive Education* entitled: 'Pedagogies: Matters of Social Justice and Inclusion, available at http://www.leeds.ac.uk/disability-studies/archiveuk/goodley/Dan, accessed on February 5, 2010.

Jahoda A., I. Markova and M. Cattermole. 1988. 'Stigma and Self-concept of People with Mild Mental Handicap', *Journal of Mental Deficiency Research*, 32(1): 103–15.

Jeffery, Roger and Nidhi Singal. 2008. 'Disability Estimates in India: A Changing Landscape of Socio-Political Struggle', *Economic and Political Weekly*, 43(12 & 13): 22–24.

Khanna, R., and A. Ghai. 2005. 'Meaning of Disability: Through the Voices of Children'. Project Report submitted in partial fulfillment of the requirement for the Bachelor of Arts (honours) degree in Psychology, University of Delhi, India.

de Lauwe, M. J. Chombart. 1984. 'Changes in the Representation of the Child in the Course of Social Transmission', in R. Farr and S. Moscovici (eds), *Social Representations*, Cambridge University Press, Cambridge.

Mitra, S. and U. Sambamoorthi. 2006. 'Disability Estimates in India: What the Census and NSS Tell Us', *Economic & Political Weekly*, 41(38): 4022–26.

NSSO. 2003. *Disabled Persons in India, NSS 58th Round (July–December 2002)*, National Sample Survey Organisation, Delhi.

Peters, Susan. 1999. Transforming Disability Identity Through Critical Literacy and the Cultural Politics of Language, in M. Corker and S. French (eds), *Disability Discourse*, pp. 103–15. Open University Press, Buckingham and Philadelphia.

Priestley, M. 2001. *Disability and the Life Course: Global Perspectives*, Cambridge University Press, Cambridge.

Roger, Hart. 1992. *Children's Participation: From tokenism to Citizenship*, UNICEF Innocenti Research Centre, Florence.

Russell, Philippa. 1996. 'Listening to Children with Disabilities and Special Educational Needs', in Davie Ron, Graham Upton and Ved Varma (eds) *The Voice of the Child: A Handbook for Professionals*, Falmer Press.

Sadgopal, Anil. 2006. 'Dilution, Distortion and Diversion: A Post-Jomtien Reflection on the Education Policy', in Ravi Kumar (ed.), *The Crisis of Elementary Education in India*, Sage, New Delhi.

Shevlin, M., M. Kenny and E. Mc Neela. 2002. 'Curriculum Access for Pupils with Disabilities: An Irish experience', *Disability & Society*, 17(2): 159–69.

Singh, Vanessa and Anita Ghai. 2009. 'Notions of Self: Lived Realities of Children with Disabilities', *Disability & Society*, 24(2): 129–45.

Swart-Kruger, J. 2002. *Children in a South African Squatter Camp Gain and Lose a Voice: Growing Up in an Urbanising World*, pp. 111–33. Unesco, Paris.

Story, M. F. 1998. Maximising Usability: The Principle of Universal Design, *Assistive Technology*, 10: 4–12.

Thomas, C. 1999. *Female Forms: Experiencing and Understanding Disability*, Open University Press, Buckingham, UK.

UN Convention on the Rights of Persons with Disabilities, available at http://www.un.org/disabilities, accessed on December 13, 2006.

Valentine, Gill. 2001. *Social Geographies: Space and Society*, Pearson Education Ltd, Harlow, Essex.

Waksler, F. C. (ed.). 1991. *Studying the Social Worlds of Children: Sociological Readings*, The Falmer Press, London.

Winnicot, D. W. 1965. *The Maturational Processes and the Facilitating Environment*, Hogarth Press, London and the Inst. of Psa; Madison, CT.

Yousafzai, Aisha K., Suzanne Filteau and Sheila Wirz. 2003. 'Feeding Difficulties in Disabled Children Leads to Malnutrition: Experience in an Indian Slum', *British Journal of Nutrition*, 90: 1097–106.

Websites:

http://timesofindia.indiatimes.com, accessed on June 28, 2007.

http://www.humsafar.org/rc/Other%20presentations%20and%20papers/Toronto%20World%20AIDS%20conference%20%20Priti.ppt, accessed on January 13, 2011.

Disabled Children Denied Their Voice, January 11, 2007, http://www.childrenssociety.org.uk/whats_happening, accessed on September 4, 2009.

http://www.ncb.org.uk/Page.asp? originx_1787ki_
27612292467612y41a_2007394050u, accessed on January 13,
2011
http://www2.futurelab.org.uk/resources/documents/other
research reports/Learner Engagement.pdf, accessed on March
17, 2011.

6

Overcoming Barriers for Getting Children Out of Work and into Schools

Shantha Sinha

Children have a right to education. The non-realisation of this right means 87 million children in India are out of school and available for the labour market. Most of them are destined to become 'little slaves'. In India, education is a fundamental right awarded by the 86th Amendment to the Indian Constitution and the enactment of the Law of Education. Following this, in 2009, the government passed the Right to Free and Compulsory Elementary Education Act (RTE). It is hoped that with the passing of this law, children in our country would no longer be out of school as part of the labour force but would all enjoy their right to education in a full-time day school. For, it is education alone that opens up possibilities for a world of opportunities and choices and without education one is inevitably drawn to the marginalised and vulnerable work force. Education leads to a path of equity and social justice which are so intrinsic to the democratic fabric of society.

For every right to be realised the state is the duty-bearer with an obligation to implement it. It therefore has to prepare and implement the agenda of governance with the child as the focal point for realisation of their rights. It is the responsibility of the state to provide schools, teachers and all other facilities to ensure that children enjoy that right. Thus the state has a huge responsibility to actualise the legal entitlements and evolve terms of clear-cut obligations of the functionaries of the state, and articulate the claims of all children especially those of the neglected child. In doing so it has to break the continuous practice of violation of this right and also simultaneously the societal norm of tacit acceptance of the violation. The actualisation of the right to education places different but primarily complementary responsibilities of trust on the state, civil society and non-government organisations (NGOs) and the community.

Community mobilisation for monitoring state performance at the local government level ensures that governance at the local level is child-sensitive and responsive, with its insistence on transparency and accountability. By initiating a process of social mobilisation and conflict resolution at the level of the family, employers and the school, the NGOs can take a lead in abolishing child labour and putting the child in school, thereby guaranteeing the child's right to education. This complex process involves building networks and appropriate norms at all levels. This essay dwells on and draws lessons from the role played by the M. Venkatarangaiya Foundation (MV Foundation or MVF), in the state of Andhra Pradesh, India, to illustrate the role of an NGO and the importance of social mobilisation to monitor the government's performance and force it to act on behalf of children. The process of working with existing law and programmes can help in understanding the problems and pitfalls within the government structure and thus we can press for change. A continuous engagement with the governance systems can make them responsive to the needs and rights of children.

The recognition of the right to free and compulsory education between the age of 6 and 14 years as a fundamental right and the enactment of the law on right to education, places the primary obligation of implementation of this right on the state.[1] Non-governmental organisations and other civil society organisations must hold the state accountable for its non-performance, and yet support the state in the delegation of its role. The NGOs have a difficult role of continuous engagement on both fronts—the state as well as the community. Yet, in the drawing of boundaries, they need to be clear that they cannot substitute for the state.

India has been witness to some large-scale movements for the right to education involving millions of volunteers. Their role in fostering social mobilisation of peace, solidarity and active citizenship has to be acknowledged. All these 'child defenders' strive to contribute to a process of empowering children to become active citizens who exercise choices, seize opportunities, discover their potential, take part in public action and demand equity and social justice.

The MV Foundation has been working since the early 1990s to eliminate child labour from villages and to ensure that children go to school through the active involvement of child defenders from the community. In getting every child out of work and into school, the MV Foundation considers that it is the state's obligation to deliver services and so it did not set up parallel institutions to the schools, social welfare hostels, Gram Panchayats and other state institutions. Instead, the MVF programme has blended with the existing government programmes, enriching rather than supplanting them. It mobilises the community to demand for better schools and facilities. The MV Foundation urges communities to accept the norm that children must not be at work, but in school. The MVF recognises that NGOs have a responsibility to engage with the system in bringing about systemic changes so that no child is excluded from school. This requires providing solutions for practical difficulties that children face and converting this into a policy. These can range from seemingly small issues such as denial of admission on frivolous grounds, demand for fees that parents cannot afford or the issue of transfer certificates, to bigger policy issues involving decisions and resources at the state level, such as filling up teacher vacancies. In fact, MVF has been involved in bringing about significant policy changes in the Indian state of Andhra Pradesh. The basic premise of such a policy should be zero tolerance for child labour as well as removing all barriers to school education. Simple as it may seem, this process of social mobilisation that enables the child's journey from work to school is ridden with conflicts, and must be resolved at various levels—home, school and employers. Parents often question the worth of education, especially for the female child, saying 'What is the use of studying, is she going to become an officer?' About the school, they complain, 'Schools don't function, teachers don't come', emphasising again the irrelevance of the engagement of their child with this institution. With the employer there may be a case of debt-bondage, where the family may have pledged the child's labour for money and the employer would be unlikely to release the child without repayment. In such circumstances, releasing even a single child out of bondage requires immense persuasion. As a last resort it also requires the officialdom and even the police to enforce the Bonded Labour Abolition Act, 1976. Even when all these fronts have been negotiated, there is still the school, where access is a hurdle. Once the institutional entry barriers are negotiated, the child may require a long period of formal preparation for school.

What is the role of the community? The approach MVF takes is based on trusting the community and its capacity to be part of the entire programme for liberating children. All that is required is a whole-hearted appeal, which could catch the imagination of the poor, and resonate with what they have always desired—education of their children. When setting out to meet families, teachers, local officials and employees, to appeal to them on the need to liberate children from work, it is important not to have any negative stereotypes of any of the stakeholders. Thus, the activities of MVF were based on trust, debate and discussion. Therefore, a recalcitrant employer was not seen as an enemy but as a potential ally who had to be engaged with till there was a change in attitude. A teacher who was irregular was contacted and persuaded for several days till he started enjoying his work as a professional. Even a parent who objected to send his child to school was persuaded endlessly till he relented.

All this was done by local youth groups who were first-generation learners themselves and were slowly able to win over resistance from all quarters. However, MVF would not have succeeded if the community was reluctant to educate its children. All that MVF did was to bring its latent demand for education to the fore and place the child rights agenda in the mainstream of community needs.

In the years that MVF has been working, over 400,000 children have been released from child labour and enrolled into school. The MV Foundation's experience shows that child labour is not inevitable and it is possible to totally abolish child labour, even among the poorest communities and areas.

However, this is only the beginning. After a child enters the education system, she has to cross many more hurdles. A rights-based approach involves identifying all such gaps in the system that make it difficult for the first-generation learner or an older child to come to school and bridge the gaps in favour of the child's right to education. This entails a continuous engagement with numerous functionaries of the state at the local level, identification of the plethora of rules and regulations that form the governance of schools, and finally of the state with respect to children. The governance agenda for children needs to evolve from an integrated view of the world of children. It must be fully equipped to withdraw children from the exploitative nexuses of the world of work that children are trapped in and make their transition to becoming students smooth and non-intimidating.

Overview of the Barriers: Child Labour is Not Inevitable

The status quo on child labour and education is maintained in a number of significant ways, the most important of which is the absence of a rights-based perspective in the policy discourse on child labour and education. Such policy thinking is reinforced by major arguments that underline an intuitive emphasis about both the 'inevitability' of child labour, and the 'uselessness' of schools. Untangling these arguments has the enabling merit of evolving a framework of meaningful thinking about children that looks at child labour and children out of school as two sides of the same coin.

◊

Children 'Missing' from Indian Policy

Children, especially children of the deprived, marginalised and disadvantaged, occupy no space in the public debate and discourse in contemporary Indian society and polity. In spite of their omni presence, and our daily lives being connected, these children are still invisible—the 'missing children'. We see them everyday, all around us, vending flowers, newspapers or cleaning car windshields at traffic signals, carrying tiffin boxes and school bags of other school-going children and in homes working as domestic help. They are in *dhabas* (highways eating joints), herding cattle and sheep, in farms, brick kilns, cycle repair works, railway bogies and platforms. They are also in places that are an anathema to an ordinary middle-class family—in sweat shops, mills, garages, in their own homes, working like robots and dangerously, in heat, unbearable noise, crowded spaces and dark rooms. We depend on their sweat and labour in every grain of rice and wheat, all the vegetables and meat we consume, the clothes we wear and the buildings we live in. Yet we pretend that they do not exist and accept the fact that nothing much can be done for them.

We rationalise the endemic problem by saying that they labour because they are poor! The predicament of such children is not even newsworthy. This pervasive ignoring of child labour has an impact in terms of the unacceptable numbers of children joining the labour force every day, yet the government persists with its lackadaisical response to abolishing child labour, once and for all.

The Child Labour (Prohibition and Regulation) Act (1986) is an instance of policy making in ignorance. The Act violates child rights and has serious limitations. It prohibits child labour in certain occupations and processes, as notified by the government from time to time. Currently, 65 processes and 18 occupations are prohibited. The Act, however, does not prohibit those processes and occupation in which the child renders work for his/her own household. The Act also excludes children working in agriculture, who form the majority of children in the labour force today. The way the Child Labour Act (1986) has defined child labour, it excludes a large number of girls working in their own households taking care of siblings, fetching water and fuel wood, cooking and washing utensils, and helping in farm work or in any other household industry. In short, the Act is based on the premise that children are poor, so it is impossible to abolish child labour.

Therefore, it is imperative to lobby for laws and policies that address the needs of those children who are at a great risk as they are out of school. Policies must be sensitive to social inequality and prioritise the needs of the most vulnerable. There are, however, some other Acts which are useful to liberate children from work. For example, the Bonded Labour System Abolition Act, 1976, enables release of a child from debt bondage and allows for cancellation of all debts. By ensuring that forcing a person to work against advances taken is unconstitutional and violates the right to freedom, this Act has freed several children from bondage. The Juvenile Justice (Care and Protection) Act, 2000 covers protection of all children including, interestingly, child labour *up to 18 years of age.*

The number of children out of school in India (87 million) and the number of children in the work force (12.6 million) are the highest in the world. This is not just a coincidence.

Why do then none of the documents on education policy make little more than a passing reference to child labour?

The Poverty Argument: Child Labour is Needed Because of Poverty

"People are poor, so they need the income from their child's labour. Therefore, to eliminate child labour you must eliminate poverty, else people will starve"—this argument may sound convincing but is erroneous. The situation persists because neither the policy makers nor the influential voices in the society believe that we can eliminate child labour. That is a problem to be solved on another day, in another realm.

Unfortunately, because the poverty argument is so widely accepted, we also think every child who is working is doing so because of poverty. The correlation between the two is belied by the rapid strides made in school access in a number of states, prominently in the states of Himachal Pradesh and Madhya Pradesh, thanks to good policy implementation.[2] When the state of Kerala is cited as a success story, the anticipated response is, 'in Kerala, anything can happen', as if the Kerala story were an outlier that cannot be replicated.[3] We tend to forget that the route to universal schooling in Kerala was a non-economic one. At a micro level, even the Ranga Reddy district in Andhra Pradesh has shown the results of continuous engagement in over a thousand villages, where children of the poor have begun to go to school. Critics will be quick to point out that this is because of MVF intervention and cannot be scaled up. The counter-point is that Ranga Reddy effort happened because of the clarity of purpose, the clarity of overall framework, trust in people and, *is* replicable.

Experience over the years has shown that in every village there are a number of poor parents sending their children to school even as some of the relatively better-off families are sending theirs to work. How does one explain this? There is no 'poverty line' or a level of poverty below which parents are compelled to send their children to work. It is difficult to calculate 'how' poor you ought to be not to send your child to school. There are thousands of parents, among the poorest in the country, who are in debt bondage, from different family sizes and backgrounds but still send their children to schools because they believe that their children must not work. If they can, many others can and should, but do not. Any new and sincere effort by the state to provide a complete measure of schooling has seen a surge in the numbers of those attending school, reaffirming the latent desire for learning.

We are dealing therefore with not an issue of bare economic need as the motivator for child labour, but a complex compact of attitudinal, social, and policy neglect that reinforces a current practice rather than question it. In aggregate data, we can perhaps make a statement that poor children do not go to school on account of poverty, but when disaggregated, the relationship does not hold. To understand the problem of child labour and education, therefore, we must actually understand 'why children are in schools', or 'why they are not going to schools'. In understanding the barriers to school, the non-economic factors also need to be fully comprehended.

Does this mean child labour and education has nothing to do with poverty? Of course it has, but not in the conventional sense of it being unaffordable. It is one more instance of the poor not being able to articulate and access what they want; one more instance of the system being unavailable to the poor simply because it is too difficult to use. In fact, the system is structured to reinforce the specious argument that education is irrelevant to the poor and child labour is inevitable. It is yet another instance of an entitlement denied.

Why then are so many children out of school and working? Mainly because no one has bothered to tell the poor parents that the schools are meant for them and it is their right and the entire government machinery will support them to send their child to school. No one has even told them that it is wrong to send their child to work. Instead, for generations the poor have been told that it is their lot to labour, and children with education will become useless for any manual work. It is in this area that the facilitating role of the state, as also a transformation of its daily practices, is most needed.

The 'Irrelevance of Education' Argument

Children of the poor don't go to school because schooling is irrelevant for them. This is another example of an exclusionary argument and comes unstuck when we view it in the context of children of the rich. This 'irrelevance' argument is never used to keep children of the rich out of school, even though the so-called elite schools that they go to have little to offer them in terms of life skills.

We also find fault with the formal day schools because

- they provide irrelevant education, i.e., they don't teach them how to be good labourers/workers,
- they run at the wrong time and in peak agriculture season.

Indeed, it also seems that the schools are being blamed for not allowing children to work! Can anything be more absurd? Instead of using the schools to eliminate child labour we want to eliminate the schools, this time using poor quality of schooling as an argument.

It is true that when we focus on every child's right to education, there is a need to focus on the quality of schools. But to define quality as a matter between teacher and student alone is to ignore all the factors that contribute for a teacher becoming a teacher and a student becoming a student. Quality means the entire process of making schooling possible. The issues, such as removing all barriers that exclude children's participation in schools, intolerance of a large number of children not attending schools, not having enough schools, teachers or classrooms, and sensitivity to poor children and first-generation learners need to be addressed. The process of uinversalisation of education is linked to the issue of quality in schools. Quality definitely need not be taken as an argument that stalls the children's entry to school.

Similarly, the argument for skill-based training is used only for the poor and keeps them out of school. Saying 'Let's give them some vocational training' instead of the same quality of education available for privileged children is a denial of equal opportunities. The fact that 'skills' are poorly integrated into the knowledge architecture is a challenge for curricular reform, affecting all children rich and poor equally. It should not be specifically used to keep poor children out of schools, citing their special need for vocational or skill-based training instead of basic education which is their right. Moreover, as a society we invent arguments that allow children to work and study at the same time, and sadly, the law as it is currently formulated, allows for that.

Is Compulsory Education the Way Out?

For years it was believed a law that made elementary education compulsory would harass parents, especially poor parents who we think make their children work because of poverty. Experience of working with the poor who despite all odds sent their children to schools challenges this argument.

Now we say that children are not in school because it is the government which cannot afford it, and therefore denies children of the poor access to schools. The costs of universalisation, as per the appropriate norms of schooling, were until recently considered too high to be able to assign it as an obligation on the statute book. And when the Right of Children to Free and Compulsory Education Act was finally passed in 2009, it was without a financial memorandum attached to it.[4] Anyone who has read the Constituent

Assembly debates knows that the same argument was made to take the right to education off the list of fundamental rights. Clearly, there is a demand for education, which the state is not in a position (or not completely willing) to provide and is worried about the enormous burden of extra work that compulsory education will entail. The best way to ensure that children are not in school but at work and reversing the existing state of affairs would be possible only if the anomaly in the Child Labour Act 1986 is addressed too.

The state of Andhra Pradesh's move to bring in The Andhra Pradesh Child Labour Abolition and Compulsory Education Bill, 2003 was one effort where the clear link between child labour and the attempt to universalise education was formulated in terms of statutory obligations. This draft was facilitated by the National Academy of Legal Services and Research, Hyderabad, and prepared by the government in consultation with academics, specialists and NGOs. The MV Foundation was a part of these deliberations. It had clearly taken a stand that all out-of-school children are to be regarded as child labour by defining child labour as 'any child who is employed or working in any employment, occupation, process or activity which interferes with her or his full-time formal schooling' and that all forms of child labour were to be abolished without making a distinction between 'hazardous' and non-hazardous work. Further, the Bill stipulated, every child must be provided with free and compulsory education till completion of 15 years of age and schools would be obligated to accept any child seeking admission any time during the academic session. In other words, children withdrawn from work and seeking admission into schools could not be refused admission on any ground.

Thus, for the first time in the country an effort was made to clearly link the legal and policy framework for abolition of child labour with the attainment of universal education. A combination of factors enabled such a radical move. At the ground level there were rights-based programmes initiated for abolition of child labour by the NGOs, led by MVF, and the district officials. They took a categorical position that 'no matter what, children must not be in work and all of them have to attend formal schools full-time. It is their fundamental right.' Since MVF's focus was on engaging with the system alongside a social mobilisation for withdrawing child labourers from work, steady changes occurred in the system of delivery of education.

There was a gradual flow of information on the success of the perspective at all layers of administration up to the state level. It was facilitated by the presence of some enlightened civil servants at the policy level who empathised with the content and processes that were initiated on the ground. They negotiated with the political functionaries and this was supported by the NGOs who lobbied with their elected representatives to take a stand on the issue of abolition of child labour. The popular demand for education was acknowledged and it was made an integral item in the *janma bhoomi* (motherland) programme, a campaign led by the then chief minister on social issues that placed a special emphasis on establishing direct contact with people on some themes in the social sector. In all the village-level interactions, rescue of child labour and right to education were articulated by the community and the children as well.

It was then felt that a legal framework would help consolidate the gains made in the campaign. Simultaneously, an all-party programme was developed and the Legislative Assembly passed a resolution unanimously to make Andhra Pradesh a child-labour-free state. But the Bill was not taken forward as elections were announced and the ruling government of the Telugu Desam Party lost in the 2004 elections putting a break on the campaign. The priorities of the new government under the new party were entirely different, and hence the legislative process came to a standstill.

Way Forward: Need for a Change in Perspective

With large numbers of children of school-going age out of school, it is inevitable that they join the labour force. Some markets are ever ready to absorb them as they are a source of cheap labour that can be compelled to work for long hours. Consequently, the child joining the labour pool is condoned. This indirectly gives a message that children may not learn and teachers need not perform because poor children in any case would not continue in schools. Under the RTE Act, no child out of school is to be tolerated and in order that older children and school dropouts catch up with their peers, children will be enrolled in the grade that corresponds to their age. It is the obligation of the state to admit a child to an age-appropriate grade and receive special training to be on par with others. This means that the RTE Act addresses the huge backlog of children who have been left out of formal schools.

What we need to recognise is that continued existence of child labour, and the inability of every child to access education means that we have failed our children. No country has ever achieved anything worthwhile on the backs of such child labour or illiteracy that we have in India. The worst pockets in some of the Indian states are worse than the worst in the world, countries such as Rwanda or Burundi in Sub-Saharan Africa. More specifically, we must acknowledge that the problem of child labour and illiteracy are two sides of the same coin, and we cannot universalise education without eliminating child labour. In the Indian context, to send a child to school is to withdraw him from work. In other words, it is not enough to just say that all children should go to school. There must be a clear commitment that no child shall work. Any form of work, unpaid work at home or wage work for an employer, must not be tolerated. For all out-of-school children—those who have never been enrolled in schools, those whose names are on the rolls of a school but are not attending, those who have dropped out of schools or been absent for a long period, those who are forced to stay at home and work after grade 5 as there are no elementary schools in the vicinity or roads and bus facilities if they were to travel, as in the case of tribal children—their only redemption is in going to school.

The journey of a child to school is not easy. It is filled with conflicts and defiance of existing social, economic and political hierarchies. As can be seen from the story of Swarupa (see Box 6.1), it is a process of breaking the nexus that encourages child labour and gains from child exploitation. By appealing to those who employ children and encourage child labour, by constant motivation and compelling all to take a stand in favour of children, and by bringing about a change in attitudes, norms will result in the child being withdrawn from work. Of course wherever necessary the local officials are to also take sides on behalf of children. If a village can say that all children in the age group 5–14 years are out of work and in formal schools, then it would be quite an achievement.

Overcoming barriers to schooling: Case of Swarupa, Parrigi Mandal, Ranga Reddy District, AP

Swarupa, a Dalit girl, lived in Chityala, a small village in Parigi mandal in Ranga Reddy district, Andhra Pradesh. When she was 12 years old in 1997, her father Mogilaiah put her to work on hybrid cottonseed farms, for ₹15 a day. Young Swarupa had to work for 12 hours on the farm (cross-pollination) and at the home of her employer (weeding cotton). She had to be at the farm by 7.00 in the morning, work in the hot sun till 7.00 in the evening, with two breaks for lunch and supper. After that, she worked from 7.00 pm to 9.00 pm at the home of her employer weeding cotton. She worked like this for two years. The seed farmers said cotton would get spoilt if grown-up women entered the farms. Swarupa's parents had been paid money in advance, so there was no way out for her. About 30 to 40 children worked with her. The employers used ingenious methods to keep them in, such as providing a TV, taking them to the occasional movie, giving them chocolates, ribbons, etc.

When MVF entered the village and collected data on out-of-school children, they discovered Swarupa and motivated her and other children to join MVF's Residential Bridge Course Camp (RBC) for working children. She joined the camp without her father's permission. When Mogilaiah came to know, he demanded release of his daughter. The volunteers spent one whole day convincing him to allow Swarupa to stay on. Local villagers also pitched in. In the camp, Swarupa sat for the 7th grade examination, after which she was admitted to grade 8 of a residential school in Vikarabad. She eventually completed her graduation. While she was studying for her graduation, villagers questioned Mogilaiah as to why he was sending his girl for education to another town. Mogilaiah felt pressured and tried to stop her education. But Swarupa was determined. Twenty-two-year-old Swarupa is now working for IDEA Cellular Phone Company, at its branch office in Shadnagar, a small town in Mahabubnagar district on the Hyderabad Bangalore Highway. Her life has changed and she is a role model for her village. Her parents now proudly tell others how she overcame hurdles and completed her education.

The programme to abolish child labour and universalise education must be a programme that covers all children in the age group 5–14 years simultaneously, not just children in hazardous occupations, or bonded labourers or street children. The 85 per cent of child labour in agriculture is the reserve army of labour force available for all sectors in the economy. There is a huge market demand for child labour as they are cheap and can be made to work for long hours. Banning child labour in a few sectors is a hidden sanction to child labour in the rest. Instead, in the best interest of the children, there must be a total abolition of child labour.

The successful accomplishment of ensuring that children's right to education is guaranteed would need a wholehearted attempt by all forces/institutions, both within the government and outside. All have a role to play in this. In fact there has to be an agreement that there is a role for all the institutions and the battle is in arriving at this agreement and commitment for children. This is certainly not an easy task. But the debate must go on and capture the imagination of one and all into partaking in the project of universalisation of education in India.

At the field level pursuance of children's right to education and actualising it through a conscious process of social mobilisation enables transformation of the family, community and the entire nation. In creating moral spaces in the community that take up the cause of children's rights, societies fractured on caste and communal lines begin to get harmonised. Undoubtedly, this march towards imagining humanity founded on plural values would be further enriched with inclusion of each of us in a literate society.

The mantra is to trust the local. It is so easy. This process of building thought and action of the local gram panchayats, youth, community, opinion makers and local officials has a profound impact on the lives of all of us. The issues of social justice and equity, access to services and state obligation, citizenship and participation, democracy no longer remain abstract notions. They become focal points of concern within the context of the concrete realities and predicament of the poor. The seeds of deepening democracy are sown in this process of articulation, debate and discussion and resolution of differences in perspectives, enabled by insisting that every child must be in school. There is something very organic about capturing the imagination of everyone in the process of making a literate society. A non-violent, silent social transformation for citizenship and rights is launched in this process.

The Micro-level Changes

Schools need to especially prepare themselves to take in first-generation learners. Then there are many seemingly innocuous issues, such as how to accommodate over-age children, or pay the nominal school fees. Many of MVF's key struggles have concerned not only getting children into school but even struggling with the schools to keep them in. Understanding the nature of micro-level changes is the starting point for developing an agenda of governance for children.

Considering that only 56 per cent of children complete grade 5 and 22 per cent finish grade 10, it seems schools have become instruments to produce child labour, not for students to become enlightened citizens. The solution lies not in abandoning the system but in accessing the system, and grappling with each of the issues that obstruct a child's participation in school. It is only then that the gaps are seen and there is a way to rectify the lacunae. In this context access to, and availability of physical infrastructure, teachers, classrooms, transportation services, scholarships, etc. becomes important. It is crucial to create an enabling environment where the child feels wanted and comfortable.

Zero Tolerance of Out-of-school Children is the First Step

While getting a child out of the labour force requires the energy of the entire community, it is a mammoth task to keep the first-generation learner in school. Once the parents have confidence in their decision to send the children to school, they begin to hope for a break in their cycle of deprivation and see education as an indispensable value. This hope gives them the power and resilience to overcome the voices of discouragement. Further, quality of education in schools begins to improve when the community shows zero tolerance to children out of school. Only when the demand for schools is expressed clearly by all as a non-negotiable right of the child, the schools will begin to show interest in their own performance and in improving quality of education. Only when there is respect and dignity for children in the society will the child become a child, the teacher a teacher, and the school a school.

It is important to recognise that the act of going to school can result in a radical shift in the child's self-perception, dignity and freedom. For the first time in her life the child is investing in her own development and growth to realise her own potential. A child in school is transformative. Once this is recognised, the quality of education has to be measured in terms of the capacity of the system to retain the first-generation learner.

Preparing Schools for First-generation Learners

The preparedness of the school for the first-generation learners and making them feel valued requires a school governance system that understands the constraints and limitations of the family in terms of coping with schools as institutions and culture. Parents know the procedures involved in engaging their children in work but they are unfamiliar with procedures involved in enrolling a child in school. In most states, there is an enrolment drive and a campaign to get every child into school. As a result, some older children, who may be working or absent from schools for two or more years, aspire to rejoin, sometimes in the middle of an academic session. This becomes a problem for the school. This is also because there is a lack of appreciation of the fact that the child had to resolve innumerable conflicts to come to school and therefore a 'no-rejection policy' for such a pupil is necessary. Ironically, while there is such rigidity about the child's entry into the school system, the schools do not show equal firmness about a child's exit from the system.

This tolerance of children being pushed out of school is universal. Children moving from one school to the next require a lot of documentation, such as transfer certificates and so on. This record is indispensable as this is the only method by which continuity in the child's education can be traced. But the issue of transfer certificates has not been institutionalised and it is the responsibility of the poor parent to procure it. This often requires frequent trips, is never smooth and the certificate is rarely error-free. This is the reason the children of migrant labour can barely afford formal schooling. Institutionalising the issue of transfer certificates and other documentation is a simple way of preventing children from dropping out of the school system. Till this is done, all children seeking admission must be given admission and all formalities completed by the school authorities later. Also, no child can be denied school admission, which is her right, on the ground of lack of seats.

Space for Older Children and Correcting the Backlog

Even when the school is generous and allows children to be admitted, there are no rules governing admission of older children into entry-level grades. There is no clarity on whether they are to be subjected to eligibility tests to gain an entry into an age-appropriate grade. And, since many of them are likely to fail such an admission test or may not be able to cope with school work even after admission, schools need to have mechanisms to prepare them during the academic session for the class. Often, children are excluded for not producing a birth certificate or not having enough attendance. Some of the processes of declaration of birth, such as filing an affidavit in a court of law, are so intimid-ating that the parents give up. In case of a child labourer admitted in the middle of an academic year how does one calculate his or her school attendance?

Some other issues poor children grapple with relate to fees and uniforms. Elementary school education is free in India and campaigns are conducted to tell this to the children. Yet, schools charge fees for sports, library and maintenance. Most families are unprepared for this investment. There are also instances of children unable to appear for the school-leaving examination, even after being in the school system for many years, due to their inability to pay the examination fees. Similarly, most poor children can ill afford the luxury of school uniforms when they are unable to afford more than two pairs of daily wear. Thus, a school uniform, which is worn as a symbol of equality, ends up perpetuating inequality when children are forced to drop out of school for not wearing one.

Schools also need to update their rosters regularly with the help of the community. Often, the list of enrolled students doesn't match with the attendance register because of frequent dropouts or transfers or even migration. Cumulatively, for all grades from 1 to 10, the dropout rate rises to at least 50 per cent of the total children in the school-going age. Yet, all official data shows that 95 per cent of children are in schools. The only way in which this can be rectified is by ensuring that the children are monitored individually by the schools in consultation with the community. The drive must ensure that every single child in the list is retained in school and promoted to the next grade. Every child should be physically identified by name and verified if she/he is in school or not.

The State and Civil Society and Future Directions for Change

In sum, schools can perform the vital role of protecting children and their rights. Poor children can ill afford the luxury of experimentation of mobile schools, part-time schools, shift schools, seasonal schools and so on. They have to be in full-time formal schools, where they can acquire friends, a peer group, a body language and confidence and the skills to negotiate and bargain with others in the society, and with the state and the market.

There can be no other instrument as powerful as the school in ensuring dignity and freedom to the child. Schools enable correcting the intergenerational imbalances in the society and ease the passage into the mainstream. Even when schools are differentiated and reflect class hierarchies, it is only when a child is in school that there is an opportunity to break those barriers. Schools bridge the gap between the rich and the poor. They are the instruments for hope and change and it is with this faith that the poor send their children to schools. Schools are sites for contests of power and denial of children's rights to education is losing a battle for equity and justice. It is in the process of democratisation of schools that there is a strengthening of democracy of the society.

Conclusion

A childhood enjoyed is the result of having state support; either direct or indirect. This requires galvanising the energies of all in society to create an atmosphere where the rights of children are protected as a state obligation and guaranteed by the state as political expression.

However, over the years, an undercurrent of cynicism about government and its capacity to deliver is slowly getting solidified. All of us are aware that there is no other institution in contemporary times that can parallel the state, especially for the protection of rights. Such a discourse does not encourage or build the capacities of the state to deliver services, instead allows for abdication of the state's obligation towards its children. More than anything else it systematically augments de-legitimisation of the state.

Therefore when the state falters and creates structures and processes that exclude children, the solution must not lie in abandoning the state, instead they should lie in re-forming its system, rethinking its policies for children, pushing it to make greater investments, and constantly bringing to the fore the rights-based perspective that reson-ates with the values of democracy, justice and equity as enshrined in the Constitution of India. It is best done through mobilising of communities that are the beneficiaries of state action, and empowering them to force the state to act through non-violent and democratic processes that are based on information, transparency and accountability. Strengthening of the community forums serves to strengthen collective democratic processes through local consensus building. The challenge of taking such movements forward has always been in institutionalising the ground swell of local action because every right attained brings changes in the existing socioeconomic formation towards greater participation and confidence of citizens of the nation. Every right attained builds state capacities for democratisation of all public institutions, giving access to one and all without discrimination, when those institutions no longer are sites for contestation of power. Every right attained indeed radicalises democracy and makes for a proud and cultured nation.

ℒ

Notes

[1] The Right of Children to Free and Compulsory Education Act was passed by the Indian parliament on August 4, 2009 which describes the modalities of the provision of free and compulsory education for children between 6 and 14 in India under Article 21-A of the Indian Constitution.

[2] The state of Himachal Pradesh has achieved universal elementary education, in spite of a hilly terrain and thinly distributed habitations.

[3] The state of Kerala has every child in school up to grade 12 in spite of its not-so-strong economy.

[4] Article 21-A, as inserted by the Constitution (Eighty-Sixth Amendment) Act, 2002, provides for free and compulsory education of all children in the age group of 6 to 14 years as a Fundamental Right.

7

Children's Impact on State Governance: Overarching Issues

Kavita Ratna

The popular understanding of the relationship between children and governments evokes the image of young passive recipients waiting to be protected and provided for by the state. Hence, the possibility of 'children impacting on state governance' is bound to raise eyebrows, to say the least. Even in the arena of social development, the perception of children as 'holders' of rights is a very recent phenomenon.

Internationally, the United Nations Convention on the Rights of the Child (UNCRC), 1989 is often referred to as the most 'complete' human rights treaty—in that it contains all the civil, political, economic, social and cultural human rights of children, and also covers some areas usually associated with international humanitarian law. The UNCRC re-emphasises that children are holders of rights, and their rights cover all aspects of their lives. It applies to all human beings under the age of 18.

The UNCRC considers children as active subjects who have a right to be not only provided for and protected, but to be active participants in determining the nature and quality of the provisions and protection they are entitled to. Historically, adults and the state are perceived as providers and protectors of children hence the 'participation of children' is, for many adults, an un-chartered territory.

Unpacking 'Children's Participation'

The Oxford English Dictionary defines 'participation' as 'To take part or become involved in an activity, share in something', not attributing any value, either positive or negative, to the word. However, it is interesting to note that in the development parlance it invariably has a positive connotation. The fact that participation varies with its motive, context and perspective, and that the nature of participation comprises a wide variety of possibilities on a continuum ranging from detrimental to beneficial is often missed; the various realms of participation are also often telescoped into one general expression, concealing the true nature of the participation (Reddy 2009).

A child participant can be a protagonist, a representative, a resource provider, a recipient or even a commodity. Her/his degree of freedom in determining her/his 'participation' may vary. She or he may be well-informed, may have a free choice, may be held to liability, may be used, may be serviced, may be exploited or may even be oppressed as a participant. The mandate she/he holds may range from being a self-appointed advocate, to being hand-picked, to being chosen by a few, to being an elected representative. Similarly, there is a vast difference between cultural participation and political participation and the manner in which one participates—be it as a passive recipient or as one who plays an active role in decision-making (ibid.).

The understanding of participation and the way it is translated into action varies and seems to be defined by the sociocultural context of the child and the ideological frame surrounding this understanding. However, it is important to arrive at a culturally neutral definition of children's participation, where the principles are common, though the manifestations may vary according to the situation of children (ibid.).

When children's participation is seen within the frame of protagonism, where children advocate on their own behalf in order to be a part of decision-making processes, it takes on another dimension. This form of participation, that is the participation of children and youth to determine their present and future, underpins the concept of rights. 'Rights' without the possibility of making choices, the ability to decide what one wants and how, defeats the very concept of rights and reduces it to mere provision. Protagonism or self-determination enhances the concept of civil society participation and strengthens democratic processes (ibid.). It becomes a running theme that weaves through every engagement with children, and for adults to understand and internalise it, it requires nothing short of a major paradigm shift.

For the children themselves, this form of participation is the opening up of a new and exciting experience. For the first time they see the world of adults, they begin to understand how this world works and what they need to do to intervene in it. This experience is often tinged with disappointment; at times they find that we, adults, haven't made such a good job of it, but there is also joy in the realisation that we do care and that we have learnt to respect them. What the children need from us is an honest, unbiased and in-depth presentation of the way things are and the tools and skills to enable them to build a better world (ibid.).

Hence, when the term 'children's participation' is used within the children's rights frame; it is critical to understand that what is being referred to, is the act/process by which 'children exercise their right to self-determination' in their own lives and in all matters that concern them.

Children's Participation as a Means to Self-Determination

The right to self-determination is the foundation of the rights discourse. Yet, it is the least recognised of children's rights—even the well-intentioned child rights activists are very often guilty of being ignorant of its full import. 'The issue of self determination is at the heart of children's liberation. It is, in fact, the only issue, a definition of the entire concept' (Farson 1974). For adults, since it challenges the power equation between them and the children, it is perhaps the most difficult concept to internalise and practise. Yet, it is important to realise that for all those who are committed to children, respecting children's right to self-determination is not an option, but an obligation, failing which we stand guilty as violators of their rights.

There are numerous examples from around the world in which this right is given scant regard by the state and civil society, resulting in a large number of rights violations ranging from aggravated hardships for children to unfulfilled expectations and dejection. Within the Convention on the Rights of the Child (CRC), Article 12 clearly articulates the right of children to express their views in matters that concern them. However, this Article cannot be interpreted in isolation.

The CRC may be divided into three areas of focus. They are the three P's, namely the articles concerning the protection of children, those related to the provision of services to children and those concerning participation or the recognition of children as political beings with both civil and political rights. Most of us find it easy to translate the articles of the Convention related to protection and provision into programmes. When these are read separately they are easier to translate into action, as it is our (adults') perception of the nature and quality of these articles that we convert into interventions and not those of the children themselves (Reddy 2009).

Many of us seem to miss the vital link between provision and protection with the right to participation. When we read them together, this third element gives a whole new dimension to the first two; that children have a right to determine the nature and quality of all protection and provision that they have a right to. In fact this would make it mandatory that all interventions must be designed with the active and informed participation of the children concerned and not by adults alone (ibid.). For instance, early this year, we learnt of a Sangkat, an urban local government unit in Cambodia, that is renowned because it has members from non-governmental organisations (NGOs) on its decision-making body. This unique positioning enables the NGOs to represent the concerns of women and children in the local government. They also provide financial assistance to the local government and this contribution is listed in the official budget line of the government and is reported on. The national and international agencies in Cambodia are appreciative of this model and are considering its replication. Examples such as these abound, showcased as 'good practices' and are often considered worthy of emulation in the children's rights arena.

Unfortunately, they are not recognised as illustrations of how adults repeatedly declare themselves as self-appointed advocates of children, position themselves as the 'spokespersons' of the young people they are engaged with and in essence, monopolise the spaces through which children should exercise their right to self-determination in order to improve the quality of their lives. For the right to self-determination to be exercised most effectively there is a need for protagonism that either leads to or is a result of 'empowerment' which ensures 'mutual' accountability between the rights holders and the duty bearers. Their participation should embody processes that empower them to negotiate with the duty bearers. This is true of any meaningful protagonism and applies to children as well. In this framework, the concept of 'children's impact on state governance' implies that children's right to self-determination applies to the decision-making processes of the state as the primary duty bearer, to ensure that their 'citizenship' is recognised.

At present children lack spaces through which they can voice their views and opinions without the fear of retaliation. At best, they end up being dependent on adult advocates, such as parents or NGOs, to 'speak on their behalf'. As a result of this situation of dependency they are most often deprived of their right to hold their adult advocates accountable.

Another area for critical consideration is the fact that the perception of children's rights by adults and by children themselves is vastly different. It is important to distinguish between the positive benefits of children's protagonism on children, their families, communities and society. What children actually benefit from may be dramatically different from what adults feel children need. Hence it is useful to define and demonstrate 'benefits', the 'best interest of the child', in terms of the enhanced quality of children's lives, improved provision and protection for survival and development through participatory decision-making and the increased capacity and opportunities for children to actively negotiate their concerns. For instance, we have faced stiff opposition from teachers who feel that a few days set aside by children to take part in processes that aid their protagonism are a 'waste' of time as they do not 'see' the true 'benefits' that children gain from such empowering processes.

It is also possible that some of the issues children raise may be contrary to the interests of some/all adults in their communities. For instance, when children's issues have required specific budgetary allocations or when children have challenged practices such as unlicensed liquor shops and child marriage, in our programme areas they have faced stiff opposition and even animosity. The adults, who have been affected by such interventions, do not consider children's protagonism beneficial.

This variation in the conceptual understanding of children's rights is quite common and the only way to bring about the 'rights' focus is to invoke the principle of the 'best interests of the child'—a concept that should govern all policies and programmes that directly or indirectly concern children. Though questions such as 'Who determines the best interest of children?' and 'What are the principles that govern such as an assessment?' are still being debated, it is apparent that when children participate in and influence decisions which affect their lives, the outcomes of such decisions are more likely to be in the best interest of the child (ibid.).

Often the advocates of children's protagonism emphasise its 'positive benefits' for society. But rights are not optional or based on the choices made by duty bearers to fulfil their obligations. Children have a 'right to self-determination' and this right is not conditional as to whether or not it benefits others in society. While experience indisputably demonstrates that children's participation is highly beneficial to the entire community, this should be seen as an added advantage and, not as the *raison d'être* of children's participation.

Examples from around the world confirm that the silence imposed on children, preventing them from voicing their concern has been detrimental to them. Most striking is the case of 'out of school' children covered by so-called 'protective' legislation relating to child labour and education who are 'rounded up' and remanded to state institutions violating several articles of the UNCRC and fundamental rights under the Indian Constitution. National laws and more specifically their corresponding Plans of Action have not been examined within a child rights framework. A case in point is the Indian National Policy on Child Labour. This state of affairs is further exacerbated by the absence of mechanisms for redressing grievances by children who are adversely affected by such laws.

Children's right to organise and participate in decisions that pertain to them does not mean that they have all the answers, nor does it mean that we, as adults, are absolved of our responsibilities towards them. Rather, it is to allow for opportunities for children to defend themselves and shape their own futures, and to enjoy the right to intervene in their environment and change elements that do not uphold their rights. We must also be prepared to face the fact that children will say things we do not necessarily agree with. They will ask embarrassing questions for which we do not have ready answers. They will disagree on the stands they take based on the differing realities they face. But we must be willing to accept this. Only if we accept this challenge will we be any closer to finding solutions that work (Reddy 2000).

Children and Democracy

The state of democracy in most developing countries is highly precarious. These are times when political accountability is at an abysmal low, fundamentalism and parochialism are flourishing, civil society movements are largely fragmented and corporate governance and privatisation are gearing up to high-jack democracy to fulfil the personal aspirations of the elite. Those who are marginalised are further impoverished as the social security nets are full of gaping holes. Some communities are appallingly marginalised. Children from these communities are the most exploited and vulnerable. Within each oppressed group, women and even more so children, are politically marginalised even though they have the right to association and right to self-determination as stated in the Human Rights Conventions as well as the CRC.

The governments closest to children and the marginalised communities either do not exist (for example, the shining IT City Bengaluru did not have elections for its urban local government for over three years) or where they do, they are constantly under the pressure of the power centres located higher up that have a vested interest in rendering the local governments ineffectual.

In such a setting, when the notion of citizenship is questionable for adults, for children it is even more elusive. They have very few, if any, 'real life' experiences of democracy either at home or in public spaces like work, school or state. As a signatory of the UNCRC, our state has a national obligation to ensure that all rights of our children are realised. In order to progressively attain that, it has to ensure that the principle of the best interest of the child and their right to self-determination—that is embodied in their right to self-expression, right to association and right to information—are upheld at all cost.

In most cultures, children and youth are kept away from 'politics' as it is considered 'bad' for them until they are 18 years old. At the dawn of this biological milestone, they are expected to attain sufficient civil and political maturity to participate directly in democracy as members of the Grama Sabha or indirectly as the electoral constituency. It is, therefore, no surprise that the young adults of India having had no prior practical experience of participatory democracy fall despairingly short of this expectation. Nurturing our young within a framework of constitutional obligations and a secular national identity is the most urgent need of our times.

Children's Right to be Heard by the State

When in reality social, political and economic structures are still very much hierarchical, children and youth are the most marginalised—even more so than women. Children lack mechanisms to hold various stakeholders accountable, including the state, the primary duty bearer.

The lack of formal platforms, structures, or spaces for children's voices and views to be heard by State Parties is the first major stumbling block for the realisation of Article 12 of the UNCRC. A notable exception is Mongolia, a relatively new democracy that in 2005 provided for groups of elected representatives of children to be linked to all levels of their government, right up to the Mongolian Parliament. It also set up an autonomous support structure with child envoys, elected by children and linked to the National Children's Commission (a division of the National Human

Rights Commission) (CWC-Dhruva 2005). It would be interesting to review how this structure is currently functioning.

Though progressive countries such as Norway have provided for Youth Councils, until very recently its members were not elected and hence were not the real representatives of the constituencies they represented. To date, young people from migrant communities or refugees remain unrepresented in the Youth Council. The Youth Council's procedures are very similar to those of the adult Council members and so it is a challenge for the young representatives to participate to their full potential. Equally importantly, the Youth Council members do not report back to the children and young people who elected them on a regular basis as they lack a clear understanding of their 'accountability' to their constituency.

Children and adolescents are critical observers of their own conditions and should be participants in decisions concerning themselves and their lives. These young people need to participate in finding solutions to the problems they face. They need to relate to society in an organised way, yet feel the protection and security needed by children. They should be encouraged to reason independently and have the courage to dissent. A practical experience of participatory democracy (learning through doing) is essential for the moulding of the 'new citizen'.

Participation can build capacity for active citizenship, good governance and sustainable development of communities. When children, especially the most marginalised, have opportunities to express their views, access information, form associations, participate in decisions that affect them and take action to fulfil their rights, they are often able to protect themselves more, claim their rights and hold adults accountable (Reddy 2004).

However, children's participation should not be seen in isolation. It is related to participation as a human right for empowering and engaging children, families and communities. The mobilisation and participation of children and communities is important for claiming child rights and addressing social norms that perpetuate acceptance of discrimination, violence, abuse, exploitation and the non-participation of children (Feinstein and O'Kane 2009).

The implementation of the CRC cannot be disconnected from the political climate available for adults to assert their rights, as the degree to which children are able to realise their rights is directly related to the degree to which their adults realise their rights. The realisation of Article 12 by children is impossible to achieve in countries where State Parties may have signed the CRC but have autocratic or authoritarian civil and political structures that do not recognise the role of civil society and even adult participation in state governance is non-existent.

Also, when the adults themselves lack spaces for their protagonism and have not experienced its strength, it is very difficult for them to comprehend the need for children's protagonism. In countries such as Cambodia where their recent political history is replete with the repression of civil society participation, or in the Democratic Republic of Congo where a war reigns, it is a challenge for the adults to visualise children's participation. However, it is our experience that even in such adverse conditions children have managed to generate spaces to articulate their views, and adults who lack such spaces for themselves are likely to invade and manipulate these spaces. We have also seen the converse, that is, adults being inspired by the initiative of children and spurned on to take charge of their own lives and begin to actively claim their rights. However, it is clear that the realisation of the CRC is closely linked to the existence of basic human and fundamental rights for adults.

Deeply rooted structures of inequality also need to be challenged at all levels for children's protagonism to become a reality in the family, community, society and the state. There is also a need to recognise and address conflicts of interest and inequalities within families where it is usually women and children who have less control over resources and decision-making, fewer choices, and greater exposure to violence. It is these, not just attitudes that make participation erratic and unequal. Hence a deep understanding of the poverty that acts as a barrier for the realisation of human rights is crucial in order to develop strategies that are unique to each context to enable children as well as adults to increase their opportunities to be heard.

Adults involved in supporting or facilitating participation must also be aware that children have an innate sense of justice and have a strong tendency to strive for 'win-win' solutions. However, in order to actualise them, their capacities to manage information and relationships have to be enhanced in a systematic and sustained manner.

All State Parties that are signatories to the Convention on the Rights of the Child have to present their periodic reports to the Committee on the Rights of the Child. The Committee had observed that Periodic Country Reports presented before it indicated a very poor understanding and reporting of the right to participation among the governments from around the world. Hence it has come out with its General Comment on Article 12 in 2009 (CRC/C/GC/12, July 1, 2009). However, the reporting mechanisms of the CRC still do not stipulate parameters—such as number of consultations held by national, state and local governments with children, especially the marginalised children represented, or the number of concerns raised by children that have been addressed and the budget expended on these issues—that demonstrate the required 'political will' to make Article 12 a reality for children.

Assertion of Citizenship by Children

In democracies adults have several means to represent themselves such as adult franchise, direct participation in local government through platforms such as the councils (or the Grama Sabhas in some states in India), legal process, protests, petitions and other forms of political dissent as individuals or members of unions or movements. Though children are citizens too, they are denied these avenues and lack formal spaces to represent themselves and their interests. They need to understand and prepare for governance and citizenship and, therefore, must be enabled to interact in a constructive, meaningful and sustainable way with the state and policy-making bodies. They need to be a part of the design, implementation and monitoring of policies and programmes intended for them.

Rakesh Rajani (2000), in his article 'Questioning How We Think about Children' writes,

> First, policies and programs designed by adults for children often go wrong, however well-intentioned. They tend to miss out key information and fail to fathom the critical priorities, constraints, influences, pathways and connections in children's lives. By leaving children out, these policies also weaken the structure if their accountability and forgo the opportunity to contribute to children's sense of belonging and influencing the world.
>
> Second, children are capable. They are increasingly competent in a wide set of issues, and can often share valuable information about their circumstances. Many children are able to reflect, analyze and weigh options and consequences. Many can organise; build powerful and thoughtful alliances with adults, and advocate for themselves.

However, for children's protagonism to be truly productive and not just tokenistic, the state must create structures such as forums and mechanisms (not child-led organisations) for children to, first of all, engage with their local governments that are closest and most accessible to them; organisations of children and youth should be enabled and given mandatory rights to participate in state governance; structures that enable this participation and link organisations of children and adolescents to local governments need to be created; these structures should have special provisions that enable children from the most marginalised communities to exercise their right to self-determination. A good example of this concept in practice is currently functioning in the state of Karnataka, India since 1996 as the Makkala Panchayats or Children's Local Governments.

Structures for Children's Participation

While introduction of legislation and policies that place obligations on social actors to provide opportunities for children to participate may be of some use, it is most important that State Parties ensure that platforms and mechanisms are in place for children to express their views where it is made mandatory that these views are taken seriously.

Children's effective participation depends largely on platforms for their participation. While such platforms created by NGOs may temporarily mitigate the situation, it is mainstream decision-making structures that have to embody the platforms through which children can exercise their right to self-determination.

The creation of such mainstream structures should start from the bottom, and the local governments are the most appropriate point to start. On the one hand, they are the policy-making bodies that are most accessible to children on a regular basis. On the other hand, they, as elected representative bodies, have to be accountable to their constituencies, which most certainly include children. They also have the political and administrative jurisdiction that mandates them to develop plans, monitor them and to manage resources.

Hence, creating spaces where children can effortlessly and confidently represent themselves in decision-making processes, in a protective and nurturing environment, is one of the most important obligations we adults shoulder.

Child-led Organisations

Experience from around the world shows that when children and young people get organised, their capacities, strength and collective bargaining power increase exponentially. The more marginalised they are, the greater their need for autonomous child-governed organisations or associations. Such children's organisations have existed even without adult facilitation or support because getting organised— based on common issues of concern—is an intrinsic need for survival.

Hence, it is no surprise that the Working Children's Movements of the world laid the real foundation for children's participation as protagonists. History shows that the newspaper boys of New York, over 120 years ago, collectively raised their voice against the newspaper baron whose payment policy hit them hard where it hurt them most, on their stomachs. After a remarkable struggle that required tremendous persistence and strength, they were victorious.[1] In the more recent past, going back a little over four decades, the working children of Latin America, of Asia and of Africa were the very first children's organisations that demonstrated the capacity of children to advocate for their rights against great odds. Even in countries such as Canada and Germany, the very first children's organisations were of working children.

The organised protagonism of children and youth, especially the more disadvantaged children, gives children strength, access to more information, confidence, an identity and ownership. Individual children or youth representing such groups voice the views and aspirations of the collective.

Experience has shown that when children come together, and deliberate about what kind of structures they would like for their own organisation, there are very few reference points to begin with. All around them they see hierarchical structures (with very few rare exceptions) and hence they need inputs regarding the different organisational structures they could consider, with discussions about the positives and negatives of each one of them. When children juxtapose what they believe in to their own organisational structure, they are able to find innovative and interesting structures, most often 'circular' with responsibilities shared on a rotational basis.

Their coming together also enables them to find collective ways to solve problems. It contributes to preserve and add a new vibrancy to a culture of egalitarianism, secularism and equity. While all these have a great value for all children, its significance is phenomenal for children who are the most marginalised. What needs to be ensured is that all children and youth have an equitable right to exercise their rights as protagonists in the development of this collective voice; if not, the hierarchies that exist in the adult world will find insidious ways to replicate themselves and to perpetuate among children as well.

Further, as most activist and developmental organisations are, by choice, engaged with the most marginalised groups of children, there are naturally more examples of children's participation emerging from these groups. Children in different parts of the world who have organised themselves unequivocally say that they have most often received immediate support from their peers and fellow members. They derive strength and moral courage from their organisations.

In the recent past, there have been suggestions related to the role of 'State Parties to consider the introduction of legislation or regulations which enable and support children to form their own associations'. It is important that while the state can create conditions favourable for children to get organised, if it begins to organise children themselves, there is a high tendency for it to control and also influence the agenda of these child-led organisations or associations. It is strongly recommended that the state should be prohibited from playing a direct facilitative or regulative role in the formation and running of children's organisations or associations that may undermine their autonomy. Many countries have state-sponsored youth movements that are also controlled by them. The same could happen with children's associations. In India, for example, government orders have been issued to schools for the formation of 'children's clubs'. In the few schools where these have been formed, the clubs are under tight scrutiny by the school faculty. While non-controversial activities by children are allowed, there seems to be a tacit understanding about 'areas that are cordoned off' for children's engagement and trespassing into these areas has several direct and indirect repercussions on the children concerned. These state-set-up organisations invariably become 'state controlled' and 'co-opted', especially in settings that promote authoritarian governance, and hence defeat their very purpose.

The protagonism of democratically formed child and youth organisations will bring about a de facto accountability on the part of the administration and a transparency in their functioning. For children and their organisations to be able to participate effectively they need structures or platforms that encourage their constructive involvement and that take their inputs seriously to be acted upon. When children's participation in state governance is enabled, they are able to exercise their right to self-determination in order to express their views and needs, hold the state accountable to its commitments and learn about democracy through their own experience of it.

Processes that Empower Children

While discussing approaches to protagonism, a clear distinction has to be made between 'events and processes'. Unfortunately, the practice of children's 'participation' is predominantly seen in the form of organising 'events' in which children take part, and not as processes that need sustained support and commitment.

There are many examples from around the world in which adults initiate programmes or projects with children that are time-bound or task-bound or both—without factoring in strategies to sustain the process. It is possible to design such programmes in a way that they may even empower young people—by enriching their attitudes and enhancing their knowledge and skills. Children do internalise learning from good processes, however brief, and can draw insights from them as and when they require.

However, to reach their full potential, they need such inputs in a timely and sustained manner. Working children in Ghana, for example, were able to carry out a highly nuanced research about children and transportation following a facilitative process by our organisation, but the adults based in the country, despite their attempts, did not have the means to take the group forward.[2]

It must also be noted that in 'child-led' processes, the adults may not always have a role. As child-led organisations become increasingly self-reliant, they are able to form 'partnerships' with adults, in which both children and adults jointly determine the nature, scope and the ground rules of that relationship. Child-led organisations that have attained a high degree of maturity and organisational development have an 'interdependent' relationship with their adult support organisations that are highly beneficial to both.[3]

Children's Impact on Policy

A few rarefied spaces that have emerged for 'children's participation' in policy matters in the last few decades have been mostly in the international arena—because children's rights have begun to gain currency, and rightly so, to a certain extent in international policy related consultations. One of the most famous examples of this has been the UN

General Assembly Special (UNGASS) of 2002. Here is the official view of the children's participation at the exalted UN level:

> The Special Session was a landmark, the first such Session devoted exclusively to children and the first to include them as official delegates. . . . For several reasons, the participation of children and adolescents at the Special Session represents a real breakthrough at the United Nations. . . . They presented their views in the statement 'A World Fit for Us', at the opening of the General Assembly debate, formally addressing the Assembly on behalf of children for the first time in the United Nations history. They participated in great numbers at the Special Session as delegates from either non-governmental organizations (NGOs) or governments. Finally, they were also actively involved in a number of official meetings and key supporting events. (United Nations General Assembly 2009)

Those of us who followed the process closely and also had a ring-side view did not experience it quite the same way. To begin with, children and young people had not been informed that by the time they had a chance to interact, in the 'unofficial' spaces with the governmental delegates, or 'view the official proceedings from the gallery', most of the important decisions related to 'A World Fit for Children' were not only taken, but also available in print.

It was a sorry sight to see children from around the world, some of whom had met their 'accompanying' adults for the first time at the airport prior to departure, carrying thick volumes of UN documentation, trying to make sense of the UN labyrinth. It was not clear through what processes many of the children who reached New York were selected and whose mandate they carried as representatives of the children of the world.

There, the only children who were able to negotiate some opportunities were the children who represented the

Working Children's Movements. They had a long history of being organised and fighting their way into the international child labour debates. So in partnership with their collaborating adults they had carried out extensive planning to organise parallel events during the UNGASS. Through these, some of their views were heard by a few policy makers, but they too were not timely enough to have a real impact on either the main document or the heated 'political' debates over semantics that were taking place in the inner chambers among diplomats.

For most children, such 'top heavy' consultative processes that have very little or no scope for real influence make a mockery of their right to self-determination. The building blocks of meaningful children's participation should be laid much lower down, closer to their own communities where they have sustained access to local level 'decision makers' and where they are recognised as 'individuals' and not just another representative sample. When their base is set firmly in the spaces closest to them, only then will children be able to engage with decision makers at higher levels from a position of strength because then they will have an unquestionable mandate, unified purpose and a high degree of accountability to the children they represent.

Children's Right to Information

Informed and organised participation is the key to effective protagonism of children, especially those who are most marginalised. Children need to have the collective strength as well as knowledge, skills and tools for accessing, analysing and using information to make logical and constructive interventions on their own behalf and also to advocate for effective solutions with policy makers.

Children's movements face great difficulties regarding access to local, national and international policy-making spaces. The members of the International Movement of Working Children have clearly expressed their views on the matter in two of our films—*Time to Listen* (International Working Group on Child Labour 1997) and *Taking Destiny in Their Hands* (The Concerned for Working Children [CWC] 2004).

Children's movements do not have information related to current policy discussions that have a direct bearing on their lives. Many of these policy discussions exclude children as they do most adults. Sometimes, as seen during the ILO consultations related to Article 182, in 1997, children are deliberately kept out of the discussions because they may express views that contradict the dominant adult thinking on the issues concerned.

In the few policy discussions that do include children, issues related to 'representation' are hardly given due importance. Some NGOs become self-appointed advocates of children and often 'choose' which children should participate. The participation of individual 'hand-picked' children or youth is loaded with discrimination and such 'representatives' represent no one but themselves. Such 'selection' processes exclude the less vocal and visible; and it gives more room for manipulation. While their individual views carry a certain weight, their views cannot be considered as the collective view of the constituency they belong to. In policy-related issues, it's the collective view that is of critical importance and most often the individual views are treated as that of the collective and that can be totally misleading. Hence, facilitating children to form their own organisations or representative groups has to figure high on our list. At times, even when such organisations exist, they are rarely provided the information, opportunities, facilities or time to carry out processes of criteria setting, of preparation for the discussion and of selection of representatives.

Children also lack access to documents related to the policy in question. The few documents they do have access to, are not child-friendly in language and presentation. Despite all these odds, children have shown tremendous courage, drive and determination in the few policy-related discussions they have been involved in, such as the UN Global Study on Violence, where for the very first time an advisory group of under-18-year-olds provided their inputs.[4] The contributions of children, where they were provided enabling environments, to the debates have been highly valuable and insightful. State Parties should consciously plan for consultations with children and should debrief children on the outcome of such discussions—as only then will their participation be meaningful.

Children's right to information should not limit itself to children 'receiving' appropriate information, in forms that are most relevant to them. As citizens, they have a right to adequate coverage of their issues and most importantly, they have a right to produce and disseminate their own media products. The average mass media scenario in relation to children is that there is widespread violation of children's rights through insensitive reportage and misrepresentation and a blatant denial of space for their opinions on issues. Children have pointed out that their programmes are not a priority for the media; their voices and perspectives are rarely heard or respected; they are regularly stereotyped by the media; information relevant to them is very sparsely available and information relevant to them is not presented in ways that can be understood by children. Children's issues are not newsworthy unless they have scope for sensationalism. Their contexts are often negated and they are rarely portrayed as protagonists.

After an extensive review of existing media codes on children in 2005, we at CWC learnt that they focused only on children's right to privacy and confidentiality. Significantly, none of the charters or codes focused on the rights of children to be 'producers' of media in society. In the same year, through an extensive consultative process with children and media persons, CWC developed the 'The Media Code to Realise Children's Rights'. This code is an effort to effect a paradigm shift in the media's approach to children—from that of being recipients of adult benevolence to being viewed as full partners in society. It has been developed to give children a say in defining the media, to outline children's rights-based standards so that children are creators of media, and to provide a tool for monitoring of children's rights violations by the media or by civil society groups.

Children Rejuvenate Local Governments: Three Examples from Karnataka, India

Despite recognising the right of children to participate in decision-making processes, it is often debated worldwide whether or not children have the potential to articulate their concerns and influence decision-making at the level of state governance.

Here are three examples from India, which have proved, for several years now, that children's participation in state governance is not only critical for children to realise their rights, but that it is also fundamental to protect, nurture and strengthen democracy. It must be noted that in general, the status of children's rights in Karnataka is not different from the rest of the country. However, in comparison with other states, the degree of political decentralisation is high in Karnataka, with only the state of Kerala scoring higher.

CWC has been an advocate for children's protagonism and their right to self-determination since the mid-1980s.[5] It facilitated the first ever working children's organisation in Asia, the Bhima Sangha. Bhima Sangha has a well-documented history of child protagonism that spans almost three decades. Its partnership with CWC has laid the foundation to our praxis of children's participation as protagonists. The examples described here, are results of a proactive partnership with children that has often pushed CWC along a steep learning curve, liberally sprinkled with challenges at every turn.

◊

Makkala Grama Sabha—Children's Grama Sabha

A Grama Sabha of a Village Panchayat is the only political space available for its citizens to directly participate in a democratic manner to plan and monitor the development of their village.[6] While such Sabhas (meetings) are pre-scribed for the adults of the village in our Decentralisation Act, they are not considered relevant to 'children' as the popular understanding is that children are 'citizens of tomorrow', not of today.

CWC organised the first children's Grama Sabha in Keradi, a Panchayat in the Udupi District of Karnataka in the year 2002. 'Makkala Grama Sabhas' are especially meant for children and are modelled on the adult Gram Sabhas. They are essentially a meeting between the local government and all the young citizens who are its con-stituency. During this meeting, children interact directly with the local government. In addition to responding to children and reporting on actions taken, the local govern-ment also presents the status of children's rights in the village to the children and the entire community.

The audience at the first children's Grama Sabha included Vinay Kumar Sorake, the then member of the Indian National Parliament as well as several members of the three tiers of the local governments. Responding to the creative and powerful presentations made by children, Mr Sorake said,

> A formal interaction between children and their governments of this kind is exemplary. Children have pointed out very specific problems and have also suggested specific solutions. All their points have been backed with detailed statistics. Most often the adult Panchayats or the concerned departments do not have such in-depth information. I highly appreciate the fact that children first conducted surveys and held

discussions among themselves before presenting the points here. This children's Grama Sabha, held in Keradi, one of the most remote Panchayats of Karnataka, should become a role model for all Panchayats.[7]

'It is now absolutely clear to me why children's participation is critical to strengthen local government,' said a Panchayat president, after the children's Grama Sabha. 'Children not only list their problems, they also describe the implications of the problems and the importance of addressing them. This has been extremely useful to us to develop our action plans.'[8]

When the Karnataka government, through its Rural Development and Panchayat Raj Department, issued a circular in 2006 that made it mandatory for all the elected members of the 5,653 Gram Panchayats of Karnataka state to conduct children's Grama Sabhas to 'listen' to their young citizens once a year and be accountable to them, it was a celebration for those of us who have been advocating for children's right to be heard for decades. Until now, the Grama Sabhas, like most other public spaces, have been denied to children. Hence, this commendable decision by the government of Karnataka to categorically recognise the citizenship of children and to place children's rights at the centre of local governance is worthy of emulation worldwide.

Damodar Acharya, executive director, CWC explains,

> The children's Gram Sabha is an interface between children and the political system, perhaps the first of its kind. Unlike the many mock-parliament sessions which children participate in, what we have here is real and will surely lay the foundation for a very sound practice of children's participation. Processes such as these that start from the grassroots bring in long lasting transformations.[9]

One of the challenges the children's Grama Sabha is going to face is from adults who may try to usurp this space that has been exclusively provided for children to make policy and programme suggestions. This is even more likely to happen where adults are not making the best use of their Grama Sabhas to impact on local government. Both children and adults who facilitate them will have to guard against this kind of manipulation that will not only violate the true spirit of the children's Grama Sabhas but also put children under tremendous risk of negative repercussions.

So there is need for extensive capacity building of the local governments, children and all the stakeholders to ensure that this space provided for the participation of children in local governance is used optimally. Processes such as the children's Grama Sabhas that evoke the true spirit of Grama Swaraj (local self-governance) by creating a generation of empowered youngsters have a very important role to play to strengthen decentralised democracy.

◊

Makkala Panchayats (Children's Councils) in Karnataka

CWC has been working in the rural areas of Karnataka through the Toofan Panchayats Programme, which is a comprehensive programme of community development aimed at creating an environment where children are not involved in any form of work that is detrimental to their development, and where all children's rights are recognised and realised. The programme works for the empowerment of all the actors in the community through partnership and participation.

In 1995 Bhima Sangha and the CWC in collaboration with the Ministry of Rural Development and Panchayat Raj (Decentralisation) initiated the formation of Makkala Panchayats (Children's Councils) in five village Panchayats in Karnataka.[10]

The Bhima Sangha had a long history of negotiating with representatives of governments in order to improve the quality of their lives and to address the causes that compelled them to labour. The rationale that led to the establishment of the Makkala Panchayats was that despite repeated interaction with local administrative and government bodies, Bhima Sangha felt that sustained impact was lacking. They felt that a permanent structure that enabled close interaction between children and decision-making bodies was required in order to inform and influence local governments in a consistent manner. It could also ensure that children had opportunities to take part in decision-making processes within their Panchayats.

During the process of creating the Makkala Panchayats, the members of Bhima Sangha noted that it was required not only by the organised 'working children' such as themselves, but by all children in order to speak up about their needs. Hence the structure of the Makkala Panchayats was designed to include different base groups of children such as working children, children with special needs, children from migrant communities and school-going children.

A few years ago, the Karnataka State Education Department issued an order to all the schools to start 'child rights clubs', however, this remains only on paper. It must be noted in this context that locating child rights clubs within school parameters will have very limited impact because its functioning and scope to raise issues related to the school will invariably be controlled by the school management.

Hence the school children's organisations facilitated by CWC are located in the community and school-going children of a community are members of it. They are thus able to take up issues concerning different schools without being personally targeted—and they are also able to see themselves as the citizens of the entire community and not only as 'school-going children'. In this wider scope they relate to a large number of stakeholders, including their elected representatives on issues that are relevant to the entire community. They are one of the four base groups of the Makkala Panchayats.

The Makkala Panchayats are elected bodies. The voters are the children resident in the Panchayat in the age group of 6 to 18 years. The children who can contest are in the age group of 12 to 16 years. The elections for this Panchayat are conducted by the Village Panchayat and the Taluk Administration through a secret ballot. Throughout the development of the Makkala Panchayats children put in great efforts for developing an appropriate protocol to define the mandate and structure of the Makkala Panchayats criteria for both the candidature and the electorate. The Makkala Panchayat election criteria are revisited each term to ensure that the socially, economically and politically most marginalised groups of children including working children, specially abled children, girls have maximum representation.

> 'Children are not only discussing and trying to solve their problems through the Makkala Panchayat, but they are also showing the adults how to run the government in harmony. This process is now underway in only 56 Panchayats; the government is trying to expand it to the rest of the state.'
>
> These are the words of C. M. Udasi, minister, Department of Rural Development and Panchayat Raj, Government of Karnataka while releasing the book *Makkala Panchayat Protocol* at a consultation entitled 'Mainstreaming Informed Participation of Children in Governance' organised by CWC.
>
> *(Press release, CWC, December 11, 2006)*

In order to link the Makkala Panchayats to the Village Panchayats, a tripartite Task Force has been set up. It consists of representatives of the Makkala Panchayats, elected members of the local government, government officials and community-based organisations. The Task Force also exists at sub-district, or Taluk level to ensure that issues raised in the Makkala Panchayats are presented at higher levels.[11] The regular involvement of high-profile government officials increases the level of bureaucratic commitment. The close interaction between children and local government bodies creates a new form of political legitimacy for children on issues regarding their own welfare (Reddy 2004).

Each Makkala Panchayat selects a Makkala Mitra or Children's Friend, an adult whom they feel they can trust and whom they can depend on for support within the Task Force and in the community. The Makkala Mitra's role is to take immediate action in cases where children request help individually or collectively. Children have, with the help of the Makkala Mitra, been able to address and solve problems independently of the Task Force (ibid.).

The Makkala Panchayats in Karnataka have given the local governments a new lease of life with their active involvement in not only identifying the problems they face, but also proposing solutions. They have made detailed presentations regarding the issues and problems they identified related to education, basic facilities, personal problems, gender discrimination, disability and child labour.

The issues collected from each ward are compiled after detailed discussions. When they list their problems, children make it amply clear that they have explored the matter thoroughly. They are able to not just raise a problem but also propose solutions that are most appropriate to them. They have clearly demonstrated how they can use political space to negotiate with the local governments and influence decision-making processes. Experience has also shown that children always aim to use spaces constructively. They avoid confrontation and always seek win-win solutions. This is a value adult politics is urgently in need of.

When children begin to access political space, they are also vulnerable to threat and pressure. These may range from subtle hints going right up to physical violence. It is the responsibility of the state and the facilitating organisations to ensure that children are protected. This understanding of vulnerability also provides an impetus for us to create and find ways and means by which children can access decision-making spaces without exposing themselves to threat. One such example is the 'Children's Post Box'.[12]

Fourteen-year-old Sukumar, vice president of the Keradi Children's Panchayat represents the feelings of the children when he says, 'Until now, hardly any one had bothered to ask us what we thought or felt. This is the first time we had such an opportunity. We can solve some of our problems. For the others, the adults will have to be responsible. We will make them responsible.'[13]

Over the years, the members of Makkala Panchayats and Bhima Sangha have conducted research studies, made interventions on the basis of the information they collected, lobbied with the officials at various levels for development in their communities, collectively fought for their rights as children. They have made themselves heard in the state, national and international policy discussions and have advocated for consulting children in matters that concern them.

CWC has played an instrumental role in capacity building for both adults and children. This has resulted in children involved with the Makkala Panchayats becoming increasingly equipped with the means to deal with local government structures. The Makkala Panchayats, the first of their kind in India, show the potential of children to articulate the problems in the village, substantiate their demands with data and to elicit responses that are rooted in a children's rights framework. Most importantly, they are a step towards recognising children's right to participate, voice concerns and ensure that the political decisions are made in partnership with them. They also demonstrate that children can think laterally and responsibly if efforts are directed towards recognising and building their capacities and giving them opportunities to participate in the decision-making process.

◈

The Panchayat Level Five Year Planning Process—Children Lead the Way

The government of Karnataka, for several years has been trying to initiate a localised planning process in which each local government is expected to asses its own needs and develop its plans for the five years ahead with active involvement of their constituencies. These plans by the local governments are to be the building blocks for a state-level planning process. However, many local governments do not have access to the required information, skills and support to develop such plans. In 2004, the state made several attempts to build capacities of the local governments to embark on a decentralised planning process. In some geographical areas, the state government requested private developmental organisations in the region to provide assistance to the local governments.

In this context, CWC was requested by the chief executive officer (CEO) of Udupi District Panchayat in Karnataka, to support the 56 Village Panchayats to develop their own plans. We accepted the invitation, with one caveat—that was the demand for high level participation of children in the planning process. The Panchayats did not hesitate to admit that they lacked the expertise to involve children in such a process, but extended their total support to our proposal.

The output was remarkable. About 20,000 children were involved in the planning process. Their plans were comprehensive and substantiated with statistics and data. Groups and issues, such as the problems of the disabled, environmental concerns and issues related to mobility and transport, were covered for the first time in a five-year plan. They also recorded the history of the village, degradation of resources, made maps of their Panchayats that were accurate and informative and in many cases, proposed solutions as well. The adults, especially the members and staff of the Gram Panchayats were astounded and in many cases shame-faced as the plans that the adults had drafted were very poor in comparison. As a result, by and large, the children's plans became the official plans of the Panchayats. But more than that, it has rejuvenated the Panchayats. The officials and elected representatives seem to be sensing a purpose and relevance to their work. They see their Panchayats in a new light and they have gained a deeper understanding of the Panchayat's needs and concerns. The gap between the local government and the people has diminished (Reddy and Acharya 2004).

An overview of the survey of 56 Panchayats shows that education and school-related issues recur in all the plans: compound walls, libraries, high school inaccessibility, school playground, drinking water, toilets, midday meals and teachers. A major difference made by school children in the planning process is that the plans used to be hijacked by powerful individuals to improve their own lives, people's participation being a mere catchphrase useful during elections. This time, women, children and entire Panchayats built up the children-led plan through regular ward meetings and data collection. For the first time, the Panchayat felt as if it owned the plan. To recall, local planning effort by Gram Panchayats is mandated, since 1992, by Article 243G of the 73rd Amendment 'to prepare village area plan for economic development and social justice'.[14]

In retrospect, the involvement of children, their enthusiasm, their unerring sense of justice and their compassionate response to people's problems is what drew adults into this process. If children had not been the prime movers, adults would not have been involved in such large numbers and as in the past the task of drawing up the plans would have remained with the secretary of the Gram Panchayat with some inputs from some of the elected members. Adults are cynical and wary of any possible change because of their conditioning to the 'real world', whereas children still have hope and the belief that they can change the world. When their efforts bear fruit, it also serves as a role model for grown ups, and adults once again begin to have hope. Children also grow up, and if they have a positive experience of participation in governance they carry that with them into adulthood. Good politics is essential for the progress of any country. Here children have been involved in defining 'good politics'. This is not only a role model for children but also for adults in the entire country. The Five Year Planning process in Udupi District is one such experience (ibid.).

The Impact

Through their engagements with the local governments, the most important impact on children has been the assertion of their citizenship and their right to question their governments, if need be. As a result, a de facto accountability on the part of the local administration and a transparency in their functioning has been created, that has not only benefited the children but the entire community.

The members of Makkala Panchayats have been resource persons in the State Capacity Building Programmes and have provided inputs on decentralised planning to over 82,000 elected adult Panchayat members. The entire Makkala Panchayat election process and governance that takes place outside the 'political party' framework has been an inspiration to many adults. All these have resulted in a paradigm shift in the way the Adult Panchayats view children. They acknowledge children's citizenship and have gained tremendous insights from the recommendations of children—which have resulted in child rights-friendly village plans.

As a result, the adult Grama Sabhas and Village Panchayats too have become revitalised. The adults in the community have recognised that due to children's participation, many of their long-standing issues have been addressed in a democratic manner. They have been a motivation for the adults to exercise their citizenship with vigour and a renewed confidence in democracy. Children, through their example, have made it possible for women to access the political space from which many of them have been excluded. This is also true for members of the extremely marginalised communities from where initially children and now adults have begun to speak up.

As an organisation, CWC finds itself at a point in time when there is heightened awareness about children's rights as a concept—yet, there are too few examples in governance that embody the true spirit of children's participation and protagonism. Though a high degree of appreciation is expressed about Makkala Panchayats—from people, organisations and governments—when the issue of going to scale arises, the questions that are posed are 'How can the capacities of adults be built to facilitate such structures and processes?' 'How can it be ensured that the Makkala Panchayats do not become corrupt?' 'How can it be ascertained that adults do not manipulate children?' These are issues that can be effectively addressed with systematic strategising, planning, capacity building and monitoring.

As CWC sees it, the key concerns are not these. The most important challenge for structures such as Makkala Panchayats today is the present political environment that is opposed to democratic decentralisation in our country. There are extremely well-orchestrated and persistent moves from the powers that be to curtail the scope and strength of local governments. Instead of making attempts to build the capacities of the local governments that are closest to people—hence most accountable—often allegations are made about their inefficiency in order to justify the efforts to undermine the local governments.

As an organisation, CWC is coordinating a state-level campaign that is countering the latest and the most blatant move by the state-level elected representatives to take away crucial powers of the local governments. As a part of its work and the campaign advocating for decentralisation, CWC is generating debates and discussions about the need for meaningful decentralised governance that activates civil society participation—not as extensions of the state but as a vibrant and alert group of people capable of countering injustice, challenging the status quo and defining development. The focus is on ensuring that the definition of 'civil society' includes children and all other groups that have been hitherto marginalised in social, economic and political spaces.

Citizenship of children and children's right to self-determination remain difficult concepts as children's political participation has not yet been recognised by a large number of adults worldwide. However, it is time that all agencies realise that children have a right to actively determine the course of their lives and not enabling them to do so, to the best of their potential, is a violation of their rights. Children who have been actively part of state governance have had an education in democracy and protagonism that no university can match. They have proved, time and again, that they are political beings, with a strong sense of justice, capable of making extremely astute observations and evolving creative solutions.

In them lies the hope for a 'real democracy'.

ℒ

Notes

[1] This movement took place in 1889, in New York. The newspaper barons in question were William Randolph Hearst, who owned the *New York Journal*, and Joseph Pulitzer who owned the *New York World*.

[2] This study was facilitated by Dhruva, the Capacity Building and Consultancy Unit of CWC.

[3] Please refer to our publication, *A Journey in Children's Participation*, for an in-depth presentation related to various forms of engagements between adults and children http://www.workingchild.org, accessed on August 21, 2009.

[4] Ms Manjula and Ms Ayyamma, both representing Bhima Sangha, were members of this Advisory Group. The Concerned for Working Children (CWC) was the adult facilitating organisation.

[5] CWC is a secular and democratic development agency committed to the empowerment of children, especially working and other marginalised children and their communities through their participation in decision making and governance on all matters that concern them (www.workingchild.org), accessed on August 21, 2009.

[6] The Village Panchayat is the lowest level of administration in the system of local government. The term Panchayat refers to both the geographical and administrative units, as well as the elected body, which acts as the local council. A Panchayat is composed of a cluster of villages and several Panchayats constitute a Taluk.

[7] Mr Soraki's quote in a TV interview, during Children's Grama Sabha, Keradi Panchayat, Karnataka, January, 2002.

[8] Shankar Narayan Chatra, President of Hallihole Panchayat, Karnataka, 2003. An interview conducted by CWC, for a process document on Children's Grama Sabha, Keradi Panchayat, Karnataka, January 2002.

[9] An interview conducted by CWC, for a process document on Children's Grama Sabha, Keradi Panchayat, Karnataka, January 2001.

[10] A union of, by and for working children in Karnataka facilitated by CWC striving for the realisation of child rights.

[11] Sub-district level administrative body consisting of a cluster of Panchayats.

[12] Children's Post Box is a facility for children to write about problems they face, be it emotional, social or physical, which they cannot share with adults or with other children directly. Children can also share their personal views and experiences with other children through this post box. The children's

council has placed such post boxes in each ward and its members review the contents of the post box and take appropriate action-seeking adult support when necessary.
[13] An interview conducted by CWC, for a process document on Children's Grama Sabha, Keradi Panchayat, Karnataka 2001.
[14] L. C. Jain, former member of Planning Commission, and former ambassador of India to South Africa.

ℒ

References

Dhruva 2005. Submission made to the Expert Group on Children's Participation, UNICEF, by Dhruva, Training and Consultancy Unit of The Concerned for Working Children, India.

Farson, Richard. 1974. 'Birthrights', in David Archard (ed.), *Children—Rights and Childhood*, Routledge, New York.

Feinstein, Clare and Clare O'Kane. 2009. 'Children's and Adolescents' Participation and Protection from Sexual Abuse and Exploitation', *Innocenti Working Papers*, Innocenti Centre, Florence, Italy.

Isin, Engin Fahri and Bryan S. Turner. 2002. *Handbook of Citizenship Studies*, Sage, United Kingdom.

Rajani, Rakesh R. 2000. *Questioning How We Think About Children*, Cultural Survival, Summer, Inc.215 Prospect Street, Cambridge, available at http://www.culturalsurvival. org/publications/cultural-survival-quarterly/none/ introduction-questioning-how-we-think-about-children, accessed on January 7, 2010.

Reddy, Nandana. 2000. *The Right to Organise: The Working Children's Movement in India*, Cultural Survival, Summer, Inc.215 Prospect Street, Cambridge.

———. 2004. National Curriculum Framework—Participation of All Children, National Council of Educational Research and Training, New Delhi, India.

Reddy, Nandana. 2009. *Introduction to Child Rights Based Programming*, Center for Child and Law, National Law School of India, Bangalore, India.

Reddy, Nandana and Damodar Acharya. 2004. *A Unique Revolution*, The Concerned for Working Children, Bangalore.

Reddy, Nandana and Kavita Ratna. 2004. *A Journey in Children's Participation*, The Concerned for Working Children, Bangalore, India.

The United Nations General Assembly Special Session website (http://www.unicef.org/specialsession) accessed in August 2009.

http://labour.nic.in/CWI/Child Labour.htm, accessed on March 21, 2011.

8

'Everywhere We Go, Our Presence is Felt': Reflections on a Governance and Budget-monitoring Project in South Africa

*Shaamela Casseim, Deborah Ewing
and Mabusi Kgwete*

For several years, child rights activists have been monitoring the implementation and realisation of the UN Convention on the Rights of the Child (CRC) in South Africa.[1] They have persistently found a failure to put the CRC into practice, and a lack of children's participation in particular. The current practice shows that children are creating spaces for participation in shaping policy and they are being trained as self-advocates to monitor policy implementation. The South African Constitution and the legal framework of South Africa have made significant strides in terms of law reform and policy development since the end of Apartheid and has been responsive to the needs and rights of children.[2] The Institute for Democracy in South Africa (IDASA) was one of the pioneers in the world to undertake analysis of budgets for children through the setting up of the Child Budget Unit (CBU). This unit was set up in 1995 to conduct research and disseminate information on the government's budgeting for children in South Africa. The CBU built capacity within government and civil society bodies in developing countries to advocate for the generation and use of resources for the realisation of children's rights. Over the first few years, the CBU was engaged in recording government's commitment to children (including those relating to the realisation of child rights and poverty reduction), tracking budget allocations and policy development for children and highlighting service delivery challenges in key government programmes providing services to children. There was no explicit attempt to link monitoring questions to the state's legal obligations to give effect to child rights. In 2001, a critical decision was taken to try and base the monitoring method more on government's obligations to deliver child rights and hence adopt an approach that holds the government accountable for its legal obligations also.

Children growing up in a young democracy have a window of opportunity to advocate for their own rights, and engage in governance issues. Children's participation in governance ensures that their perspectives, experiences and priorities inform, *inter alia*, economic policy and budget allocations. This process has many benefits. In particular, it ensures that:

- Policy and budgets are responsive to children's actual needs—not just their needs as perceived by adults.
- Our society and its economy are shaped by the young people who will one day run it.
- Good citizens are nurtured for the future.

This essay is motivated by two articles from the CRC: Article 4 (available resources) and Article 12: 'State Parties shall assure to the child who is capable of forming his or her views the right to express those views freely in all matters affecting the child, the views of the child being given due weight in accordance with the age and maturity of the child.' It is further motivated by a history of children's leadership in shaping public political discourse in South Africa, which took place long before South Africa ratified the CRC.

This was also the context for the decision taken by IDASA's Children's Budget Unit to initiate a budget monitoring project for children in 2004. The project was entitled 'Budget Monitoring within a Rights-Based Framework: Children Participating in Governance' (CPG).

Its objectives were:
- To create opportunities for children in South Africa to monitor government budgets.
- To improve children's participation in, and monitoring of, budgets for the realisation of rights in a way that ultimately informs policy.
- To contribute to the alignment of government budgeting with rights realisation.

During the first few years of democratic rule in South Africa, the government took a number of significant steps that reflected a strong commitment to reducing child poverty and advancing socioeconomic rights. Budget reform processes since 1996 have also provided the opportunity to promote budget transparency, accountability and public participation. The initiators of the CPG project had both previously worked in youth development initiatives and were able to establish an easy rapport and relationships of trust with children.

This essay documents the involvement of children in budget monitoring in the context of their rights guaranteed to them by the constitution and laws and policies made. It examines the process and lessons learnt from the CPG project. The intention is to provide information to similar projects by reflecting on the experiences of both facilitators and participants. To ensure that the views of children who participated in the project are correctly represented, their voices have been documented throughout.

A Brief History of Children's Leadership and Shaping Politics

South African children have a history of participation, including leadership.[3] Children were instrumental in the struggle against apartheid. 'Organised youth' was a common phrase used during apartheid. Organisations such as the Azanian Students Organisation (AZASO), the South African Youth Congress (SAYCO), Congress of South African

Students (COSAS) and the Soweto Student Representative Council (SSRC) were at the forefront of the liberation struggle. These student organisations had members and leaders from schools and tertiary institutions. They mobilised people across South Africa to protest in different ways against oppressive apartheid laws. It is significant that student organisations were the first to adopt the Freedom Charter. A turning point in the struggle against South Africa was the Soweto uprising of June 16, 1976, which was led by the SSRC. Students, dominated by children between 11 and 18 years, had organised a peaceful march to protest against the 'Afrikaans Medium Decree'. This decree made it mandatory for all African schools to use Afrikaans as the medium of instruction.[4] It was very unpopular because Afrikaans was the language of the oppressor. The protest march began peacefully, but police opened fire on the protesters, predominantly unarmed children. The first casualty of this brutality was 15-year-old Hastings Ndlovu. The photograph of 12-year-old Hector Pietersen's body carried by a fellow student down a Soweto street during this protest made international headlines. The Soweto uprisings, of June 16, 1976 in particular, symbolised the role of children and youth in the struggle against apartheid and saw the emergence of a new set of young leaders.

While students were becoming activists, young people were also recruited into the military wings of the African National Congress (ANC) and the Pan African Congress (PAC). About 100,000 children from coloured and African schools, as well as students from African colleges boycotted classes between 1980 and 1981. This mass school boycott was repeated across South Africa in 1985, when young activists organised marches, rallies and alternative education programmes. By this time, the focus had broadened to include community issues and children and youth took part in rent-increase protests and consumer boycotts.

The political credibility and importance of children during the anti-apartheid struggle were recognised and acknowledged by adult leaders of the struggle during and after apartheid. So much so that, in 1993, Nelson Mandela advocated for the voting age to be 14 years. This proposal was rejected and the voting age was set at 18 years. The rejection was based on the consideration of the political milieu during apartheid and the responsiveness of children to a brutally oppressive regime, which was clearly absent during the 1990s in South Africa.

South African history has witnessed the influence of a politically informed, organised and conscientised cadre of children during apartheid who were instrumental in changing the laws of the land. Today, the South African political landscape—albeit a different one to apartheid—is almost oblivious to the importance and credibility of children's participation.

Citizenship Participation: From Apartheid to Democracy

The majority of the people living in South Africa during apartheid were not regarded as citizens, that is, they were not allowed to vote, had no civil and political rights, and no socioeconomic and cultural rights either. The anti-apartheid struggle was the fight for the right for all South Africans to be recognised, for respect for human rights and good governance. Anti-apartheid activists and leaders ensured that human rights and good governance were enshrined in South Africa's first democratic constitution. The role of civil society during the creation of the world's most liberal constitution ensured that these fundamentals were prevalent through legislation.

After an overhaul of policies and laws, civil society turned its attention to monitoring government service delivery. South Africa's civil society is strong and able to raise its voice, mobilise and question government. A few years after a Mandela-led government was elected, South Africa witnessed growing civil society discontent over the government's lack of service delivery. A common focus of civil society advocacy remains public service delivery. Rising poverty, unemployment, poor performance on housing delivery, the government's weak response to HIV/AIDS, lack of access to clean water, lack of primary health care services and social security grant corruption are some of the areas that have received vehement criticism from activists. In some instances, organised protests by civil society—including unions, social movements, students and residents' groups—have borne stark similarities to the protests organised against the apartheid regime, with mass protests and burnings in townships, police firing at protesting crowds and marches to parliament.[5] At times, civil society has vigorously objected to the government's lack of consultation and failure to facilitate meaningful civic participation in key national-level decision-making processes.

However, government invitations to schools and children's organisations to engage in decision-making processes have been inconsistent and resemble tokenism more than meaningful participation. This essay aims to contribute to a body of knowledge of the experiences of children preparing to monitor their local government budget and service delivery. These experiences of children are located in a theoretical framework of 'rights', 'citizenship' and 'participation'.[6]

From Commitment to Action: Writing Rights into Law in South Africa

The South African Constitution is widely lauded as one of the most progressive and rights-focused in the world and is quoted often by politicians in support of their claims that government is fully committed to children's rights. Commitment is an essential but early step on the road to realising the spectrum of civil, political and socioeconomic rights of children. However, the provisions of the Constitution can yield a decent life for children, and adults, only if legislation, policy, programmes and budgets are put in place. South Africa has made significant strides in terms of law reform and policy development since the end of apartheid.

- *Children's Act and Children's Amendment Act*
  These two pieces of legislation, which took years to draft and have been the subject of intensive and targeted lobbying and advocacy by child rights organisations, help to bring South African law in line with the Constitution. They address many gaps in social service policy for children. Parts of the Children's Act came into effect in 2007 and the rest became law with the passing of the Children's Amendment Act in 2008. They greatly strengthen protection for children and entrench the right to participation.

- *Child Justice Bill*
  This Bill was tabled in 2002 but is still going through public hearings on the latest draft. Among a wide range of provisions, it raises the age of criminal capacity. Although a child of 10 may be found to have criminal capacity, there is a focus on diversion and restorative justice. There are several concerns about measures in the current draft regarding children in conflict with the law. Among them, children over 16 who are convicted of serious offences could be sentenced to life imprisonment.

- *Sexual Offences Act*
  This Act also came into effect over 2007 and 2008. It also represents great advances in the effort to combat a broad range of sexual crimes against children. However, significant provisions relating to prosecution of such crimes and to the protection of children in the criminal justice system were removed or diluted. For example, children are not automatically protected from direct questioning by an accused and the

common law 'cautionary rule' that children's evidence should be treated with caution compared to adults' testimony, remains. Further, the Act does not make all necessary services to children following sexual offences mandatory.

* ***The Education Laws Amendment Act***
  This became law in December 2007. It improves the process for developing education law and policy, and introduces norms and standards, with reporting and monitoring requirements, to promote equal access to quality education.

The lives of many children are lost in the gap between policy and practice. There is an ongoing need to monitor the actions of the state, advocate for measures to realise children's rights and hold government to account for delivery.

Participation, Partnership and Power

There are assumptions about the relationship between 'young people and the world of politics' (Wyness et al. 2004: 81). One of these assumptions is that 'children and young people do not ordinarily inhabit civic or political spheres' (ibid.). Another assumption is that children's 'imputed intellectual and moral incompetence means that they cannot account for themselves in the world and are therefore unable to make judgements on political matters' (ibid.: 82). However, experience has shown that when children are active participants in planning and making decisions, the results are often surprisingly different from when adults decide everything by themselves. That is both the magic and the 'risk' of children's participation.

> 'Power relations pervade any spaces for participation'
>
> *(Cornwall 2002: 8)*

'Children's participation' has gained significant currency in the market of rights, governance and democracy, so that many adults, especially politicians, support it in principle. However, many decision-makers are only comfortable with the stage-managed, performance-style of 'participation' that sees children pleasingly present at events conceived and controlled by adults. The idea of children influencing what, how and why anything is done on their behalf is in itself a serious threat to most decision-makers, be they parents or presidents. Ironically, resistance can be even greater when decision-makers *invite* children to participate, in a public event or process, and those children then have the temerity to express opinions, ask questions or make demands that challenge adult assumptions. This is not surprising—adult members of civil society attempting to engage in public and political processes often face the same reactions as political decision-making is like a members-only club with entry criteria that screen for age, gender, education level, socio-economic status, appearance, language, ability, political and sexual persuasion, and all the other unconstitutional grounds of social exclusion.

In effect, it is, of course, all about power over others. In the case of child participation, the impulse of adults to retain control is reinforced by complex, intertwined notions of protectiveness, responsibility, authority, respect, appropriateness, hierarchy, tradition (that cipher for bad habits), indignation and fear. Suddenly there are boundaries, limits, contexts, unrealistic expectations. Children may participate as long as they don't . . . well, *participate*. Stir the soup but don't add anything to it. Shake hands with the mayor but don't comment on her speech.

We almost forgot about the magic. When children are able to seize opportunities to share insights and experiences, to apply their young minds to old, intractable problems, they often present perspectives and possibilities that have eluded those of us who thought we knew best. Even where child and adult analyses coincide, perceptions of urgency and priority may collide; children may highlight immediate threats to their safety at home, school, or in the community that adults have seen as distant clouds.

We recount here a children's participation initiative, the Children Participating in Governance project, set up through the Children's Budget Unit of Institute for Democracy in South Africa. Much of the reflection comes from participants in the project. This was a concerted effort to promote active, informed and skilled engagement of a diverse group of children in analysing and monitoring budgets from a child rights perspective, and their involvement in local governance. This reflection is prefaced by some sweeping observations about attitudes to children's participation, since the many achievements and few disappointments of the project played out in this ambivalent context. In the project, children and adults learned to function as equal partners in an inclusive, transparent process characterised by robust debate and head-on challenges to preconceptions. Then the children ventured out to engage in environments and processes that were often highly unequal, not at all transparent and where debate was curtailed.

Activating Citizenship: Acquiring 'Skills to Govern'

Citizenship should be an active process. The ability to be part of decision-making processes that include government requires that citizens understand how government works, know who the key stakeholders are, and when best to participate in these processes based on knowledge, abilities and disposition to activate citizenship (Merrifield 2002). Merrifield describes 'knowledge' as an important attribute because 'active citizens need to have a broad framework of understanding that enables them to make judgements in the political sphere'. In order to exercise their rights they must know them, while 'abilities' implies 'that a range of different abilities can all contribute to active citizenship'. The ability to fully participate requires negotiation, reflection, debate and voicing opinion. Merrifield describes 'disposition' as a sense of justice, fairness, and care for others (ibid.: 4). Meaningful participatory citizenship also requires a process of 'active engagement in nurturing voice, building critical consensus, advocating for the inclusion of women, children, illiterate, poor, (people with disabilities) and excluded people, levering open chinks to widen spaces for involvement in decision-making, and building the political capabilities for democratic engagement' (Cornwall 2002: 28).

However, citizen participation linked to good governance is about power and for the most part, citizen participation implies 'adult' participation.[7] In most countries, children are not legally citizens and they do not have the knowledge, ability or the disposition to participate.

The Children Participating in Governance project was started in 2004, with the aim of encouraging children's inclusion in public political discourse and their contribution to governance processes. It is best expressed by one of the participants:

'By learning today, we can acquire the skills to govern a successful nation, when it is handed down to our generation'.[8] (Louise Steyl)

The CPG operated through a partnership with four children's organisations: the Youth Development Programme of the City of Cape Town (YDP); the national Disabled Children's Action Group (DICAG); It's Your Move, a subsidiary of the NGO Molo Songololo (based in Cape Town) and Life Hunters, operating under the auspices of Practical Ministries, an NGO in Port Shepstone, KwaZulu-Natal province. A core group of child facilitators was selected from the membership of these groups. It brought together children from urban, rural and peri-urban areas, from different socioeconomic backgrounds, from communities still geographically separated by apartheid racial planning into black, white, coloured and Indian areas. The group included children with disabilities and children from different linguistic, cultural and religious communities.

> 'I was recruited from my school. . . . I would say I was lucky because my Physics educator informed me that I was selected to participate. Bear in mind I knew nothing about accounting but I think they saw the potential in me!'
>
> *Life Hunters participant Senzo Mkhungo*

The project recognised the need to ensure that, as the children gained knowledge and skills and they were able to advocate on their own behalf, there would be a favourable environment for them to become partners in governance. Therefore, parents, caregivers, educators, NGO patrons and government stakeholders were kept informed of the activities of the children, introduced to budget advocacy and 'primed' for the children's involvement in governance. The children were trained in facilitation skills, including life skills such as self-esteem enhancement, in children's socio-economic rights and in budget analysis and monitoring. They then facilitated workshops with their membership, or constituencies, and other focus groups.

The peer facilitators were trained in three intensive workshops. The first, 'Linking Budgets and Rights', focused on the concept and implications of the progressive realis-ation of socioeconomic rights for children, as entrenched in the South African Constitution, the process for the division of revenue and the competencies of local, provincial and national government. The children also acquired facilitation and gender analysis skills. The second workshop focused on 'Budget Analysis as a Monitoring Tool' and also included budget analysis from a gender perspective. During this workshop, the peer facilitators spent a day visiting com-munity development projects to analyse their budgets and financial management. They visited one of the traditional leaders to learn about how they work alongside elected representatives in local government (there are traditional leaders in six of South Africa's nine provinces). Some of the children and a representative from IDASA also met with the deputy mayor, the youth coordinator of the local municipality and officials to introduce the project and to ask the municipality to involve children in the Integrated Development Planning (IDP) process, including reviewing and commenting on the IDP document.[9] In the final workshop, the children developed a Strategic Budget Advocacy Campaign. They learned about advocacy strategies and strategic planning techniques. This workshop was timed to coincide with the 2006 national budget speech and civil society budget advocacy initiatives. The children participated in a press conference and handed a petition supporting the extension of the Child Support Grant (to include children aged 14–18 years) to officials at Parliament. Some of the

'My duty was to gather all the information that we were trained in so that I would be able to share it with my constituency through workshops. The information also expanded to our families by telling them about the importance of the household budget. We mobilised people in our communities to participate in IDP forums and we told them what to look at. Our aim was to make sure that children's rights issues and what we wanted the local government to do for us as children were covered.'

Smanga Mzindle, peer facilitator from Life Hunters

'I gained a lot of skills, like facilitation skills, how to do a presentation and how to communicate and interact with people who are regarded as of high authority or superiors. I also know that the budget is important to all of us; before I thought it was only for the people who are on grants, taxpayers, people who use alcohol and cigarettes. My involvement taught me a lot about the budget.'

Khanyisile Mbhele, a fellow Life Hunters

group watched the budget speech in Parliament and had the opportunity to ask the minister of finance questions live on national television. The whole group attended a meeting of the Joint Monitoring Committee on Finance and posed further questions to the minister.

To gain a better understanding of the role that they could play in budget monitoring, five peer facilitators travelled to Brazil in December 2005 for a learning exchange with Centre for the Defence of Children and Adolescents (CEDECA) in Fortaleza, Ceará. The Brazilian child budget advocacy network, Rede OPA, arranged meetings with government officials who explained their participation processes and the two groups exchanged information about children's participation in different spheres of life.

◊

'Knowing Ourselves and Representing Others'

The process of involving children was as significant as the content of their training and intervention, and it was important that they understood their roles. Children were selected to be trained as peer facilitators based on recommendations from their organisations and educators, their own potential as also their commitment to passing forward and sharing with other children what they learned. They took this very seriously. The children selected to represent the project in Brazil were very mindful that they were acting as ambassadors.

'Going to Brazil, flying outside the country, I was shocked at first. On this trip, we were all excited but our facilitators made us focus on and not lose sight of our goal even if we were experiencing something new and beyond our expectations. I learned that it was not about me, I was representing other children so I had to gather as much information as I could so that I could give feedback to others and they would be satisfied.'

Zakithi Dlamini, Life Hunters

**Monitoring government's budget for children's rights—
The Case of the Children's Budget Unit at IDASA**
A government's budget is an important instrument for civil society to use to examine government's commitment to its legal obligations to good governance and poverty alleviation. The budget tells civil society how far government has turned rhetoric into reality. This is a persistent challenge for all governments that have ratified the CRC; the challenge is even more persistent when a country like South Africa has a Constitution that moves towards 'domestication' of the CRC. Domestication requires budgeting for implementation and service delivery; and, budgeting for implementation and service delivery, in turn, creates the opportunity for civil society to monitor government's performance.

The Children's Budget Unit at Institute for Democracy in South Africa was created to monitor the South African budget in relation to the domestication of children's rights in South Africa. The CBU started its work around 1996, during the budget transformation process in the country, amid policy and legal reform. These processes and reforms aimed to give effect to the South African Constitution. The Bill of Rights in the Constitution applies to all residents but Section 28 spells out the rights of all children to social security, basic social services, health services and shelter, *inter alia*. The reality for most South African children, however, does not reflect the high ideals of the Constitution. It was the sharp contrast between paper rights and reality that gave the impetus to research the government's budget obligations for fulfilling, protecting and promoting the rights of children, and monitoring the government's budgets to comment on whether the government is meeting these obligations.

A fundamental for the CBU was to work with organisations and to support their advocacy efforts to realise the children's rights. One of these advocacy projects focused on improving the coverage of government's key child poverty alleviation programme, the Child Support Grant (CSG). The Child Support Grant (CSG) was introduced in 1998 and targeted the poorest of children aged 0–6 years. The poorest children were defined as children living in the bottom 30 per cent of South Africa's households when ranked according to income. On the basis of this definition, the government's original aim, when it introduced the grant in April 2008, was to reach 3 million children in the said age cohort by April 2003. The CBU worked with advocacy and research institutions in South Africa to advocate for:

(i) An inflation-related increase per fiscal year for the grant;
(ii) An increase in the age cohort to all children under the age of 18 years;
(iii) An adjustment in the means test so as to better target, and include, all poor children;
(iv) Better information about intra-provincial targeting of poor children and,
(v) Better information about the income status of CSG beneficiaries.[10]

A key driver of the advocacy for changing the CSG was the Alliance for Children's Entitlement to Social Security (ACESS), which is made up of more than 1,200 children's sector organisations across South Africa. The CBU, along with other research organisations, provided research information that could support ACESS in its advocacy. During 2000–2006, the CBU persistently produced credible information that showed that government has the resources available to budget for

(i) Year-on-year inflation-related increases for all social security grants;
(ii) Child support grants for all children under 18 years, and
(iii) An adjustment in the means test so as to address the inflation-related erosion since April 1998.

In 2001, the Ministry of Finance announced that all grants would receive year-on-year inflation-related increases and, since 2002, the government of South Africa has progressively increased the age cohort receiving these grants from 0–6 years to 14 years. At the time of writing, the Ministries of Finance and Social Development, and various provincial ministers, were respondents in a case in the High Court of South Africa, brought by civil society, to challenge as unconstitutional the government's failure to extend the CSG to all children under the age of 18 years,* despite the fact that *it has the resources to do so.*

The CBU is no longer functioning as a single unit in Idasa but has been mainstreamed into the organisation's Economic Governance Programme. The value of using budgets as a tool to monitor government's obligations and commitments has spread to many organisations and has been used to support civil society advocacy campaigns, as well as court cases. The impact of civil society engaging with budgets as an advocacy tool can be far-reaching for policy and legal reform; the goal should be good governance and a reduction of poverty and marginalisation.

*Note: In 2011, the CSC was extended to include children upto 18 years.

Apart from the excitement of Brazil, there were many 'firsts' for the children. The training workshops took place in Johannesburg, Cape Town and Durban, so all the participants had to fly at least once. It was their first time on a plane; for some it was the first time anyone in their family had flown; and for most, it was the first time they had left their home town. More importantly, it was the first time that the children had encountered other children from such diverse backgrounds, living and working together on equal terms.

Handling statistics and stereotypes

There was a lot to absorb, in terms of information and personal and group dynamics. Getting to grips with revenue flows, budget shares and balance statements in English, the common but second language for most participants, was challenging enough. Then there were assumptions and stereotypes to work through. Looking back, many of the children felt enriched by the exposure.

Smanga, one of the young participants observed:

'I benefited a lot. Being informed that I was selected to be part of this, being at the airport knowing that I will be leaving my province for the first time in my life, having people who are organising everything for me and being the first person in my family to be on a flight. The most important part of the project was gaining knowledge, and knowing that it was not for me but for other children in our constituencies. I gained a lot of skills, accounting, leadership, facilitation and communication. We also learned how to communicate with different people since our group was diverse and in our first workshop there was a lot of tension. We grew up with an idea that Black and White people don't sit and share their experiences but this project changed all that.'

> 'We are all the same, if you are in a wheelchair or you use both legs. This training helped me mentally and emotionally as I used to feel pity for a disabled person and I know now that we have lots in common. I shouldn't pity as people need no pity but fair treatment.'
>
> *Khanyisile, a participant*

However, as the children learned about each other's lives, some barriers came down and others went up. Language differences proved divisive, with groups and individuals feeling excluded by use of home languages outside of the training. A session in which children shared information about their family lives and circumstances evoked painful emotions. Smanga observed how people tended to hide the fact that they lived in impoverished circumstances and tried to give the impression that they were superior, because they were ashamed to be open. 'We all hide where we're coming [from] because we're buying each people's faces' (meaning putting on a front or a mask).

The skills and personal qualities of the participants shattered a lot of stereotypes about race, colour, gender and disability. For example, tracking allocations in the huge budget book and debating spending priorities with children using sign language was a revelation to many. Being challenged about views on gender by assertive young rural women was a wake-up call for others. Ideas about 'typical' irresponsible boys who get schoolgirls pregnant and leave them to face the consequences alone were shifted by the 17-year-old father who proudly brought his son to one workshop and spoke of his plans for supporting him with his girlfriend.

Youth Development Programme participant Louise Steyl said that working with the DICAG group especially taught her how to deal with diversity: 'I learnt a lot about myself and how I react to others. I honestly felt ashamed of how I used to think. Because I had never been exposed to so many different people before, I didn't know exactly how to react, or understand children with disabilities.' Alex Henry, one of the DICAG representatives, who uses a wheelchair due to cerebral palsy, saw the project not as a personal opportunity to be 'included' but as a chance to raise awareness about diversity with mainstream youth and to encourage youth with disabilities to reach for their dreams. According to Alex Henry, 'Part of my dream is to show disabled youth—yes, it may take you a longer time, but you can get what you want and be where you want to be. . . . I find that the mainstream youth do know someone who is disabled but they don't know how to interact with them. Then you get someone like me that does what he does.... It shows them "disabled but still able", hence differently able.' One of the girls summed up her experience after the training, 'Ever since I've been part of this project I have grown to be another person, all good. I've learnt so much in different ways, spiritually, mentally, and emotionally but the list is endless. I cannot put what I feel in words. Yes I come from a home and I'm raised by a disabled mother but I have never worked closely with disabled teenagers . . . at first it wasn't easy, 'cause we live under expectations but today I stand in awe of the things I've learnt from them.' Changing expectations, extending perceptions of the possible, is a key element of successful advocacy. These encounters taught the children to look beyond their immediate realities. Embracing diversity was not just a matter of personal growth, it was critical for the objectives of the project. As Zakithi described, 'Working together with children from other parts of the country was good knowing that you are not only representing your province but children of South Africa. I believe that was the best strategy to be used to work together as children of our country because if we approach government as children they will recognise that what we are doing is important. South Africa is a very diverse country so you must learn to work and deal with different people, to work towards a common goal that as a group you would like to achieve.'

An ideology about children, and adults' relationships with children, was fundamental to the facilitators' design of all the workshops, and the relationship development between the facilitators and the children participating in this project. Alderson states that, 'Treating children with respect can markedly increase their competence' (Alderson in Lister 2007: 711). Lister further states that 'like adults, children build competence and confidence through direct experience: participation leads to greater levels of confidence, which in turn enhances the quality of participation.' Over the 18-month period that the facilitators worked with the children, the changes in the children were apparent. These changes were not only regarding their confidence to assert and voice their opinions, but also their ability to self-reflect on attitudes and prejudices towards children in the CPG who were initially regarded as 'other', that is, children with disabilities, poorer children, children living in rural areas, children who were less confident speaking in English. Smanga's remark, 'We all hide where we come from' captures the mood and the facilitators worked hard to create a safe environment for the children participating in this project since this was the key to children voicing their opinions about feeling violated and discriminated against by peers in the project. The emotive and painful session alluded to above, was an eye opener for many children. During that session, children reflected, voiced opinion, stood up for their rights and were able to communicate with each other.

Expanding Budget Literacy:
Facilitating knowledge and advocacy
for monitoring public budgets

Facilitating workshops for children between the ages of 12 and 18 years is usually challenged by the level of interest of the participants and maintaining the interest of the participants. These challenges are combined with the facilitators' ability to steer away from a 'teaching-orientated' style of learning and instead, create a learning environment of conscientisation, critical thinking, questioning, reflection, self-discovery and voicing opinion. The facilitators of the CPG designed the project bearing in mind these challenges. In addition, there was that other, very obvious challenge: the looming threat of adults rejecting the knowledge and abilities of the children.

The three workshops followed a routine of facilitating information by first, using common games, simulation exercises, collages, drawings, jigsaw and crossword puzzles, visiting government institutions and meeting officials, watching videos and conducting interviews; second, reflecting on the knowledge created during the first step; and third, applying the knowledge to different situations important for budget advocacy. However, training children to learn to read budget books, to read the story behind the numbers, to do budget calculations, and to tell their story from the budget books, was a highlight for facilitators and participants. Like their adult counterparts in budget analysis and budget advocacy workshops, the children were unsure if they had the ability to do the number crunching. At the start of the second workshop, 'Budget Analysis as a Monitoring Tool', many participants were anxious because they were 'not good at maths', had 'failed accountancy' or 'not good with numbers'.

This workshop marked a turning point in the participants' understanding of their own abilities, and opening up a space of confidence and self-discovery. Once some of the participants understood that the analyses were easy to do, that they were able to read the budget books and understand where to get the information they sought, they became peer facilitators and supported the learning of their peers in that workshop. Participants were surprised at their own abilities to do the basic budget calculations—'my teacher told me I was not good at math' was heard from more than one participant—and to connect the calculations with the information they were looking for to support their advocacy. After the first day, participants did not want to stop working because of their excitement and their amazement at their abilities to do budget analysis. Participants worked until ten o' clock that night, because they wanted to learn and put their learning to test.

> *'It is really not that difficult' was a common*
> *cry at the end of this workshop.*

Standing Up to Rights Violations

One of the many challenges of children's participation is to realise the right to participate without jeopardising other rights. Beyond responsibilities to ensure children's physical security and comfort, one must protect dignity and emotional well-being. Challenging the status quo is rarely conducive to this.

During the Johannesburg training, one of the female participants, away from her family for the first time, was sexually harassed and intimidated in her hotel room by a participant attending another conference at the same venue. One of the boys went to her aid and eventually gave evidence in a disciplinary hearing that resulted in the man being dismissed and the company paying compensation. The girl's parents had initially opposed her participation and after this incident withdrew her from the group.

The children and adults who made the trip to Brazil were treated with great warmth and respect by their hosts. Sadly, they endured obduracy, ignorance and insult from Home Affairs in South Africa, both in securing passports and in seeking assistance for the children with disabilities. A further blow was that efforts by the reference group, including one of the disabled children, to publicly challenge Home Affairs from a disability rights stance were dissuaded by IDASA, which wanted the matter dealt with discreetly.

The participants were generally strengthened in the face of such challenges by the support they received from the project and each other. They went on to run workshops for their own organisations and broader constituencies. They also began to engage in advocacy at school and with local government structures.

Being Heard

The CPG project was motivated by the general sentiment that children lack the capacities to participate in public policy debates and advocacy. The project was keen to work with children who were already leaders in other projects and who were keen to be self-advocates for children's rights. The CPG project used the children's existing, foundational knowledge of rights and responsibilities. The project coordinators deemed this knowledge to be an essential foundation and reference on which to build knowledge of advocacy in the budget process relative to children's rights advocacy. This was the relatively easy part; getting government officials to recognise the knowledge and capabilities of children was the more difficult challenge. Merrifield (2002: 4) states that '(we) need to ask both *what* knowledge is essential, and *whose* knowledge is deemed important. In order to exercise rights citizens must know them. In order to participate and have their voice heard, citizens need to understand power and how to have impact.'

Children's capacities evolve with age; in practice, the actual ages at which a child acquires competencies vary according to her life experiences, and social and cultural environment on the one hand, and the nature of the competencies and the situation in which they are required to be exercised on the other (Lister 2007). At every stage there must be regard for 'children's right to respect for their capacities' and for children's agency. In practice, adults consistently underestimate children's capacities, raising questions about their ability to assess them (ibid.).

Gaventa argues that the development of critical consciousness is important for full citizenship. A critical or questioning attitude, scepticism toward authority, can be seen as a disposition that is essential to good governance. Connected to this is the citizen's sense of efficacy—a sense that one can have an impact, and the self-confidence to attempt it (Gaventa 1999). In the CPG project, children were delighted to find they were listened to. They became confident in gathering facts and developing arguments to make their case. Children were represented on the national reference group, which gave guidance and support to the initiative. The KwaZulu-Natal group made presentations on children's needs and how they would like to be included in decision-making, to representatives of their local and district municipalities, and the Department of Health. One of the representatives said: 'We attended a meeting at IDASA offices where I met adults from different organisations who were full of great ideas and also listened to our ideas.' Another commented, 'I learnt that children do have a voice and that there are people willing to listen to us. . . . I learnt to use my power I have as a child and I've become confident around a lot of people.'

Khanyisile was proud that their input led to the establishment of an Office on the Rights of the Child at the district municipality.

I learned the importance of knowing the past and present situation or state of what you want to talk about if you are approaching government officials, and to make your point based on those facts. Activism is important; you must know what is happening in your municipality and be known by role players so that you will be able to monitor the budget. Budget monitoring was the focus point in this project but it helped me to monitor other programmes or services that the government is providing for the communities.

Senzo felt their engagement with the municipality opened the door for other children. 'It enabled us to get involved in making decisions that affect our lives because there is a youth desk. Although we may not be participating in it now, we hope that children who are invited to participate are there to represent other children's needs.'

Alex was among the few who had the chance to ask Finance Minister Trevor Manual a question about the national budget. He recalls,

I commented that it was good that he was increasing disability grants, social welfare provisions, etc. Then I said there was a need to invest more in accessible transport because once a disabled person is given access that person can provide for himself and earn a gainful salary, thus lessening the burden on welfare and grants. Then I asked what percentage of the taxi recapitalisation programme budget was being used in this regard. He and the DG [Director General] weren't sure how to respond but eventually said that they were investigating the matter and funds would be allocated.

Smanga could not be in Parliament for the budget speech but he made sure that no one in his class missed it, 'At school, I initiated that when the national budget speech was delivered, all the Grade 12 learners must be given an opportunity to watch it, so the school organised television sets for this.'

Real Politics

Alongside these individual and collective achievements, there were some disappointments and frustrations. It proved difficult to keep up the momentum of engagement with local government and involvement from the NGOs was erratic. In Cape Town, politics impeded the integration of YDP into the city's youth participation processes and one of the NGOs failed to give the children's group any back-up. In KwaZulu-Natal, efforts to establish Life Hunters as an autonomous youth organisation faltered for lack of support from the parent NGO. At home, school and in the community, some children encountered resistance to the notion of children's rights, as somehow undermining adults' rights. T. H. Marshall, renowned author on 'citizenship' wrote about children and young people as 'citizens in the making' (quoted in Lister 2007: 696). Khanyisile Mbhele from the Life Hunters group challenged this notion when she wrote:

> *I am told that I have freedom of speech*
> *But also told that I am showing disrespect*
> *In fact they should remember that*
> *I am the future but also the present.*
> (Khanyisile Mbhele, 2005, aged 17)

Three years on, Smanga says:

> About the decision-makers, especially government officials, I would say most of them don't take us seriously; they still look at us as children. I think that is where we still need to fight as children. I remember at one of the IDP forums in my ward where the local municipality mayor misquoted something from the national budget. I'd just been trained on budget analysis. I raised my hand so that I could correct what she said. They gave me the opportunity, I introduced

myself, and the project, then I started to correct what the mayor had said. They did not allow me to finish that; I was intimidated and just imagine how many people went home with wrong information thinking it was correct because the mayor said so.

Government officials have a problem. They don't want to listen. They think they know it all, especially when they are at work but when they meet you in town or other places they would ask you what you wanted to say or what you meant in a certain meeting, then they understand, which makes no difference because it ends there.

Khanyisile was disappointed that the initial positive response from the municipality did not lead anywhere, 'After our presentation, nothing much came out of it. We are not blaming the municipality; both sides did not make a follow-up. However, when we had our trainings and invited the municipality to do presentations they did not attend.'

Kulynych asserts that it is critical that debates over children's citizenship recognise the development of citizenship as a political entity and 'recognition of children as politically relevant beings' (Kulynych 2001: 231). Similarly, Roche (1999) equates 'being counted as a member of the community' with participation and proposes that the 'the demand that children be included in citizenship is simply a request that children be seen as members of society with a legitimate and valuable voice and perspective' (quoted in Lister 2007: 701).

Lister says that:

> while on one level, all children are members of the community and therefore have the status of citizens in a thin sense, recognition of children as citizens in the thicker sense of active membership requires facilitating their participation as political and social actors. This is about more than just participation in

> individual decisions about a child's own life made by
> parents and professionals. It also means participation
> in wider collective decision-making. (Lister 2007: 708)

In almost every circumstance, children have less power than adults because society and its institutions are organised by adults. It is not our argument that children should enjoy exactly the same civil and political rights as adults but that there should be acknowledgement of the responsibilities that children exercise, the abilities of children to provide credible information and to make judgements in the decision-making process. Recognising the power of children to participate is as important as respecting the right of the child not to participate.

We are not advocating for changing the children's right to be children (as understood in particular contexts) but asking adults to 'transform their relationship to children particularly in terms of respectful behaviour and changes in the way participatory citizenship is practised in order to accommodate children' (Lister 2007: 715).

Older children and young people are expected to assume 'adult modes of behaving and communicating' so that 'it requires little change on the part of adults'. 'Citizenship for young children, on the other hand, requires some effort on the part of adults to accommodate children's varied modes of doing, saying and being' (B. Neale quoted in Lister 2007: 711). There is an expectation that children should fit with the adult way of thinking and doing. Khanyisile went on to conclude, 'People have lost hope in the government, especially youth. Many times when the municipality or another forum is doing an outreach, people don't attend. In order to mobilise, they ask for our assistance to achieve that goal and they would vanish after that.'

Although the children were highly motivated to pass on what they had learned and encourage other children to become involved in budget advocacy, they felt they needed ongoing support. However, towards the end of the funding period, IDASA relocated the Children's Budget Unit and the project managers left. Of course, children move on too. They become adults, they leave school and home. They join new groups and take on new causes. At the same time, many of the 'graduates' of the CPG claim that their experiences in the project have influenced what they are doing today.

Being the Change They Want to See

Khanyisile is employed by a bank and has been appointed to the staff committee. Smanga is in his last year of school and is active in youth and community committees, representing children's needs. He says, 'At home, I think being listened to depends on how you carry yourself. Showing respect towards adults and all that can give you the advantage to suggest how the budget should be drafted.'

He suggests that successful children's participation projects should be integrated into governance rather than closing when funding ends. Zakithi feels that young people should be given support to access funding for their own projects. Trained youth should set goals and pursue opportunities to participate, 'rather than wait for adults to give a go ahead'.

Children's participation initiatives, including the CPG, are time-bound funded programmes, and do not change the way societies operate. The best hope is that the individuals who participate will motivate and educate others to engage actively in governance practices, wherever adults have been sensitised to the concept and the possibilities of child participation.

The 'CPG generation' spent most of their time in environments controlled and managed by adults but they too are now adults, with the potential to promote the active citizenship of children, if they don't fall into the perennial 'we know best' trap. Several of the group, and the former project managers, made presentations at the launch of an initiative to make children partners in city planning in KwaZulu-Natal. Zakithi believes that all who took part in the project continue to influence attitudes and behaviour towards child participation in governance: 'Everywhere we go, our presence is felt.'

Conclusion

The CPG project aimed to increase children's commitment by being members of children's rights organisations, to encourage their participation in the budget process and to advocate for children's rights in the budget. The participation required a process that provided children with the tools to engage in different public political spaces. This not only required direct interaction with public officials, but also that children reflect on their knowledge of rights and responsibilities and how these were indeed internalised.

Advocating children's active citizenship and participation requires more than opening spaces for children in the decision-making process. Simultaneous to this advocacy is to support children's ability to be self-advocates, to change adult spaces of decision-making so that they enable citizenship participation and create public political spaces for children, persons with disabilities, women, illiterate persons, excluded people, people living in poverty, people living outside of cities. Children's citizenship participation requires a change in the processes of participation, and increasing the knowledge and abilities of children.

The voices of Zakithi Dlamini, Alex Henry, Khanyisile Mbhele, Senzo Mkhungo, Smanga Mzindle, Louise Steyl and others are testimony to children's citizenship participation and the processes that contribute to reinforce children's sense of belonging to a community as well as building their skills and capacities vital for strong and effective citizenship.

ℬ

Notes

[1] The authors wish to thank and acknowledge the time given by all the young people consulted for this essay. Their insights on and reflection of their participation in the CPG project are the foundation of this contribution and the impetus for advocating for children citizenship and participation in governance. In addition, we acknowledge the intellectual resource and commitment to civic education of the project manager and co-facilitator of the CPG project, Christina Nomdo.

[2] Additional information for this section is drawn from *Child Gauge 2007*, a barometer of child rights published by the South African research and advocacy body the Children's Institute, Cape Town (http://www.ci.org.za). The authors of this chapter take responsibility for any errors.

[3] Children are recognised as persons under the age of 18 years.

[4] The apartheid system classified the South African population into racial groups, the primary ones being African (referring to the indigenous peoples from groups such as the Xhosa and the Zulu); Coloureds (referring to those of mixed origin); Indians (referring to persons of Indian descent); and Whites (referring to descendents of European settlers). These race labels were used to delineate a hierarchy of citizenship and privilege, with Whites being the preferred class of citizens; Indians, Coloureds and Africans being discriminated against and oppressed in varying degrees; and Africans being the worst off. Although South Africa is no longer segregated according to race labels, one of the residual effects of the apartheid system is the continued existence of racially homogenous communities (Christopher 1994: 103–16).

[5] Townships are planned, contained and enclosed areas far from South African cities created during apartheid for African, Indian and Coloured populations. In post-apartheid South Africa, townships remain the home for the majority of working-class people, and typically contain a mix of low-cost houses and informal structures (shacks). They are high in population density and are under resourced.

⁶ The authors understand that citizenship is informed by relationships between the state and the individual, relationships between individuals, freedom of association and the ability to express identity, and a sense of belonging. The authors' understanding of a 'sociologically informed' definition of citizenship is with reference to Isin and Turner as stated in the *Handbook of Citizenship Studies* (Isin and Turner 2002). This understanding is based on articulating citizenship 'as a social process through which individuals and social groups engage in claiming, expanding or losing rights'.

⁷ The authors understand the fundamental elements of good governance to mean respect for human rights and the rule of law, transparency, accountability, participation and legitimacy.

⁸ Louise Steyl was a peer facilitator from the Cape Town Youth Development Programme and shares her experiences of the project.

⁹ A statutory process for participatory planning, implementation and monitoring of local government service delivery.

¹⁰ This would give insight into the extent to which inputs and outputs in the CSG are flowing to the poorest of children.

𝄢

References

Cornwall, A. 2002. 'Making Spaces, Changing Places: Situating Participation in Development', *IDS Working Paper No. 170*, Institute for Development Studies, Brighton.

Christopher, A. J. 1994. *The Atlas of Apartheid*. Routledge, London and Witwatersrand University Press, Johannesburg.

Gaventa, J. 1999. 'Citizen Knowledge, Citizen Competence, and Democracy Building', in S. I. Elkin and K. E. Sotan (eds), *Citizen Competence and Democratic Institutions*, The Pennsylvania State University Press, University Park PA.

Isin, Engin F. and Bryan S. Turner. 2002. *Handbook of Citizenship Studies*, Sage Publications, USA.

Kulynych, J. 2001. 'No Playing in the Public Sphere: Democratic Theory and the Exclusion of Children', in *Social Theory and Practice*, 27(2): 231.

Lister, R. 2007. 'Why Citizenship: Where, When and How Children?' in *Theoretical Inquiries in Law* 8(2), Article 13, available at http://www.bepress.com/til/default/vol8/iss2/art13, accessed on March 17, 2011.

Merrifield, J. 2002. 'Learning Citizenship', IDS Working Paper 158, Institute of Development Studies, Brighton, UK.

Roche, J. 1999. 'Children: Rights, Participation and Citizenship', in R. Lister, 'Why Citizenship: Where, When and How Children?', in *Theoretical Inquiries in Law* 8(2), Article 13, available at http://www.bepress.com/til/default/vol8/iss2/art13, accessed on March 17, 2011.

Wyness, Michael, Lisa Harrison and Ian Buchanan. 2004. 'Childhood, Politics and Ambiguity: Towards an Agenda for Children's Political Inclusion', *Sociology*, 38 (February): 81–99.

9

Monitoring the Public Budget with Adolescents: The Experience of Cedeca-Ceará

Margarida Maria Marques

Introduction

In 1999, The Centre for the Defence of Children and Adolescents, (Cedeca) in the state of Ceará, Brazil, initiated its programme of monitoring the Fortaleza city budget. This was based on the understanding that the struggle for the human rights of children and young people must find space in the discussion of public policies that give effect to these rights.The Brazilian Constitution had already declared protection of children's rights as a priority. Laws too carried a clear stipulation to have first call for children on public resources. In 2003, Cedeca initiated a project for empowering children and young people in public budgeting. This essay is based on this project. Brazilian society has managed, through a process of broad social mobilisation, to have written into the 1988 Federal Constitution that children and young people have rights and that these need to be fully protected as a matter of absolute priority. Further, the Children and Adolescents Act (ECA), stipulates that meeting this priority envisages children having first call on public resources. Unfortunately, the democratic culture of the country does not fully recognise the rights of children and young people nor does it allow for the exercising of social control on public budgets. The issues raised in this essay are fundamentally about the social control of the state and the right of participation of children and adolescents and the role of the state and society in 'invisibilisation' of infancy. The essay also discusses the contradictions between the improvements in institutions and the effectiveness of the law, with special reference to guaranteeing the rights of children and adolescents. Ceará is located in the north-east of Brazil, South America, which is a country with the fifth largest population in the world—187.2 million—and the fifth biggest territory. The north-east is the poorest region in Brazil and characterised by gross social inequalities. Between 1994 and 2004, they dropped by 32.6 per cent to 26.6 per cent thousand live births (UNICEF 2005). Ceará has a total population of 8.2 million, including about 2.8 million children up to 17 years of age. That represents approximately 35 per cent of the people born in Ceará (*called cearenses*). According to the National Household Sample Survey (PNAD) 2006 of the Brazilian Institute of Geography and Statistics (IBGE), an overwhelming 56.3 per cent of the population is below the poverty line, which also means that more than half the people live below half the minimum wage per month.

The reality of the children in Ceará is hard: an infant mortality rate of 29.9 per thousand live births, worse than the country average of 28.4, which itself is very high. Diarrhoea-related diseases, usually easily fought, account for 5.2 per cent of the under-5 infant mortality rate in Ceará; while it is 3.4 per cent for Brazil. According to the State of Ceará Government Accountability Office (Tribunal de Contas do Estado do Ceará—TCE), the hospital bed occupancy rate of children between 0 and 5 years for diarrhoea was 27.5 per cent of the total in 2006, higher than 25 per cent in 2005.[1]

These figures give the essential backdrop in which Brazilian children and adolescents live and are needed to understand the places in the society destined for them as well as the challenges faced by the state in exercising social control. What is particularly distressing is that the state itself violates the rights of children and adolescents.

Who is CEDECA-CEARÁ?

The Centre for the Defence of Children and Adolescents Cedeca-Ceará is a non-governmental organisation which fights for the rights of children and adolescents. It was established in 1994 as a result of several organisations concerned for the rights of children and adolescents coming together in the city of Fortaleza. Cedeca-Ceará, was an answer to the extreme violation of rights at that time. Because of its historical exclusion from the rest of Brazil, the state of Ceará still bears the scars of this neglect.

The years that preceded the establishment of Cedeca-Ceará were characterised by the struggle for democratisation of the country. Like the whole of Latin America, Brazil suffered for more than 20 years under a military dictatorship. Many social movements emerged at that time, such as the women's movements, movement against high prices, the popular organisations in the city districts, human rights groups, environmentalists, among others.

It was around this time that a movement aimed at combating the violation of children and adolescents' rights was structured, motivated especially by the great number of children and adolescents living on the streets, directly exposed to all forms of violence and exploitation. This movement gained momentum as the situation became serious, especially in the big Brazilian cities, as a result of a model of development that pushed several people out of the country to the cities. Children and adolescents were the most affected by this migration.

From this process of social mobilisation emerged two important national legal references that are directly linked to the establishment of Cedeca-Ceará: the Brazilian Federal Constitution of 1988 and the Statute of the Child and Adolescent—ECA (Law no. 8069) in 1990. The ratification by Brazil of the UN Convention on the Rights of the Child (CRC), too led to some major changes.[2]

In the Constitution of 1988, the social movement and the movement for infants' rights in particular, managed to introduce a precept which profoundly altered the way that the country had so far looked at infancy, thus bringing in a formal recognition of children and adolescents as citizens in their own right. It is Article 227 which establishes that children and adolescents are a priority.[3]

The adoption of this law was deeply influenced by the discussions and the world-wide acceptance of the CRC—the first international law to recognise children and adolescents as subjects of rights.[4]

It is this context that led to the establishment of Cedeca-Ceará and also guided its emergence as an organisation for the defence of children and adolescents' human rights. Thus Cedeca-Ceará's interventions are based on a legal framework that has emerged out of the social struggles, taking into consideration both the structural and historical causes of the violations of children and adolescents' rights. This approach is also based on the knowledge that the violation of rights which affects children in the country (and in the world) is the result of a social and historical construction of a concept of infancy and of its place in the society. It is understood that the violation affects some social groups differently such as black people, homosexuals, women, as well as, of course, the different social classes. All these factors cause inequalities and exclusion that affect children and adolescents strongly.

It is based on this understanding that Cedeca-Ceará formulates its mission, which is to defend children and adolescents' rights, especially when the violation is a direct act of commission or omission of the state or of public authorities. To act based on this perspective means to understand that since its formation the Brazilian state has had the mark of Portuguese colonisation, which suppressed the local Indian population, expropriated the country's natural resources, smuggled millions of Africans to slave on Brazilian soil, thus creating a history of exclusion and inequalities which persists until today. It is also necessary to highlight the issue of gender as power is remarkably male, therefore patriarchal, and that determines the social relations.

A state built on these foundations is not only at the service of the dominant elite but this historical heritage brings consequences to the public administration as well as to the public policies, and in particular to the policies aimed at the socially invisible majorities such as children, adolescents, women, black people and homosexuals. It is based on this understanding of the state, where there is an institutionalisation of violence and where some groups including adolescents and children continue to be voiceless, that Cedeca-Ceará was based on the following three rights:

- **Right to protection—fighting institutional violence:** The organisation plans actions against police violence, abuse of children under the responsibility of the state, lack of assistance from the public service, defence of the rights of adolescents with problems with the law and control for the attribution of responsibilities for sexual offenders.
- **Right to participation: Social control of the state and of the public administration:** As part of this, the focus is on the monitoring of the public budget. Cedeca-Ceará defends the right to participation of children and adolescents as a human right; therefore, it encourages the political participation of the infant-juvenile population.
- **Right to development: Defence of the Cultural, Social and Economic Rights of Children and Adolescents:** This includes all the actions of mobilisation and legal protection of these rights focusing on the right to education.

Social Control of the State and of the Public Administration: Public Budget and a Political Tool

The process of the Brazilian budgetary projection occurs through a cycle called budgetary cycle which is guided by a federal law (Law no. 4.320/64) at the three administration levels: city, state and federal. This projection has three phases:

First, a strategic projection for the whole administration period is made, that is, four years. This phase is called Pluri-annual Plan (Plano Plurianual, PPA) and is always made in the first year of the administration with its validity starting in the second year and finishing in the first year of the next administration.

The following phase is the Organic Budget Law (*Lei de Diretrizes Orçamentárias, LDO*), which is the phase in which the public administrator explains the strategic projection included in the PPA for the period of one year and determines the policies for each year.

The final phase is the Annual Budget Law (*Lei Orçamentária Annual, LOA*). It is in this phase that the budget will be detailed and the amount of money and goals for the financial year established.

The executive power in the government has the initiative for the three budget laws and it must send the proposed budget bill to the legislative power which will discuss the proposal, alter some points through amendments and approve it.[5] Until recently, the only way for the society to intervene in the setting up of the public budget was by proposing amendments along with some members of parliament or by political pressure for the approval of the amendment.

In the 1980s, in some Brazilian cities, left-wing parties managed to have candidates elected and a new experience of participatory budget discussion started. In the places in which it was implemented, the population had the opportunity to voice their opinion about what should be the priorities in the public budget. It is important to highlight that this change in the process was a victory for the population that had always fought for transparency and democracy. However, there are still many hurdles to overcome, principal among which is that the public administrator does not have the obligation to strictly obey what is approved.

For the organised social movements, it has become clearer that much more than a public administration planning tool, the public budget is the expression of a political option of the administrators and it expresses a model of economic development. This is true of Brazil as well.

In the last few years, the governments have tried to adjust the budgets in order to accumulate a financial surplus and thus guarantee the resources to honour the commitments with the public debt.[6] In Brazil, the financial surplus has been growing and it reached 6.51 per cent of the country's GDP in April 2007. In order to create this surplus, taxes have to be raised, the burden of which falls on the working class because the taxes are collected on consumption rather than on income. This model has also guaranteed incentives with public resources by means of fiscal renouncement, that is, companies and industries are given specific tax exemption in order to encourage them to take root in very poor regions with high unemployment rates where the work force is very cheap. Such a policy favours the economic groups corporate rather than the local people and their development.

Another example of the use of the public budget by the government is the curtailment of the public resources, which is a mechanism through which the government decides which areas or programmes will have less or no funds at all. With these mechanisms, the government has failed to fully execute the budget for the social sectors.

Therefore, despite the fact that Brazil has one of the most modern legal systems in the world as far as children and adolescents are concerned, with the legal provision of priorities in the definitions of the public policies and resources, it is precisely the analysis of the budget execution and of the economic policies that enables us to verify the exact priorities of our country's government.[7]

Unfortunately, 17 years after the approval of the Statute of the Child and Adolescent (ECA) and 20 years after the UN Convention on the Rights of the Child, this legal recognition is not visible in investments and in public policies and this makes the state the greatest violator of children's and adolescents' rights. This situation justifies the need for surveillance of the public administration by society, monitoring of public expenditures, the quality of public policies and the discussion on the role of the state.

Monitoring the Public Budget: The Experience of Cedeca-Ceará

◈

When and How it Started

Undoubtedly, Brazil has one of the most modern legal systems as far as human rights are concerned. However, it is only through public investment that the rights won through social movements and stated in the legislation will be effectively guaranteed. It was this understanding that made Cedeca-Ceará initiate the monitoring of the resources available for children's and adolescents' programmes. To do that, it used a concept formulated by the Institute of Applied Research (Instituto de Pesquisas Aplicadas, IPEA) named 'child budget' which is defined as *all the activities and projects of the public budgets aimed exclusively at or those that prioritise children and adolescents.*

Between 1999 and 2002, Cedeca-Ceará focused on two main areas: the analysis of the public budgets for the production of information and the capacity building of civil society to use the budget as a political tool through *lobbying* and *advocacy*. After analysing the public budgets, all the resources aimed at children's and adolescents' policies were highlighted and a report called *Child Budget Report* was written. In this report a critical analysis of the proposals presented by the executive power for the children and adolescents was made.

This report was made available to all organisations that fought for the rights of children and adolescents to use it as a pressure tool to intervene in the formulation of the budget proposal, with the presentation of amendments and the action inside the parliament.

After some time other action fronts were put up: monitoring of the participatory budget in Fortaleza; a state network through which non-governmental organisations monitor the state budget; an alliance of individuals and organisations in the cities of Ibicuitinga and Sobral in the interior of Ceará; participation in the Child Budget Theme Group of the National Association of Centres for Defence of Children and Adolescents (ANCED) which has the responsibility of monitoring the expenditures at a federal level; and also supporting a group of adolescents to discuss the public budget and children's policies. It was through these groups and alliances that the Budget and Active Participation Network (Rede OPA – Rede de Orçamento e Participação Ativa), that Cedeca-Ceará was able to monitor the expenditures on children and adolescents at the city, state and federal levels and the project, together with the adolescents from the OPA Network.

The production of information and the capacity building of the civil society is still a priority for the Cedeca-Ceará because it is only through this we can *lobby* and *advocate* to the public administration. However, this essay focuses on the incorporation of adolescents in the monitoring of the public budget.

◈

The Recognition of the Importance and of the Need of the Participation for the Adolescents

In 2003, the Cedeca-Ceará started bringing adolescents into the process of monitoring the public policies through a project of empowering them to work with the public budget. This initiative counted at first with the participation of organised groups in communities from the outskirts of Fortaleza.

This decision represented the recognition of children's and adolescents' rights to participate in accordance with the UN Convention on the Rights of the Child, Article 12:

> State Parties shall assure to the child who is capable of forming his or her own views the right to express those views freely in all matters affecting the child, the views of the child being given due weight in accordance with the age and maturity of the child.

Besides legal recognition, there was a need to ensure that these children and adolescents were also politically recognised and their concerns and opinions were incorporated in decisions, thus breaking the invisibility barrier in which they were historically consigned because of our adult-centred culture. This would create the possibility of having their opinions and proposals taken into consideration at the discussions of public policies.

However, it must be considered that this experience of effective participation of adolescents in the monitoring of public policies was taking place in one of the states with the greatest social and political inequalities in Brazil; a place with the highest income rate concentration in the country. If it has been said that the formation of the Brazilian state was characterised by a process of oppression and slavery, we can also affirm that in some regions like Ceará, the relations of power were clearly influenced by the social condition, gender and generation, in such a way that it would be impossible to consider that adolescents, and in this case poor adolescents, could take part in a discussion on public budgets, make their own proposals, and put those up for discussions. That is because in such structured and unequal societies, the child is an object of tutelage and, therefore, someone to be silenced. Their participation, especially in the political area, involves a slow process of cultural reformulation and democratic radicalisation by the state because the authoritarian attitude of the state that deals with public affairs as something private, is still very common.

Therefore, we must remember that Brazilian society has a political culture which considers representative democracy as the most democratic form of democracy, which is characterised by electoral and political clientelism and paternalism, as well as by individualistic and patriarchal social relations. In its true from, the Brazilian state was formed bureaucratically, with little democracy in practice. Such characteristics of the Brazilian state and society are the main obstacles to overcome in order for us to evolve a participatory and democratic political practice.

When we seek the participation of children, we seek that children and adolescents be recognised and included as subjects of rights, which can only be effective if we create real spaces of participation It also means that we do not speak on their behalf any longer but we speak along with them. Clearly, to include children and adolescents in the process of monitoring the public budget in such adverse cultural, social and political conditions, means the breaking of a way of functioning of the public administration.

◊

How it Started

It all started with a partnership with two non-governmental organisations in the city of Fortaleza which already had projects with adolescents and had also organised groups in the communities. In this first year, 50 adolescents who came from three communities in the city's outskirts were qualified. In the following year, 2004, 40 adolescents from two other communities were also qualified and another partnership with two other non-governmental organisations was formed. In this year we tried to work on the formation of the adolescents who participated in the previous year. For that purpose, the group chose 10 adolescents who started to contribute to the project activities and workshops.

◊

Methodology/Contents

When we started training and empowering the students, there were more questions than answers, more doubts than certainties. How would we deal with topics which seemed very difficult even for the social educators and the NGO that we worked with—topics which initially seemed unattractive and uncommon for them? Besides that we had to deal with the challenges we were able to realise only after a certain time of working with these children.

Our state-governed schools, as they are, do not offer quality education, and hence there were constraints that the children faced because of their formal education. That is an element that had to be taken into consideration in the preparation of the workshops and activities. However, it is important to reinforce the belief in the potential of each and every one of the adolescents involved in the project.

Our choice was to always work confronting the contents with an analysis of the ground reality, trying to create an idea that by entering in contact with some topics, a link with their real life experiences could be made, be it in their district, in their school, or in their city. This strategy was correct.

In a broader way, the training project is divided into three phases with specific contents. Each phase, besides the workshops, has a series of complementary activities that reinforce not only the qualification but also the feeling of being part of a group, the co-responsibility, the group initiatives, and the interaction with society and with other groups of adolescents.

Between the training phases, visits to the City Council as well as to public-financed projects for children and adolescents were organised. Seminars, debates were held; videos were produced. Generally, this is the pattern that is followed:

First phase—An evaluation of the reality

This involved a diagnosis of the rights violation. In this phase, the contents we worked with tried to provoke a critical analysis of the reality. Part of the training was done through workshops and field work.

The contents of the workshops were: the city history, human rights, children's and adolescents rights, Statute of the Child and Adolescent, Convention on the Rights of the Child. In the fieldwork we used what we called 'urban circuit'. In the first year, we worked with photography, the adolescents were divided into groups based on different rights and prepared a photographic work about the violation of their rights. This work should have been used initially for a group reflection of the reality; however, it became an exhibition to celebrate the anniversary of the Statute of the Child and Adolescent. Besides that, a video was also produced by the adolescents themselves, diagnosing the rights violations.

We worked with different mediums such as theatre, dance, arts, music, poetry, etc. These have been fundamental in each phase of growth and in the whole development of the project; using child-friendly or playful mediums has been very useful when dealing with an apparently harsh topic such as public budget.

Second phase—Training on public budget

In this phase the topics we worked with were related to the public budget: how the exaction of tribute is made; how the public administration expenditure is organised; legislation and political incidence, public administration; concepts of state, society and social class. We worked with theoretical concepts so that later we could analyse the budget. We always tried to steer the discussion as close to the reality as possible, so we always approached the concepts of public budget by drawing upon something more familiar such as a family, school or trip budget. After this phase, the analysis of the actual public budget proposed by the executive power (the public administrator) was made.

Third phase—Mobilisation and Lobbying

In this phase the political actions to be carried out by the adolescents were prepared such as the presentation of amendments, demonstrations, seminars with other adolescents for the formulation of proposals of the public budget.

While the whole process is very dynamic and always linked with the ground reality, the children were guided to think and plan for themselves.

Besides using different pedagogical resources such as art, we also tried to bring some political principles to the project because we had two main objectives: monitor the resources for the children and guarantee their right of participation. Therefore, other contents and practices were adjoined aiming at creating new relations, different from the socially prevailing ones. Hence it was important to discuss topics such as the inclusion of disabled children and adolescents, gender, ethnicity, and violence, among others.

Throughout the whole process the group defines and redefines itself and this itself works as an element of learning and respect, of fostering new values, new relations so that the representations are decentralised. They are able to speak out, raise questions of gender, among other topics, and that is important to guarantee a transforming process.

Results

We can state that important results were achieved since the Cedeca-Ceará started monitoring the child budget. These results do not refer only to the increase of investments for the children, but also the political changes that are fundamental to guarantee the social control of the state by monitoring the public budgets. There was a raising of social awareness on the need for understanding, monitoring and participating in the budget process, and that contributed to the strengthening of the civil society. The following were some of the outcomes:

◈

Changes of Quantitative Character: The Increase of Investments for the Children and Adolescents

Between 2003 and 2004, the adolescents managed to approve the addition of R$ 2 million (US$ 1.1 million) for children's development and these resources were allocated for education and social care.[8] Such resources were mostly transferred from the areas of infrastructure and advertising thus ensuring a better state budget priority.[9]

◈

Changes of Political Character

Combining the political mobilisation of the adolescents from the poorer communities as well as other adolescents from the city of Fortaleza, made it possible to gain political mileage for the adolescents' organisation so that they became a political force for the public power as well as for other social movements in the city. They were heard in several participatory processes in the city and also vociferously objected when their interests were not compatible with the government ones. They held meetings, assemblies and demonstrations claiming rights that were being violated in Fortaleza.[10] That was a new experience in the city because, for the first time, adolescents were analysing the public budget, mobilising other adolescents and pressurising for alterations in the budget law to ensure more resources for public policies for children and adolescents.

◊

Changes of Pedagogical Character

With this project it was possible to develop a participatory methodology of capacity building on an apparently difficult theme, using lucid and creative methods and most of all, using the concept of popular education which sees education as process of dialogue in which the adolescents and educators learn and teach, thus giving them the freedom to think and the freedom to develop critical knowledge about their own situation.

This methodology taught the adults who were facilitating this process that it was necessary to break the paradigm of child tutelage and that instead of working on the premise that children belong to adults, there was a need to work on building the autonomy of adolescents themselves.

The use of educational media as a fundamental mechanism for the process of organisation and mobilisation of the adolescents was an important aspect of this project. It initiated a new and permanent process of communication between the group we worked with, and the society as a whole. The result of this experience was the production of videos, exhibition of photographs about the violation of the rights of children and adolescents, seminars, debates, among other experiments carried out by the adolescents.

Although the experience described here is focused on the participation of the adolescents in monitoring public budget and some of the difficulties they faced, it is important to highlight them because despite the gains made by civil society in institutionalising participation, there are still many obstacles to overcome in the process of social participation and control.

Access to real-time information on the execution of the budget is one of the greatest difficulties in guaranteeing the monitoring of the public budget because the legal instruments that ensure the government shares expenditures, functions as an obstacle to the rendering of accounts. Because of this, we have adopted other strategies such as the use of juridical instruments. We have already filed three lawsuits; in two of them we denounce irregularities in the execution of the budget (2006) and in the other one we request that the budget execution as far as children and adolescents are concerned is shown in detail and in real time (2002). Besides that, we made a presentation in the prosecuting counsel in 2007 that notified the city administration forcing them to provide all the required information.

Other obstacles were overcome by the adolescents themselves and this has contributed to increase in the levels of participation. An example of this was the right to participate in the discussions of the city's master plan which initially was denied to those under the age of 16.[11] After several meetings and mobilisation, this obstruction was overcome and children and adolescents were able to take part in the whole process.

Evolution

Perhaps the main result of this project is the existence of a network of adolescents. The OPA Network or the Budget and Active Participation Network (Rede OPA—Rede de Orçamento e Participação Ativa) emerged in 2005 from the need of the adolescents to change from a project of capacity building to a political organisation of adolescents with guidelines and mobilisations in the city. Today it is a movement of adolescents with an effective participation in the city's political life and is recognised by the public administration as well as civil society organisations. A concrete contribution of this group in the fight for the rights of children and adolescents is the fact that while they speak as agents of rights, they are heard also as subjects of rights. As the organisation of the adolescents began to get spaces to intervene in the implementation of the participatory budget, new challenges for the monitoring of the public budget were presented. To be able to participate effectively in all of the discussions of the participatory budget, including as members of the participatory budget council, it was fundamental that the adolescents and children, as well as the other members of public bodies are prepared adequately. Here too Cedeca-Ceará had to play a definitive role.

Besides the discussion on the budget, the adolescents take part in other events for the defining public policies, such as conferences, events for the elaboration of plans in some areas like urban development, educational policy, etc. They also take part in international events such as the Latin-America Children and Adolescents Network (Rede Latino Americana de Crianças e Adolescentes) and the Brazil-Angola Exchange Programme.

Conclusion

A project that works to contribute to guarantee children's and adolescents' right to participate in an adult-centred society faces many difficulties. At the same time, it is clear that the project will contribute to alter this culture of neglect and therefore, it will provoke changes in the political culture. The participation of adolescents in the monitoring of public policies shows us that it is effective because it questions a model, ethical practices and values as well. So, besides objective results which we may achieve, we can assert that a changing process is in progress with the direct intervention of adolescents.

ℐ

Notes

[1] The audit, evaluation and investigative arm of the state is responsible for the control of the budget execution of the state government.

[2] Brazil has failed to comply with the obligations assumed on the international ambit, especially regarding the UNCRC. That happens because it only presented the first report on the monitoring of the implementation of the Convention in the end of 2003, that is, after a delay of almost 10 years. It was the Committee on Rights of the Child that made it possible for the presentation a report formulated by the civil society. There was then a great national articulation and in the following year an alternative report written by the Associação Nacional de Centros de Defesa da Criança e do Adolescente—ANCED (National Association of Centers for the Defence of Children and Adolescents) and by the Fórum Permanente de Entidades Não Governamentais de Defesa dos Direitos da Criança e do Adolescente—Fórum Nacional DCA (Permanent Forum of Non-governmental Organisations for the Defence of Children and Adolescents) was presented.

From the analysis of these reports, the committee made a series of recommendations that the Brazilian state should follow in order to guarantee the rights of children and adolescents in the country.

[3] Article 227: It is the duty of the family, the society and the state to ensure children and adolescents, with absolute priority, the right to life, health, nourishment, education, leisure, professional training, culture, dignity, respect, freedom and family and community life, as well as to guard them from all forms of negligence, discrimination, exploitation, violence and oppression.

[4] For the purpose of the Convention on the Rights of the Child a child is recognised as a person under 18, unless national laws recognise the age of majority earlier. For the Brazilian Statute of the Child and Adolescent, the child is considered as the person who has not yet completed 12 years of age and the adolescent as that between 12 and 18 years of age.

5 Amendment is the legal procedure used by legislators or the civil society in order to add to or revise or improve a proposal or document (a bill or constitution, etc). In the case of the public budget, an amendment is a proposal to transfer resources from one area to another that is considered more important.

6 In budget execution it is necessary to maintain a balance between government revenues and spending. However, the administration curtails the resources thus generating a financial balance that is called surplus, that is, the revenues exceed the spending. In most cases, this excess is destined to payment of public debts.

Brazil has a historical public debt with European countries and especially with the United States as well as with multilateral banks. This debt is imposed by governments and speculators at extremely high interest rates and the country is paying this debt very submissively.

7 Brazilian Statute of the Child and Adolescent, Article 4. 'The guaranty of priority encompasses:
(i) precedence in receiving protection and aid in any circumstances;
(ii) precedence in receiving public services and those of public relevance;
(iii) preference in the formulation and execution of public social policies;
(iv) privileged allocation of public resources in areas related to the protection of infancy and youth.'

8 Rand is the Brazilian currency.

9 Three amendments were approved in 2003 for the 2004 budget. The amendments anticipate an increase in the resources for the following projects of the city of Fortaleza public administration: Strengthening of Citizen Family Project—US$ 417.2 thousand; Psychological assistance for children and adolescents (NUAPSI)—US$ 20.2 thousand; Assistance to sexual exploitation victims—US$ 23.6 thousand.

Nine amendments were approved in 2004 for the 2005 budget. The amendments anticipate an increase in the resources for the following projects of the city of Fortaleza public administration: Maintenance of the Therapeutic Community for children and adolescents drug users—US$ 166.6 thousand; Psychological Assistance for Children and Adolescents—US$

24.6 thousand; Assistance to victims of sexual exploitation—US$ 111.1 thousand; Project Grow up with Art—US$ 111.1 thousand; Citizen Family Project—US$ 138.8 thousand; Physical activities for children with disabilities—US$ 27.7 thousand; Shelter for children who live on the streets—US$ 112.6 thousand; Information Science at schools—US$ 166.6 thousand; School Transportation—US$ 222.2 thousand.

[10] A group of people gathered together with common interests in order to approve political actions, claiming for the granting of some right.

[11] The councils are organs created by the Statute of the Child and Adolescent (Law no. 8069/90) and they must be part of the executive power. They exist at the city, state and federal level with an equal participation of the civil society and the public power. Their objective is to establish parameters for the public policies of each city and state related to the rights of children and adolescents.

⚗

References

Brazilian Institution of Geography and Statistics (IBGE). 2006. *National Household Survey Sample (PNAD)*, Brazil. Available at www.ibge.gov.br/english/estatistica/populacao/condicadevida/incadoresminimos/sinteseindicsociais2006/default.shtm, accesed on March 21, 2011.

Child Budget Report, Cedeca-Ceará, Brazil.

UNICEF. 2005. *The State of Brazil's Children 2006: Children up to the Age of 6 years — The Right to Survival and Development*. Available at http://www.unicef.org/sitan/index43351.httml, accessed on March 18, 2011.

About the Editor

Enakshi Ganguly Thukral is founder co-director of HAQ: Centre for Child Rights, New Delhi. She is a sociologist by training and a human rights activist in her heart and practice. She has researched, lobbied, advocated and fought for rights of affected persons on a range of issues since she started working 25 years ago. These include the rights of displaced persons, women's rights, housing rights and child rights. She has a number of publications, which include edited books, contributions to books, newspapers and journals on diverse subjects including issues concerning children, women, and displacement of people due to development projects.

Notes on Contributors

Assefa Bequele is executive director, African Child Policy Forum, Addis Ababa, Ethiopia. A leading pan-African policy research and advocacy centre on child well-being, ACPF has brought out *The African Report on Child Wellbeing 2008*, which shows how states can quantitatively and statistically monitor national commitment and progress on the UNCRC. It uses a child-friendliness index and a common set of CRC-inspired indicators to assess and rank the performance of all 52 African governments and to analyse differences in child well-being outcomes among countries.

Shaamela Casseim joined the International Budget Partnership (IBP) in October 2006 and is based at IBP-Cape Town. She previously worked at the Children's Budget Unit at Idasa in South Africa, where, together with her colleagues, she was instrumental in pioneering a rights-based approach to budget monitoring. During her time at Idasa she set up and coordinated Imali ye Mwana, a civil society network monitoring children's rights and public budgets in the southern Africa region. She has a background in adult education and training, children's rights activism and applied budget work.

Deborah Ewing is a writer, researcher and editor on development issues. She has a particular focus on children's rights, participation, HIV and AIDS, and poverty. Deborah has published on a range of development issues internationally and has designed and conducted participatory research on issues including development cooperation, land reform, tourism, poverty, HIV and AIDS, children's participation, child labour and budgeting.

She has developed training materials on local government, advocacy, participation, communications, leadership, education and conflict management. Deborah facilitates training workshops and designs training materials for children and adults, geared to increasing meaningful participation. She also writes books for children and young people addressing contemporary social issues. Deborah trained in journalism and edited an award-winning development magazine in London. She was editor of the children's rights journal published by Children First in South Africa and initiated a children's participation programme for the organisation. She served on the Reference Group for the Idasa Children Participating in Governance programme.

Anita Ghai is a prominent advocate for the rights of women with disabilities. Trained in psychology, she practices as a clinical psychologist and has taught and researched in the Department of Psychology at Jesus and Mary College in New Delhi, India for over two decades. Her postdoctoral research was on 'Cognitive Modifiability in Mentally Handicapped Children'. She has worked extensively on educational issues of children as a teacher fellow to Bharat Jan Vigyan Jatha in collaboration with Malauna Azad Centre for Elementary and Social Education, to work on the Lokshala project. She was nominated as the fellow for Developing Countries Research centre to coordinate the Disability Research Programme in June 2001 and selected as visiting research fellow for a duration of three months by the Disability Research Unit at the University of Leeds, Leeds. She is at present a fellow at the Nehru Memorial Museum, New Delhi.

Mabusi Kgwete has worked in facilitation, training, administration, information and research within the NGO sector since 2002, focusing on child and youth development and participation. Mabusi has been working for iMEDIATE Development Communications in South Africa since June 2006. She is involved in research, materials development and facilitation, and writes on issues of gender and HIV. She also works part-time editing websites. Mabusi worked for a South African NGO coordinating Gender and Children and Youth Programmes, and she was a debate groundbreaker at Ziphakamise, a franchise of the Love Life HIV prevention programme. Mabusi facilitated workshops with the KwaZulu-Natal peer facilitators in the Children Participating in Governance programme.

Maria Margarida Marques is a member of the Co-ordination Collegiate of CEDECA-Ceará and also member of the National Coordination of Centers of Defense-ANCED. She is a graduate in communications, and has specialisation in art and education. At CEDECA she is the coordinator of the Programme of Social Control of State and Public Management, where she develops the project 'Monitoring the Budget—Children', with the participation of children and adolescents, and the project of human rights training for children and adolescents (this programme is designed for different audiences and opinion leaders). She also conducts courses, workshops and gives lectures on human rights, children and adolescents issues.

Kavita Ratna is director, Communications, The Concerned for Working Children (CWC), India. Concerned for Working Children works in partnership with children and other marginalised communities for the realisation of their rights through participation. Kavita works closely with Makkala Panchayats (children's councils) of Karnataka and Bhima Sangha, a union of working children. She is engaged in policy and advocacy related to child labour, children's rights, education and decentralisation. She has directed several films and edited the Media Code to Realise Children's Rights 2005, and assisted children to bring out several publications. She has been developing training modules, conducting workshops and designing strategies that enable civil society participation, protaganism and governance.

Nevena Vuckovic Sahovic is a human lawyer focusing on children's rights. Beginning her career as an advisor to the Serbian government in matters of international relations from 1985 to 1992, she began practice as a human rights lawyer. In 1997, she founded the Children's Law Center of Belgrade, and was the director for 10 years. From 2003 to 2009 she was a member of the UN Committee on the Rights of the Child, and continued as a board member of the Rights of the Child Center. Since 2007, Nevena Vuckovic-Sahovic has been associate professor at the Law Faculty of the University UNION in Belgrade.

Shantha Sinha is chairperson, National Commission for Protection of Child Rights (NCPCR). She is also a professor of political science, University of Hyderabad, and a pioneer in the field of child rights in India. She was awarded the Padma Shri in 1998 and the Ramon Magsaysay Award for Community Leadership in 2003. She is the founder secretary and trustee of the MV Foundation, an Andhra Pradesh-based non-profit started in 1991, which has withdrawn over 600,000 children from work and mainstreamed them into schools.

Enrique Vásquez is director of development, professor of Economics and senior researcher in Social Policy and Human Development at the Universidad del Pacífico. He specialises in design, implementation and monitoring of anti-poverty programmes and social management. Professor Vásquez has lectured at international fora in 39 different countries in America, Africa, Asia and Europe and has been a consultant to the World Bank, Inter-American Development Bank, Swiss Development Cooperation (SDC), Belgian Technical Cooperation (CTB), German Cooperation (GTZ), Japanese Cooperation (JICA), Canadian Cooperation (IDRC) and other non-governmental organisations such as Save the Children Sweden and UNICEF. He is author and editor of 25 publications which include *Strategic Manage-*

ment of Social Investment, Indigenous Children and Bilingual Intercultural Education in Peru, Looking for the Well-being of Poor People: How Far We Are?, Fighting Against Poverty: A Market Approach, Children . . . first? Vol.I, II and III, *The Challenges of the Anti-extreme-poverty Fight in Peru, Social Investment for a Good Government,* among others.

Index

person-hood, 129. *See also*
citizenship
Persons with Disabilities
(PWD) Act, 1995, 134
Peru: child mortality rates,
94; diminishing rate, of
investment returns, 95;
inequality among rural
and urban areas, 92; key
areas, for development of
education for boys and
girls: awareness raising
programmes, 111;
designing of nutrition
programmes, 110;
education, for food
programmes, 110;
improving of education
quality, 111; investment in
infrastructure, 109;
making of schooling, a
practical possibility, 110–
11; making schools girl-
friendly, 111; reduction of
education cost, 110;
strengthening of,
educational management
agencies, 111; upgradation
of skills and change in
attitudes, 112;
malnourished children, in
school-going age, 94;
management of public
resources, 91; negligence
towards poor children, 96;
participative balanced
budget (PEP), publication
of, 112; state of education
in, 94
Prabhughate, Priti, 138

Priyam, Manisha, xxiii
Programme for International
Student Assessment
(PISA), 116
Public Budgeting: principles
of: efficacy, 95–98;
efficiency, 99; equity, 99–
100; transparency, 100–1

Rajani, Rakesh, 191
realisation of rights of
children: and governance
(*see* governance and
realisation of rights of
children)
Right of Education:
actualisation of, 157;
connection with
Fundamental Right, 135
Rights of the People with
Disabilities, 2006, 134
Right to Free and
Compulsory Elementary
Education Act (RTE), 156,
169; recognition of, 157
Right to Information,
children, of, 198–201
Right to self-determination,
children, of, 181–82
rural girls education, Peru,
in, 108

Sarva Shiksha Abhiyan
(SSA), 134
Save the Children, 8, 84, 115
self-determination, 22. *See
also* children, in
governance
self-hood, 129. *See also*
citizenship

For Product Safety Concerns and Information please contact our EU
representative GPSR@taylorandfrancis.com
Taylor & Francis Verlag GmbH, Kaufingerstraße 24, 80331 München, Germany